T0293419

Get the eBook FREE!

(PDF, ePub, Kindle, and liveBook all included)

We believe that once you buy a book from us, you should be able to read it in any format we have available. To get electronic versions of this book at no additional cost to you, purchase and then register this book at the Manning website.

Go to https://www.manning.com/freebook and follow the instructions to complete your pBook registration.

That's it!
Thanks from Manning!

Build a Website with ChatGPT

Build a Website with ChatGPT

PAUL MCFEDRIES

MANNING
SHELTER ISLAND

Manning Publications Co.
20 Baldwin Road
PO Box 761
Shelter Island, NY 11964

Development editor:	Karen Miller
Technical editor:	Anirudh Prabhu
Review editor:	Kishor Rit
Production editor:	Kathy Rossland
Copy editor:	Tiffany Taylor
Proofreader:	Keri Hales
Technical proofreader:	Adam London
Typesetter:	Tamara Švelić Sabljić
Cover designer:	Monica Kamsvaag

ISBN 9781633436961
Printed in the United States of America

To Karen and Chase, my preferred chatting partners

brief contents

contents

preface

"O brave new world, that has such people in it!" That quote is from William Shakespeare's play *The Tempest* and is spoken by the child Miranda when she encounters a crowd of people for the first time. You're unlikely to have been banished to a remote island as a child, but you may still find yourself echoing Miranda's words when you encounter any of the current crop of *artificial intelligence* (AI) apps for the first time. It's a brave new world, indeed, that has such chatbots in it.

Tools such as ChatGPT seem wondrous at first because they appear to be quite good at putting words together. Ask ChatGPT to `Write a Shakespearean sonnet that summarizes the plot of Cormac McCarthy's novel "The Road"`, and it will comply. No, the resulting poem won't be Shakespeare-quality, but it *will* be entertaining. But after a while, this kind of cheap entertainment wears thin, and most ChatGPT users find themselves asking a question along the lines of "What is ChatGPT *truly* useful for?"

That's generally a tough question to answer, with one exception: code. ChatGPT is genuinely useful for turning text instructions into programming code. In particular, ChatGPT is good at converting text into the code required to construct a web page. This is extraordinary, and it means now *anyone* can build a presence on the web, even if they can't or don't want to learn the intricacies of web development.

There are, however, a couple of catches to this newfangled way of getting on the web. First, yes, ChatGPT is very good at turning text into web page code, but only if you know how to formulate that text with detailed instructions for ChatGPT to follow. Second, even once ChatGPT has successfully generated all the code you need for a web page, you still need to save that code somewhere and then get it on the web somehow.

Those may seem like high hurdles to jump, but that's where this book comes in. In the pages that follow, you learn not only how to instruct ChatGPT like a pro to get exactly the web page you want but also how to save that code and then deploy it to the web for all the world to see. Welcome, then, to the brave new world of building your very own website with the help of ChatGPT.

acknowledgments

The American essayist and poet E. B. White once described an editor as "a person who knows more about writing than writers do but who has escaped the terrible desire to write." I believe this to be true not only because E. B. White was a wise person but also because I've come to rely on my editors to make me look like a better writer than I am!

I'm sure the editors of novels and memoirs and such have their hands full whipping their manuscripts into shape, but spare a moment for the poor editors of computer books. They have to make sure a computer book reads well and isn't festooned with spelling errors and grammatical gaffes, and they also have to ensure that the book is technically accurate. Why? Because even the teensiest authorial (or editorial) lapse could result in a book that sows confusion and consternation rather than certainty and delight.

The good folks at Manning Publications ensure that each book reads well and is accurate by subjecting each manuscript to a barrage of reviews, not only by editorial professionals but also by a team of dedicated outsiders. Instead of a process in which single-digit numbers of eyeballs look at the manuscript, a Manning book is scrutinized by dozens. The result? The book you're reading contains accurate and relevant information that has passed muster with some of the sharpest eyes and ears in the business. Yes, my name may be the only one on the cover, but tons of people had a big role in creating what appears between the covers (be they physical or virtual). Those reviewers were Adam Wan, Andres Sacco, Andriani Stylianou, Ashwin Mhatre, Beardsley Ruml, Bruno Sonnino, Charles Lam, Drew Leon, Erim Ertürk, Ganesh Falak, Halil Karakose, James Coates, Jeff Smith, José Alberto Reyes Quevedo, Julien Pohie, Lars Pesch, Marvin Schwarze, Matteo Battista, Mikhail Karaashev, Ozren Harlovic, Radhakrishna MV, Ranjit Sahai, Rui Liu, Saravanan Muniraj, Steve Prior, Swapneelkumar Deshpande, and Tony Holdroyd.

Many thanks to technical editor Anirudh Prabhu, who is a seasoned user interface developer boasting over a decade of experience in the field. His career has been punctuated by noteworthy achievements, including the publication of four acclaimed books. In addition, he has served as a technical reviewer for various titles under esteemed publishers and has taken an active role in shaping the future of web development by creating comprehensive training materials for HTML, CSS, and jQuery.

I'd like to extend warm thanks to publisher Marjan Bace, acquisitions editor Brian Sawyer, development editor Karen Miller, project coordinator Malena Selić, copy editor Tiffany Taylor, and all the rest of the production staff at Manning who helped bring this book to fruition.

Finally, I'd also like to thank all the people who took the time to review the early manuscripts of the book and to offer comments and suggestions. Your couple of cents' worth was very much appreciated.

about this book

In this book, you learn how to instruct ChatGPT to generate the necessary web page code to deploy a page to your specifications. No experience with either ChatGPT or web development is required. Everything you need to know is provided as you need it, and you won't find any long-winded technical discussions or philosophical arguments in these pages. My goal is to get you on the web with ChatGPT's assistance, and everything in the book is in service of that goal. If you've ever wanted to put up a web page but couldn't or didn't want to learn how to code, this book will get you there with a powerful assist from ChatGPT.

I'm assuming that you have a life away from your computer screen, so this book is organized in such a way that you don't have to read it from cover to cover. If you're just getting started, read chapter 1 to get a solid foundation, and then try the simple project in chapter 2 to get an honest-to-goodness ChatGPT-generated page on the web. From there, you can try any of the projects in chapters 3–12 in any order. To make things easier to find, the section "How this book is organized: A road map" gives you a summary of the book's 13 chapters (and 3 appendixes).

Who should read this book

This book is aimed first and foremost at anyone who wants to build a presence on the web, whether that presence is a humble home page, a page to show off a hobby or interest, or a website for a book club, event, organization, or team. More specifically, I aimed this book at three types of readers:

- *Someone who doesn't know how to code web pages and doesn't want to learn*—The specifics of web development have long been a barrier to many people establishing a presence on the web. This book aims to show how ChatGPT changes all that for people with no interest in learning how to code.

- *Someone who doesn't know how to code web pages and wants to learn*—This book is mostly concerned with the instructions you have to provide ChatGPT to get it to generate the web page code you want. However, I also give some background about each of the web page code technologies used in the book. Combine that background knowledge with this book's hands-on approach to projects, and you'll learn quite a bit about web development.

- *Someone who knows how to code web pages*—Even if you already know at least the basics of web development, you can use ChatGPT to speed up your development work and can delegate some of the more tedious tasks to ChatGPT. This book shows you the prompts you can use to cajole ChatGPT into being your programming assistant.

How this book is organized: A road map

Chapter 1 introduces you to ChatGPT in general and to using ChatGPT to generate web page code in particular. You learn what types of pages you can build with the help of ChatGPT, and you get a high-level view of the process.

Chapter 2 takes you on a journey to create and deploy your first web page with the help of ChatGPT. You learn how to prompt ChatGPT to generate the code, copy that code, and save the code to a file. From there, you test the code in a web browser and then deploy it for free to the web.

Chapter 3 shows you how to prompt ChatGPT to use fonts, colors, and headings on a web page. You learn how to ask ChatGPT to supply you with suggestions for your site title and tagline, the fonts to use, and the color scheme to apply. You then put all this together in a prompt that asks ChatGPT to generate the code for a personal home page.

Chapter 4 focuses on the structure of a web page, so you learn about headers, footers, padding, borders, and margins. You also learn how to add images and social media links to the page. The chapter culminates in prompting ChatGPT for the code to build a book club page.

Chapter 5 covers publishing posts to a page as well as using AI to turn text prompts into images. You put all this together in a prompt that instructs ChatGPT to generate the code for an online journal page.

Chapter 6 is all about links and navigation. You learn how the code for links works so you can create links manually instead of always asking ChatGPT to do it. You also learn how to instruct ChatGPT to create a page navigation bar with links to other site pages. This chapter's project is an information site.

Chapter 7 examines ChatGPT's writing prowess as you learn how to prompt the chatbot for topic ideas, writing guidelines, and research suggestions. You even learn the best way to prompt ChatGPT to produce writing in your own voice. Later in the chapter, you construct a prompt for ChatGPT to generate the code for an interest or hobby page.

Chapter 8 gives you the tools you need to instruct ChatGPT to build web page forms that include text boxes, check boxes, radio buttons, lists, and more. You also learn how to sign up with a service that enables you to get form data sent to your email address.

You combine all this in a prompt that asks ChatGPT to generate the code for an event sign-up page.

Chapter 9 introduces you to two common web page features: bulleted lists and numbered lists. You learn how to instruct ChatGPT to build these lists, and you learn various ways to customize them to suit your needs. The chapter concludes by prompting ChatGPT for the code to build a recipe page.

Chapter 10 takes you through a more detailed look at working with images on a web page. You learn how to code images manually, how to use placeholder images, and how to work with thumbnail versions of images. The chapter project is a sophisticated photo gallery page.

Chapter 11 introduces you to one of the most popular web page patterns: the card, which you can use to showcase items such as works of art, hobbies, people, or events. You put this card know-how to good use when getting ChatGPT to help you build this chapter's project: a portfolio page.

Chapter 12 gives you a complete tutorial on using web page layout tags, as well as showing you how to mark up important words and how to emphasize words on the page. You also learn a powerful technique for making your pages look good on smaller screens. This chapter's project is a page that displays a long article with a sidebar.

Chapter 13 introduces you to data-driven web pages, where most of the page content is rendered from a separate data file. You first learn how to get ChatGPT to create the data file from your Excel data. Then you learn how to enable your users to interact with the data by filtering, sorting, and searching it. This chapter's project is a page that displays an online course catalog for a fictional university.

Appendix A provides you with useful background information for getting ready to use ChatGPT to build web pages. You learn how to set up a ChatGPT account, test your code, and work with web page files.

Appendix B is devoted to getting your web code online. You learn how to deploy your code to two free sites—Netlify and Cloudflare—as well as other sites.

Appendix C raises your ChatGPT game by taking you through an extensive list of best practices for prompting ChatGPT and handling any errors that come up.

About the code

Not surprisingly, a book about getting an AI chatbot to generate web page code contains quite a bit of code! To help differentiate the web page code from the rest of the text, throughout this book, the code is formatted in a `fixed-width font`. The book also has many separate code listings. In these listings, I've tried as much as possible to make each line fit into the available page width. However, there are some cases where a line is too long to fit the page width, so the line carries over to a second line, and that second line is preceded with a line-continuation marker (➡).

You may be tempted to describe the amount of ChatGPT-generated code in this book as daunting if you're operating under the assumption that you're going to need to type all that code by hand. Not so! All the book's web page code, as well as all the book's ChatGPT prompts, are available to view, download, and copy as you see fit from the book's GitHub repository at https://github.com/paulmcfe/websites-with-chatgpt. To download everything, click the green Code button, and then click Download ZIP. Otherwise, click a chapter and then click the file you want to view.

You can get executable snippets of code from the liveBook (online) version of this book at https://livebook.manning.com/book/build-a-website-with-chatgpt. The complete code for the examples in the book is also available for download from the Manning website at www.manning.com/books/build-a-website-with-chatgpt.

liveBook discussion forum

Purchase of *Build a Website with ChatGPT* includes free access to liveBook, Manning's online reading platform. Using liveBook's exclusive discussion features, you can attach comments to the book globally or to specific sections or paragraphs. It's a snap to make notes for yourself, ask and answer technical questions, and receive help from the author and other users. To access the forum, go to https://livebook.manning.com/book/build-a-website-with-chatgpt/discussion. You can also learn more about Manning's forums and the rules of conduct at https://livebook.manning.com/discussion.

Manning's commitment to our readers is to provide a venue where a meaningful dialogue between individual readers and between readers and the author can take place. It is not a commitment to any specific amount of participation on the part of the author, whose contribution to the forum remains voluntary (and unpaid). We suggest you try asking the author some challenging questions lest his interest stray! The forum and the archives of previous discussions will be accessible from the publisher's website as long as the book is in print.

about the author

PAUL McFEDRIES has been a professional technical writer for more than 30 years. He has more than 100 books to his credit, which collectively have sold more than 4 million copies worldwide. His other Manning title is *Web Design Playground, Second Edition.* When he's not writing books, Paul is building web pages, which he's been doing since 1996, and he has intimate knowledge of both HTML and CSS. Paul has hand-coded many sites, including his web home (https://paulmcfedries. com), Word Spy (https://wordspy.com), WebDev Workshop (https://webdevworkshop.io), and Web Design Playground (https://webdesignplayground.io/2). Paul loves to teach, his writing is clear and logical, and he has the empathy that comes from remembering what it was like to first learn a subject.

Introducing website creation with ChatGPT

1

This chapter covers

- Introducing ChatGPT
- Understanding what kinds of web pages you can create with the help of ChatGPT
- Getting to know the limitations of making web pages with ChatGPT
- Learning how ChatGPT enables you to create your own web pages

The British science fiction writer Arthur C. Clarke once formulated three truisms that came to be known as *Clarke's three laws*, the third of which is the one most often cited: "Any sufficiently advanced technology is indistinguishable from magic." If you've always wanted to create web pages but were daunted by the technology, then the premise of this book—that you *can* create your own website with the help of ChatGPT—may seem like magic to you. That's no surprise, because if any technology in recent memory deserves the description "sufficiently advanced," it's ChatGPT and similar so-called *generative AI*—artificial intelligence applications that can create poetry, prose, and, yes, web pages.

1

In this chapter, my aim is to demystify ChatGPT and make it seem a little less magical and a whole lot more practical. In the next few pages, you get a short explanation of the basics of ChatGPT, an overview of the kinds of pages you can create with ChatGPT's help (and, for balance, some notes on the kinds of pages you *can't* create), and a behind-the-scenes and mercifully nontechnical tour of how you can use ChatGPT to perform the seemingly magical—but in reality, merely mathematical—feat of taking a simple, typed request and turning it into a full-fledged, ready-to-be-surfed web page.

1.1   What is ChatGPT?

Unless you've been hunkered down in a hermitage over the past year or two, you've likely heard about GPT and/or ChatGPT, the artificial intelligence agents that have taken the world (or, at least, that part of the world that pays attention to social media) by storm. However, knowing *about* ChatGPT is one thing, but knowing what ChatGPT actually *is*, is quite another.

To help you get a feel for what ChatGPT is and what it does, it helps to break down each component of the name to see what it means. I'll begin with GPT:

- *G*—The *G* in *GPT* stands for *generative*, which means GPT can create—or *generate*—new content. GPT is a *large language model* (LLM), which generally means it's designed to generate text, such as essays, stories, and even poems. More specifically for our purposes in this book, GPT's generative capabilities also extend to programming code, particularly the code that underlies web pages.

- *P*—The *P* in *GPT* stands for *pretrained*, which means GPT was exposed to huge amounts of text (that's what the "large" in *large language model* is referring to). During this *pretraining* process, GPT learned the patterns and structures in the language, such as how sentences are typically formed. In particular, given some existing text, pretraining enables GPT to predict what word or phrase usually comes next. In a sense, that's all GPT is really doing: predicting the next word! GPT was also trained on an unimaginably large set of programming data; so, because programming code is usually more predictable than regular writing, GPT excels at generating code.

- *T*—The *T* in *GPT* stands for *transformer*, which means GPT is able to take some text input (such as a request to create a web page) and transform that text into its most important components while ignoring or giving lower priority to less important components of the text. This enables GPT to produce results with greater relevance and accuracy.

The *Chat* part of *ChatGPT* means you have conversational access to GPT, which means you can exchange messages with GPT more or less as you do in a chat conversation. In the context of creating web pages, these "conversations" will amount to you requesting some page component and ChatGPT providing the required code. However, ChatGPT also has a limited ability to "remember" previous messages in the current conversation, which can occasionally be useful in your website creation tasks.

As I write this, two main versions of GPT are available: GPT-3.5, released in November 2022, and GPT-4, released in March 2023. If you use the OpenAI app (discussed in a moment) either with a free ChatGPT account (learn more in appendix A) or with no account, you have access only to GPT-3.5; if you have a paid ChatGPT Plus account and you use the OpenAI app, you have access to both GPT-3.5 and GPT-4.

To access ChatGPT to help you create web pages, you have three preferred choices:

- *OpenAI app*—This is an online app operated by OpenAI, the creators of GPT and ChatGPT. The app is available at https://chat.openai.com. You don't need an OpenAI account to access it, but having an account removes certain restrictions (check out appendix A to learn how to create an account to access ChatGPT). If you have a paid ChatGPT Plus account, you get to choose between GPT-3.5 and GPT-4, as shown in figure 1.1.

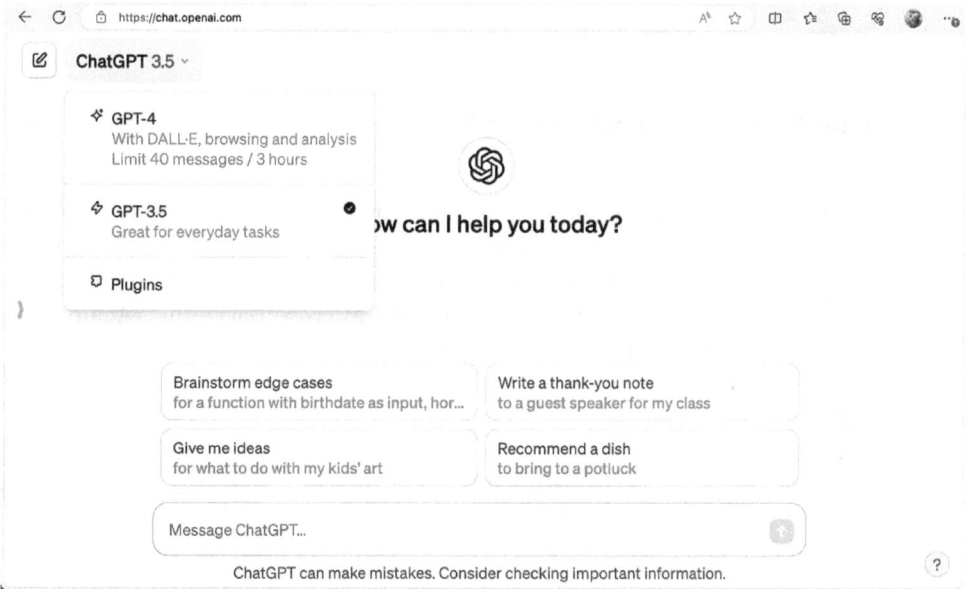

Figure 1.1   With a ChatGPT Plus account, the OpenAI app gives you access to both GPT-3.5 and GPT-4.

- *Microsoft Copilot in Bing*—This is the AI-enhanced version of Microsoft's search engine, which offers a chat feature that uses GPT-4 behind the scenes and also has access to the web. Navigate to https://bing.com and select the Copilot tab to get started, as shown in figure 1.2. Note that you don't need a ChatGPT account to use Bing Copilot. (If you're wondering about the three "conversation style" choices, I explain them in detail in appendix A.)

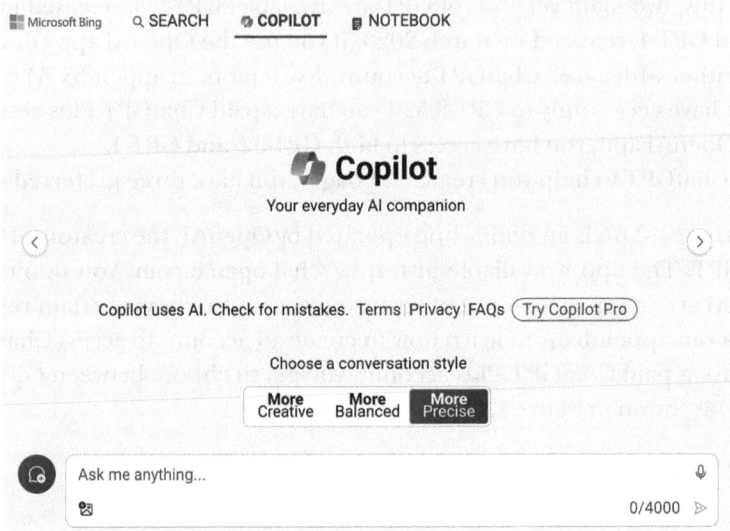

Figure 1.2   Use Bing Copilot to work with GPT-4.

- *Microsoft Copilot*—This is the standalone implementation of Microsoft's version of ChatGPT, which uses the GPT-4 model. Navigate to https://copilot.microsoft .com, as shown in figure 1.3. Note that you don't need a ChatGPT account to use Microsoft Copilot, but you do need a Microsoft account. (Again, I explain the three "conversation style" choices in appendix A.)

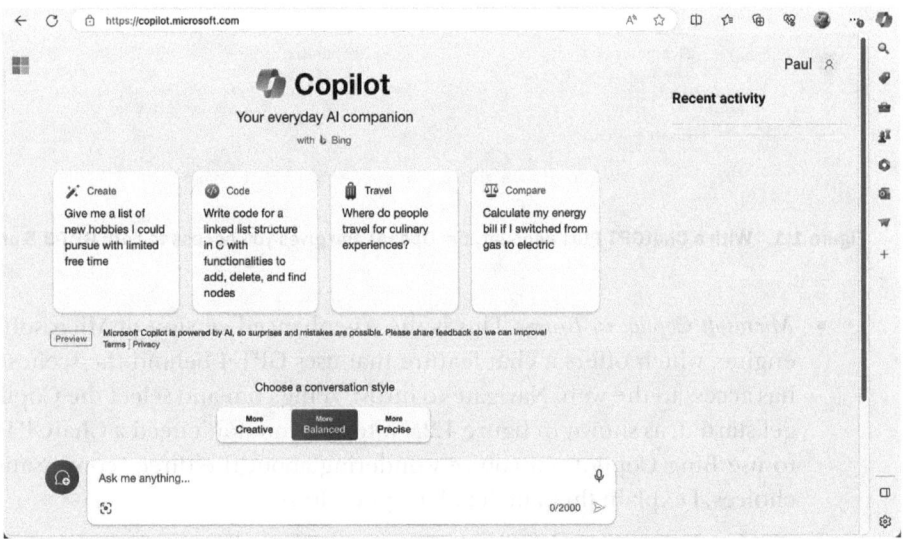

Figure 1.3   If you have a Microsoft account, use Copilot to work with GPT-4.

NOTE There are quite a few other ways to access ChatGPT, either directly or indirectly. For example, there are ChatGPT apps for iOS and Android. These other methods are fine for messing around with ChatGPT, but for creating web pages, it's best to stick with the OpenAI app, Bing Copilot, or Microsoft Copilot because they give you easy access to the code generated by ChatGPT.

Which method should you use to access ChatGPT? When it comes to creating the relatively simple web page code that's covered in this book, it doesn't matter all that much. GPT-4 tends to produce more "modern" code, which is generally a good thing. (However, this may mean your pages don't work well in older browsers such as Internet Explorer. My advice? Ignore those ancient browsers and embrace the modern web!) If you don't have a ChatGPT account and don't want the restrictions that the Open AI app imposes on non-account holders, Bing Copilot is the way to go.

1.2 *ChatGPT enables anyone to create web pages*

I've never been lucky enough to have an assistant, but I can imagine that it's a sweet deal. After all, who wouldn't be happy to have someone dedicated to performing necessary but mundane tasks such as setting up virtual meetings; arranging flights, hotels, and other travel details; and putting together presentations? Having an assistant is even more valuable if you don't know (and don't want to know) how to set up a Zoom meeting, navigate the Expedia website, or build a PowerPoint presentation.

These tasks are nontrivial, for sure, but they seem like kindergarten exercises compared to designing, coding, and deploying a web page or even an entire website. Sure, there are templates and similar page-building tools out there that offer ready-to-roll web pages, but the results are almost always disappointing because you get only a limited amount of control over the output. You have a great topic for a site, and you have a mental image of how it should look, but there's a barrier between you and your vision: the web page code.

The three main types of web page code—HTML, CSS, and JavaScript—reside on a steep learning curve: a slope that for many people is too onerous a climb when all they want is to put up a page or three for themselves or for a team, hobby, project, charity, or event. If you want to create a presence on the web but have either been disappointed in the available prefabricated solutions or shuddered at the thought of learning HTML, CSS, and JavaScript, all is not lost, because now you can "hire" (for free, if you prefer) an assistant to generate web page code to your exact specifications. That assistant is ChatGPT, which sits well on the other side of the web development learning curve and is ready, willing, and very able to help you turn your web page vision into web page reality. By providing the model with a few simple, plain-English instructions, you can cajole ChatGPT into translating those instructions into working web page code. You then upload that code to the web (ChatGPT can even help you with that step), and you're done!

Okay, it's perhaps not quite as easy as all that (otherwise, there wouldn't have been much point in writing the rest of this book!). But the basic procedure is every bit as straightforward as I've outlined it here.

1.3   Understanding the types of pages you can (and can't) create

By now, you may be thinking that transforming ChatGPT into a website-building robot assistant must come with some sort of catch. After all, to the uninitiated, building web pages seems like an almost quintessentially complex task, so claiming that you can farm out almost all that labor to an AI model without having to learn to code yourself must come with a rather large "gotcha." Surprisingly, there are no such flies in the ChatGPT ointment, but there are a few provisos to bear in mind.

First, you need to know that the types of web pages most easily created with the help of ChatGPT are those described as *static* in the web development trade. A static web page is one that contains text and data that don't change after the page is loaded. That may sound restrictive, but there's really no limit on the types of static pages you can ask ChatGPT to help you build. Here are 10 ideas:

- Personal home page
- Information page for a team, organization, or event
- Product landing page
- Hobby page
- Photo gallery
- Portfolio page
- Post page (essay, review, fan fiction, or whatever)
- Top-10 list
- How-to instructions
- Travel guide

I bet you can easily come up with 10 more on your own. These are the types of pages you learn how to create with the help of ChatGPT in this book. And the really great news is that unless you opt for a paid ChatGPT Plus subscription, you can do everything—from accessing ChatGPT to saving the generated code to deploying your pages—completely free.

Second, one of the characteristics of the types of pages I just listed is that they only require what web development geeks call *frontend* code, which means code (HTML, CSS, and JavaScript) that runs in the web browser. A much different beast is *backend* code, which means code that runs on a web server and is generally used to supply text and data for a *dynamic* web page, where the text and data change on the fly.

Technically, it's possible to ask ChatGPT to supply such backend code, but practically speaking, you're talking about setup tasks that are an order of magnitude more complicated, far more complex in terms of organizing and deploying the generated code, *huge* security risks because web servers are vulnerable to many types of attacks and advanced coding techniques must be used to harden backend code against malicious users, and almost always added costs because web hosting accounts that enable access to a server usually require a paid subscription plan. For all these reasons, you don't learn how to use ChatGPT to generate backend code in this book.

1.4 Using ChatGPT to help you build web pages

Fritterware is an old computing term that refers to any software that seduces the user into spending inordinate amounts of time playing around with the program's features and options. Once you have a ChatGPT account (which I cover in appendix A; however, remember that having an account is optional), you have instant access to one of the all-time great pieces of fritterware ever invented! It's easy to spend huge hunks of time getting ChatGPT to do all kinds of fun and silly things, but eventually, you'll want to stop frittering and start creating.

The ChatGPT creative process varies depending on what you're making, but for our purposes here, you need to know the overall process of getting ChatGPT to help you create web pages. The simplified version of that process is summarized in figure 1.4. The next few sections explain each step, and chapter 2 takes you through a complete example of the process.

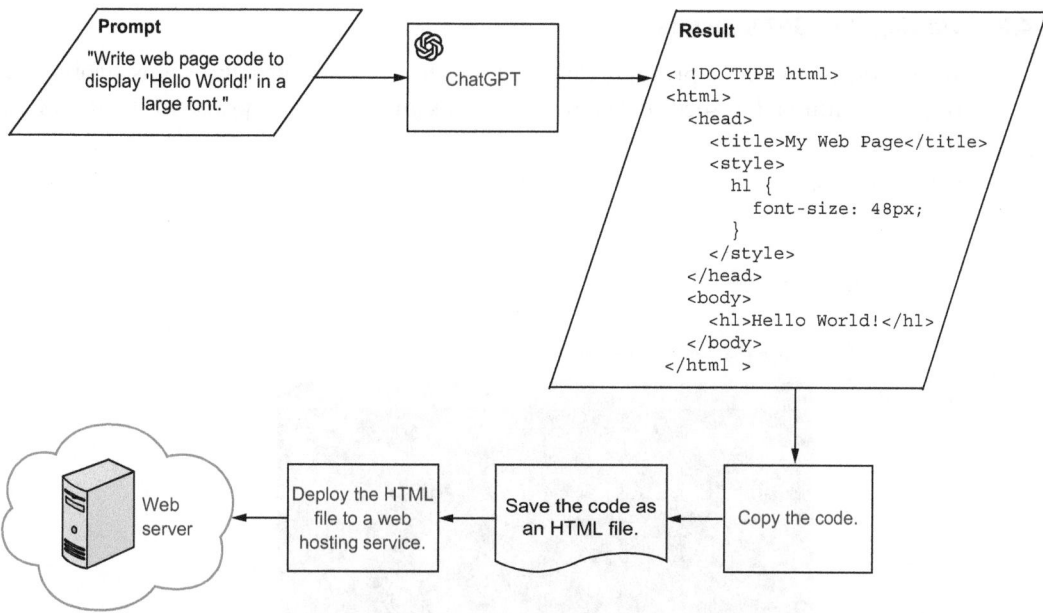

Figure 1.4　A simplified diagram of the process you use to get ChatGPT to help you create a web page

1.4.1 Prompting ChatGPT

The process always begins with a request that specifies what you want ChatGPT to create for you. This request is called a *prompt*. When you log in to the ChatGPT app (refer to figure 1.1) or navigate to Bing Copilot (refer to figure 1.2), you see a text box where you type your prompt.

Prompts can be as simple as a single sentence (as demonstrated in figure 1.3) or as complex as multiple paragraphs. However, the sky is definitely not the limit here because most versions of ChatGPT will accept only up to 4,000 characters per prompt. That's a good 500 words or so, which ought to be more than enough for most of your web creation prompts.

It's no exaggeration to say that prompting ChatGPT is the most important step because the quality of your prompt directly determines the quality of the result returned by ChatGPT. In a sense, this entire book is about providing you with high-quality prompts that get ChatGPT to perform specific web page creation tasks. I also devote quite a few pages in appendix C to explaining some best practices associated with prompting ChatGPT (a process called *prompt engineering* by the cognoscenti).

> **WARNING**   Although it's generally true that ChatGPT is a quality-in, quality-out model, it is, like all large language models, prone to occasionally producing unusable or downright weird results even when the prompt is a good one. I talk about some ways to troubleshoot such problems in appendix A.

1.4.2   Viewing ChatGPT's results

When you submit your prompt, ChatGPT sets to work and usually begins "typing" its response within a few seconds. Figure 1.5 shows an example response to the following prompt:

```
Write web page code to display "Hello World!" in a large font.
```

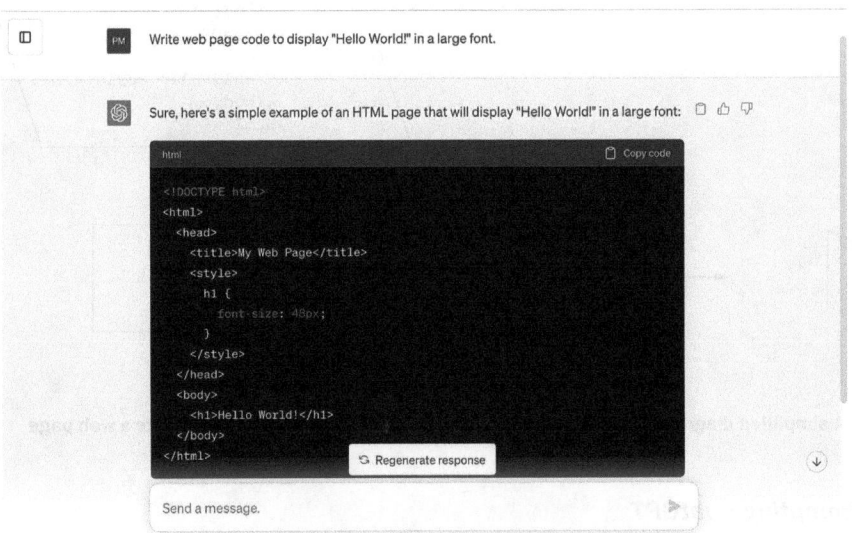

Figure 1.5   In this example, ChatGPT's response to the prompt includes the requested code.

As shown in figure 1.5, the result in this case consists of a friendly response to your prompt followed by a box titled `html` that includes the web page code that was requested. This code will no doubt seem like near-gibberish to you, but trust me when I tell you that it does exactly what the prompt asked for: it displays the message `Hello World!` in a large (in this case, 48-point) font. Note that, for various technical reasons, ChatGPT may not return the same code each time you run the prompt. However, because there are often several ways to achieve the same result with HTML and CSS, the generated code will still produce a web page that looks the same (or at least very similar).

1.4.3 Getting the code into a file

The example prompt I used in the previous section is a simple one, for sure, but it's still more than a little awesome that within a few seconds of submitting this prompt, ChatGPT generated some workable web page code that satisfied the request. As you work on your web page projects with ChatGPT at your side, as it were, that sense of amazement will come up again and again as the model quickly and seemingly effortlessly generates the code you asked for.

However, the web page code produced by ChatGPT, no matter how accurate it is or how suitable to your needs, doesn't do anything. That's because, on its own, web page code is inert; it's just a collection of words and odd-looking symbols. For web page code to come alive, it must be displayed in a web browser; and before you can do that, you must get the code into a file that a browser can access.

Appendix A dives into the ins and outs of web page files in just the right amount of detail. Figure 1.6 shows the code generated by ChatGPT (refer to figure 1.5) pasted into an HTML file, which has been saved as index.html. At this point, you could load the saved HTML file into your favorite web browser (see chapter 2 for the details), but a true web project requires one more step: deploying the code to the web itself.

Figure 1.6 The code copied from ChatGPT and saved to an HTML file

1.4.4 *Deploying the HTML file*

The only way other people can view your pages is for you to put them on the web. For the relatively simple projects you create in this book, this deployment process involves copying the file or files that ChatGPT helped you create to a service that hosts web pages. I go into this process in more detail in appendix B, but for the most part, it just means uploading the folder in which you've stored your web page files to the host. Figure 1.7 shows an example of the process where I've dragged the hello-world folder from the Finder window on the right and am about to drop it on the window on the left. With your web page files uploaded, you can view them right away in your favorite web browser, as shown in figure 1.8.

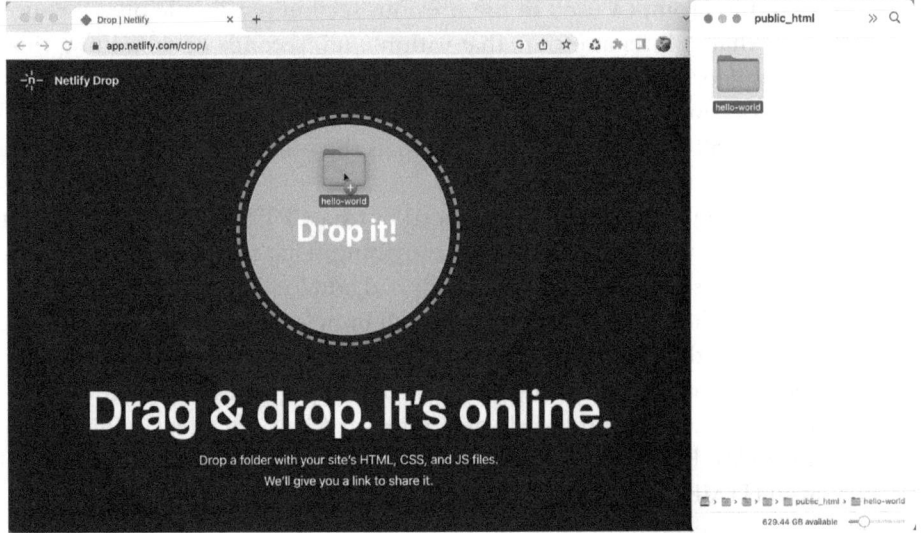

Figure 1.7   With some services, such as Netlify shown here, deploying is a simple drag-and-drop affair.

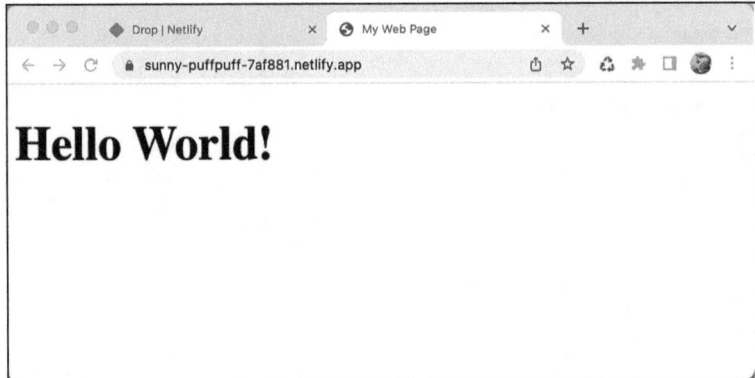

Figure 1.8   The web page created by ChatGPT is on the web.

The previous few sections took you through a prompt-copy-save-deploy process that has, I think you'll agree, a satisfying—and more than a little surprising—straightforwardness to it. However, not all of your projects will be this uncomplicated, particularly as you venture into creating web pages that go well beyond saying "Hello World!" For these more ambitious projects, you'll most often use two extra techniques: repeating the prompt-copy-save-deploy process to create multiple pages and page components; and refining and revising your ChatGPT prompts.

1.4.5 Repeating as needed

A single prompt that creates a single web page will be relatively rare in your web page creation career. It's far more likely that you'll have to perform the prompt-copy-save-deploy cycle multiple times before you end up with all the content you need. There are two scenarios to consider:

- *Creating multiple pages*—Lots of websites consist of a single page, but the far more common case is a website that consists of multiple pages. Even a modest website may consist of a home page, an About page (that describes you or your site), a Contact page (that lists the various ways site visitors can get in touch with you), and separate pages for content such as essays, photos, and portfolios. For such a website, you'll need to repeat the prompt-copy-save-deploy cycle for each page.
- *Creating multiple components for a single page*—Most modern web pages consist of multiple components, such as a header, a navigation bar or menu, a content area, a sidebar, and a footer. It's possible to include all the components you need in a single prompt, but you'll get more satisfying results if you use a separate prompt for each component. In this case, the process becomes one where you repeat the prompt-copy-save part of the cycle for each component, and the copied code gets inserted into the same HTML file. You then deploy the code only after you've added all your page components.

If all this seems a bit abstract or confusing now, don't worry: the rest of this book is all about getting you comfortable with the specifics of creating multiple pages and page components.

1.4.6 Refining and revising your prompts

The ChatGPT-assisted page creation process depicted earlier in figure 1.3 works for uncomplicated web pages and for those times when ChatGPT nails your request. But as your web pages—and your prompts—grow more complex, you'll almost certainly find yourself adding a few more steps to the process. I've included these extra steps in the shaded area of the process diagram shown in figure 1.9.

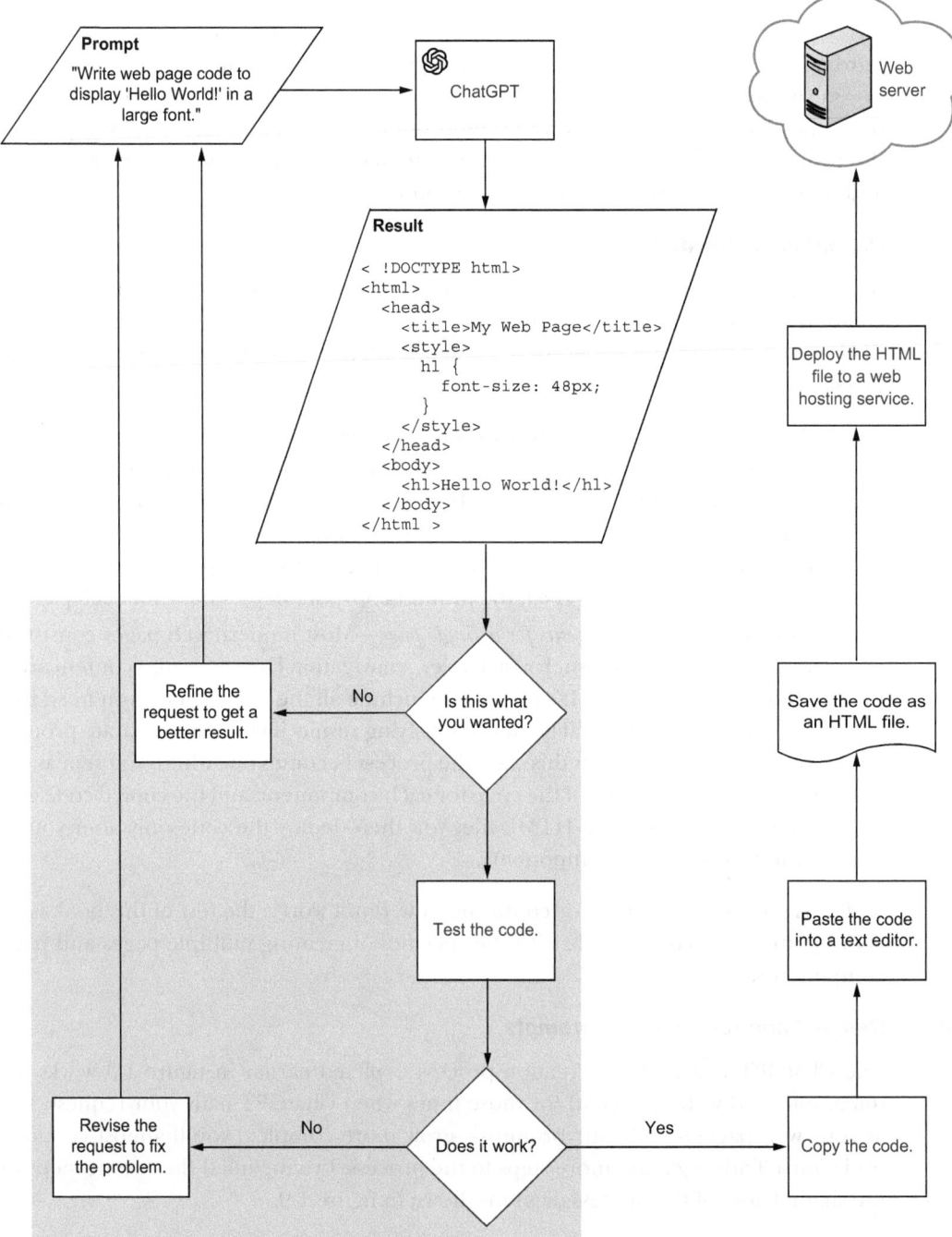

Figure 1.9   Refining and revising your web page prompts

At first glance, this likely appears to be a much more complex process, but really, there are just two extra paths this new process can take. These two paths come in the form of questions:

- *Is this what you wanted?* You ask this question immediately after ChatGPT generates the code you requested in your prompt. Basically, you're examining the code (as best you can, anyway) to make sure it does the job for you. If the answer is "Yes," you move on to the next question; if the answer is "No," you refine the prompt in some way (for example, by making it more specific) and try again.
- *Does it work?* This question requires that you test the code by copying it and then pasting it into an online site designed for testing web page code, as I describe in appendix A. If the code checks out, you can proceed with saving it to an HTML file. If the code is wrong somehow, you need to fix the error by revising your prompt in some way and then resubmitting it; again, appendix A is the place to go for some troubleshooting suggestions.

Sure, it would be great if ChatGPT generated awesome code every time. And it's great that each new release of ChatGPT gets better not only at producing accurate code but also at creating code that matches even vague or general prompts. But although ChatGPT may someday routinely crank out perfect web page code every time, it's not there yet, so you'll need to refine and revise your prompts to get the pages you want.

Summary

- GPT stands for *generative* (it's designed to generate text), *pretrained* (it was exposed to large amounts of text to learn language patterns and structures), *transformer* (it analyzes requests to give higher priority to the most important components).
- ChatGPT is an app that enables conversational access to GPT via the OpenAI app at https://chat.openai.com, via Bing Copilot at https://bing.com (select the Copilot tab), or via Microsoft Copilot at https://copilot.microsoft.com.
- GPT has been trained on massive amounts of programming code, including the code used to build web pages: HTML, CSS, and JavaScript. This training enables ChatGPT to generate web page code from plain-English instructions.
- ChatGPT is best used to create static web pages that don't require or rely on data stored on a web server.
- ChatGPT helps you create web pages using a basic prompt-copy-save-deploy cycle, where the *prompt* is the instruction that tells ChatGPT what type of page you want, *copy* means to copy the code generated by ChatGPT and paste it into a file, *save* means to save the code as an HTML file, and *deploy* means to upload the HTML file to a web hosting provider.
- For best results, you'll usually have to refine your prompts to get the structure and content of your page just right, and you'll usually have to revise your prompts to fix page problems.

Creating and deploying your first web page

2

2

This chapter covers

- Understanding the process of creating and deploying a web page
- Using a ChatGPT prompt to generate a complete web page
- Copying the generated web page code
- Saving the code to an HTML file
- Getting your web page file on the web

It may still seem too good to be true that you can get ChatGPT to help you create a fully functional website without having to learn any web development code. If you remain skeptical, I hear you: even knowing a bit about how ChatGPT does its thing, there's still an undeniable whiff of magic about the whole enterprise. After all, it's not like you're asking ChatGPT to tell you a knock-knock joke or write a haiku extolling the nutritional value of the rutabaga. No, we're talking about all the code necessary to build a web page that actually does something semi-useful. That's a complex ask by any criteria, so whatever remaining skepticism you have is totally warranted.

In this chapter, my aim is to show you that it's possible to create a web page with ChatGPT's help. I'm not going to do this by exploring more ChatGPT theory. No, there's been enough of that. Instead, I'll take you through a complete example where I cajole ChatGPT into creating the code for a functional web page that, by the end of the chapter, will have its own home on the web. To get this done in a single chapter, the web page will out of necessity be extremely simple, but it will work, and it will even provide a bit of fun (depending, as you'll see, on your taste for puns).

2.1   *Understanding the process*

To create this chapter's functioning web page, I'm going to use the prompt-copy-save-deploy cycle that I introduced in chapter 1 (refer to figure 2.1):

1 Prompt ChatGPT to generate the web page code.
2 Copy the resulting code.
3 Paste the code into a text editor, and then save the code as an HTML file.
4 Deploy the HTML file to a web host.

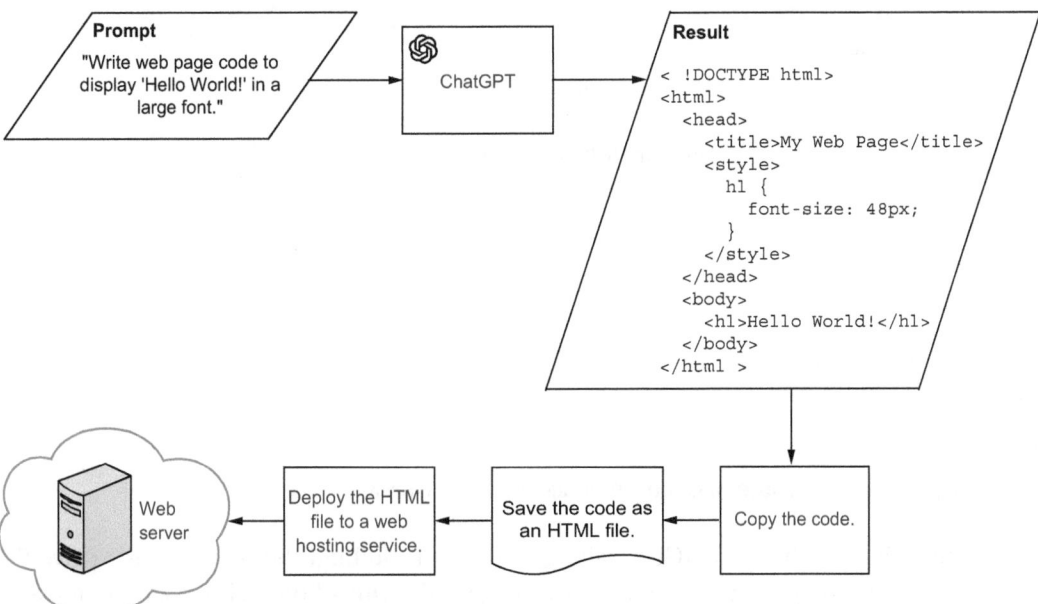

Figure 2.1   The prompt-copy-save-deploy cycle that you'll be using in this chapter

The sections in the rest of this chapter expand on each of these steps.

2.2   *Prompting ChatGPT to generate your web page code*

To get started, you first need to get ChatGPT onscreen. You have the following choices:

- If you don't have an OpenAI account, go to https://chat.openai.com to use GPT-3.5 as the model.
- If you have an OpenAI account but don't have a ChatGPT Plus subscription, go to https://chat.openai.com to use GPT-3.5 as the model.
- If you have a ChatGPT Plus subscription, go to https://chat.openai.com and then click the GPT-4 button.
- If you prefer to use Bing Copilot, go to https://bing.com, click Copilot, and then click the Precise conversation style.
- If you have a Microsoft account, go to https://copilot.microsoft.com and click the Precise conversation style.

For my own prompting, I used the ChatGPT app with GPT-4 as the model, as shown in figure 2.2.

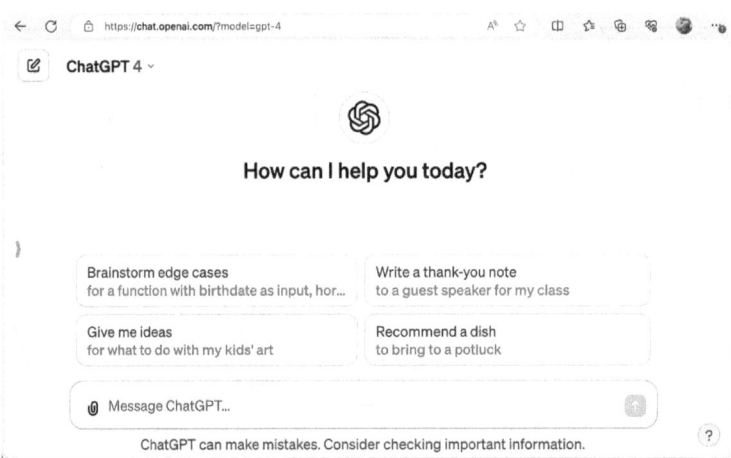

Figure 2.2   The ChatGPT app with GPT-4 selected as the language model

Now that you have ChatGPT waiting to do your bidding, the next step is to give the model a prompt to generate some web page code. One of the points I want to make in this chapter is that it's possible to get ChatGPT to output the code for a functional web page with a single prompt. To get there, we have to greatly simplify things, so this can't be a complicated, multifunction page with a ton of bells and whistles.

However, it doesn't have to be a bottom-of-the-barrel "Hello World!" page, either. In general, if you have an idea for a simple page, just ask ChatGPT to generate the code for the page and include a description of what you want. That description will vary depending on the idea, but you may want to include some or all of the following:

- *Goal*—What you want ChatGPT to generate (in this case, a web page)
- *Data*—The data you want ChatGPT to use, if any
- *Action*—What you want the web page to do, generally or with the data you specified
- *Interface*—How you want the user to initiate the action or otherwise interface with the page

Here's the prompt for the page I want (refer to figure 2.3):

```
Create web page code that stores 50 puns and displays a random pun each time
the user clicks a button.
```

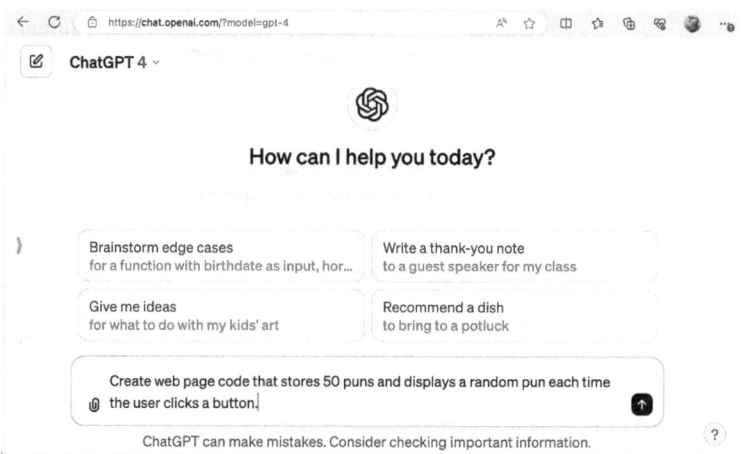

Figure 2.3   The ChatGPT app with my prompt ready to send

Here's how this prompt fits into the goal-data-action-interface schema:

- `Create web page code`—This part of the prompt tells ChatGPT to generate the code for an entire web page.
- `that stores 50 puns`—Tells ChatGPT to create 50 puns to use as the page data.
- `and displays a random pun`—Tells ChatGPT to select a pun randomly from the data.
- `each time the user clicks a button`—Tells ChatGPT to provide a button that, when clicked, displays another random pun.

Enter the prompt into the ChatGPT text box, click the Send Message icon, and wait for the result.

2.2.1   Examining the result

The following code shows the first response I received from ChatGPT (the code that ChatGPT generates for you may be different):

```
<!DOCTYPE html>
<html>
<head>
    <title>Pun Generator</title>                    ◄──── Page title

    <style>
        body {
            font-family: Arial, sans-serif;         Applies the Arial typeface
        }                                            to the page
        #displayPun {
            font-size: 24px;                         Displays each pun in a 24-pixel
            margin-top: 20px;                        font with a 20-pixel margin on top
        }
    </style>
</head>
<body>                                               Button the user
    <h1>Welcome to Pun Generator!</h1>    ◄──── Page's main heading   clicks to get a
                                                   new random pun
    <button id="generatePun">Generate Pun</button>  ◄──────

    <p id="displayPun"></p>    ◄──────  Section of the page where
                                        each random pun appears
    <script>
        var puns = [
            "Time flies like an arrow; fruit flies like a banana.",
            "I used to be a baker because I kneaded dough.",     (Partial) page
            "I used to play piano by ear, but now I use my hands.",  data, which is a
            // Add the rest of the 50 puns here...              collection of puns
        ];

        document.getElementById("generatePun").
addEventListener("click", function() {
            var randomPunIndex = Math.floor(Math.random() * puns.length);
            document.getElementById("displayPun").innerText = puns[randomPunIndex];
        });
    </script>                                        JavaScript code that extracts
</body>                                              a random pun from the data
</html>
```

There are three things to note here:

- Even though this is a simple page, the code itself is fairly complex, so don't worry if it all seems like a foreign language to you. You don't need to know how this code works, just that it does (taking into account my third point in this list).
- Remember that ChatGPT is nondeterministic, which means it won't generate the same code every time, even when you use the same prompt. Therefore, if you run my prompt in ChatGPT, there's a good chance you'll end up with code that's different than what you see in listing 2.1.
- Instead of creating 50 puns, ChatGPT created just three puns and then passed the buck:

```
// Add the rest of the 50 puns here...
```

This doesn't happen every time, but you should know that this is very common ChatGPT behavior. Fortunately, it doesn't mean you're stuck. I got ChatGPT to complete its mission with a simple prompt:

```
Can you fill in the rest of the puns for me?
```

ChatGPT regenerated the code with the complete set of puns (although I did have to click the Continue Generating button—check out figure 2.4—once when ChatGPT got stuck). That's a fair amount of data to generate, so it took a couple of minutes for the full code to appear.

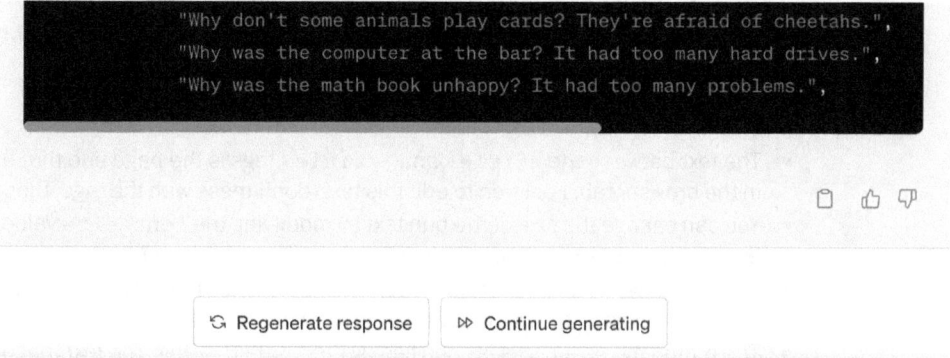

```
"Why don't some animals play cards? They're afraid of cheetahs.",
"Why was the computer at the bar? It had too many hard drives.",
"Why was the math book unhappy? It had too many problems.",
```

↻ Regenerate response   ⏩ Continue generating

Figure 2.4   If ChatGPT gets stuck, you may have to click Continue Generating to get it unstuck.

Understanding and customizing the code (optional)

If you want to understand and/or customize the code generated by ChatGPT (this is entirely optional), here are some notes:

- HTML consists of a collection of items called *tags* for specifying page objects such as paragraphs, headings, bulleted lists, and links. Most HTML tags are alphabetic codes surrounded by angle brackets (< and >). For example, you designate the start of a paragraph with the `<p>` tag and the end of the paragraph with the `</p>` tag. As another example, the ChatGPT-generated HTML code from the previous section included the following line:

  ```
  <h1>Welcome to Pun Generator!</h1>
  ```

  The `<h1>` and `</h1>` tags mark up a first-level heading (refer to chapter 3 to learn more about headings), so in this case, the text `Welcome to Pun Generator!` appears on the page as such a heading.

- CSS consists of a collection of items called *properties* for specifying the styling applied to page objects. For example, the `font-size` property determines the size of the text for a specified object, so to set the size to `24px` (24 pixels), you use the following CSS declaration:

  ```
  font-size: 24px;
  ```

(continued)

Note the colon (:) after the property name and the semicolon (;) at the end. CSS declarations are grouped into *rules*, which consist of the object to which the declarations are applied and with those declarations surrounded by braces ({ and }), as in this example from the ChatGPT-generated code shown earlier:

```
#displayPun {
    font-size: 24px;
    margin-top: 20px;
}
```

In this example, #displayPun is a reference to the following element in the HTML code:

```
<p id="displayPun"></p>
```

- The text between the <title> and </title> tags is the page title that appears in the browser tab. Feel free to edit this text (don't mess with the tags, though).
- You can change the size of the pun text by modifying the font-size value. Whatever value you use, just be sure to follow it with px (for pixels).
- The text between the <h1> and </h1> tags is the main page heading. You can edit this text (but don't touch the tags).
- The button the user clicks is specified by the <button> tag. The text that appears between that tag and the </button> tag is what appears on the button. You can edit this text if you feel like it.
- ChatGPT stores the page data in a special data object called an *array*. In this case, each item in the array is text (specifically, a pun) surrounded by double quotation marks (" ") and followed by a comma. You can edit, add, or delete array items as needed; just make sure that when you're done, each array item is surrounded by double quotation marks and followed by a comma. Also, don't delete the square brackets ([and]) that start and end the array.

Before moving on to the next step, I'm going to take a moment to give you a few other prompt suggestions for a simple one-page website.

2.2.2 *Checking out a few other prompts for single-page websites*

If you're following along and want to create your own single-page website with ChatGPT's help, you can use my prompt from the previous section, or you can use your own prompt if you have an idea you've always wanted to try. If you're not sure what to do, here are a few suggestions:

> **WARNING** ChatGPT has a kind of "memory" for what you prompted and for what it generated earlier in the same chat session. Before trying any of the following prompts, be sure to start a new chat so that ChatGPT's results aren't tainted by anything from earlier in the session.

- "Create web page code that displays a list of ten X things to do in Y" (where X is an adjective, such as *fun* or *interesting,* and Y is the name of a city or neighborhood). Example:

```
Create web page code that displays a list of ten entertaining things to
do in Miami's South Beach area.
```

- "Generate the code for a web page that provides a recipe for making X" (where X is a dinner, dessert, or other type of dish that can be cooked from scratch). Example:

```
Generate the code for a web page that provides a recipe for making
panna cotta.
```

- "Provide web page code that lists the steps required to X" (where X is a project, repair job, maintenance chore, or other task). Example:

```
Provide web page code that lists the steps required to replace a
bathroom faucet.
```

- "Create web page code that explains how X works" (where X is a machine, gadget, scientific principle, or, really, just about anything). Example:

```
Create web page code that explains how a hologram works.
```

- "Generate the code for a web page that stores X and displays a random Y when the user clicks a button" (where X is some data, and Y is the data combined in some way). Example:

```
Generate the code for a web page that stores a dozen each of the
following: names, verbs, colors, adjectives, and nouns. When the user
clicks a button, the code should assemble and display a random sentence
that uses the template "Name verb the color, adjective noun."
```

- "Provide web page code that displays X in a list and stores a Y associated with each X. When the user chooses X from the list, the page displays the associated Y" (where X could be a word, person, or object and Y could be a poem, biography, or description).

```
Provide web page code that displays six rarely used adjectives in a
dropdown list and stores a limerick associated with each adjective.
When the user chooses an adjective from the list, the page displays the
associated limerick.
```

Feel free to use the example prompts as is or by customizing them to suit the page you want.

2.3   *Copying ChatGPT's web page code*

Once ChatGPT has finished generating your code, your next step is to copy the code. How you copy the generated code depends on whether you're using the ChatGPT app, Bing Copilot, or the Copilot sidebar in Microsoft Edge. Each interface offers a Copy

Code feature in the form of an icon or button. For the complete details of how to copy code in each interface, see appendix A. If, like me, you're using the ChatGPT app, the code appears in a separate HTML code window that has a Copy Code button in the upper-right corner, as shown in figure 2.5.

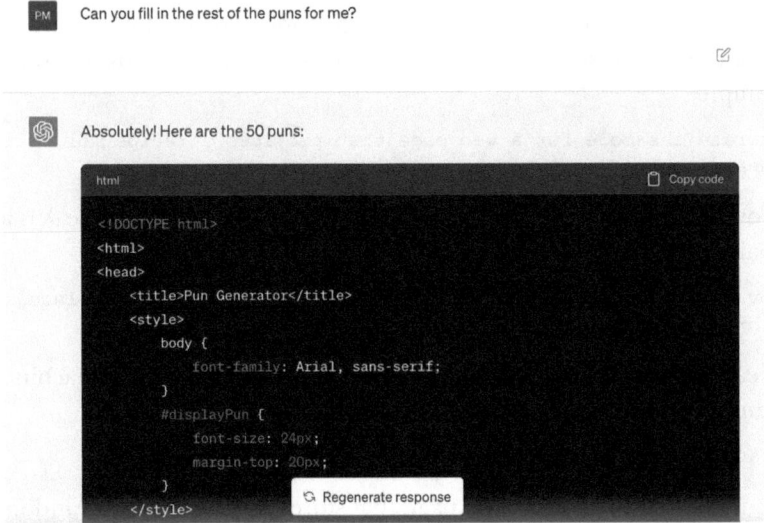

Figure 2.5   To copy generated code in the ChatGPT app, click Copy Code in the upper-right corner of the code window.

The copied code now resides in your computer's Clipboard, which is a special memory area that stores the most recently copied data. To avoid having the copied code overwritten in the Clipboard, be sure to move on to the next step before doing anything else on your computer (especially copying or cutting any other data).

2.3.1   Saving the web page code to an HTML file

Now that you've copied the ChatGPT-generated web page code, your next order of business is to paste the copied code into a text file and then save that document as an HTML file. Before getting started, use File Explorer (Windows) or Finder (macOS) to create a subfolder to store all your web projects. For example, you may want to create a folder named sites or public_html in your user account's Documents folder.

With that done, here are the steps to follow to save the copied ChatGPT code to an HTML file:

1 Open your text editor.
2 Start a new text file. In most text editors, you choose File > New (or, depending on the app, you may have to choose a different command, such as New File, New

Text File, or New Document). You can also usually press either Ctrl-N (in Windows) or Cmd-N (macOS).

3 Choose Edit > Paste to paste the copied code into the new text file. You can also press either Ctrl-V (in Windows) or Cmd-V (macOS).

4 Choose File > Save. You can also press either Ctrl-S (in Windows) or Cmd-S (macOS). The app displays the Save As dialog.

5 Navigate to the folder you created earlier (the one named sites or public_html or whatever) to store your web projects.

6 Click the New Folder button, and then enter a name for the folder. You're going to upload this folder to the web in the next section, so the name you use should consist of just lowercase letters, numbers, dashes (-), and/or underscores (_). No spaces allowed.

7 For the filename, type `index.html`.

8 Click Save. The app saves your HTML file. Figure 2.6 shows my Pun Generator code saved as an HTML file.

```
index.html
paul / Documents / public_html / pun-generator / index.html / (no symbol)
1    <!DOCTYPE html>
2    <html>
3    <head>
4        <title>Pun Generator</title>
5        <style>
6            body {
7                font-family: Arial, sans-serif;
8            }
9            #displayPun {
10               font-size: 24px;
11               margin-top: 20px;
12           }
13       </style>
14   </head>
15   <body>
16       <h1>Welcome to Pun Generator!</h1>
17
18       <button id="generatePun">Generate Pun</button>
19
20       <p id="displayPun"></p>
21
22       <script>
23           var puns = [
24               "Time flies like an arrow; fruit flies like a banana.",
25               "I used to be a baker because I kneaded dough.",
26               "I used to play piano by ear, but now I use my hands.",
27               "I'm reading a book about anti-gravity. It's impossible to put down!
```

Figure 2.6 The ChatGPT-generated code saved as an HTML file

Near the top of figure 2.6, note that my text editor displays the path of the HTML file:

```
paul/Documents/public_html/pun-generator/index.html
```

This path means that in my user account's Documents folder, I created a subfolder named public_html to hold all my websites. Using the previous steps, I first navigated to public_html, created the new pun-generator subfolder, and then saved the code as index.html in that new folder.

You're now ready to give your page a test drive in a web browser.

2.4 Testing your web page in the browser

With your web page code saved to a file on your computer, it's always a good idea to give the page a quick check before deploying it. The easiest way to test a web page is to open the HTML file in your favorite web browser. Here are the steps to follow:

1 In your web browser, display the Open dialog:
    – Windows web browser: Press Ctrl-O.
    – Mac web browser: Choose File > Open File or press Cmd-O.
2 In the Open dialog, navigate to the folder where you stored your HTML file in the previous section.
3 Select the HTML file.
4 Click Open.

The web browser opens the HTML file and displays the web page according to the HTML tags and CSS properties.

Opening the web page from your computer is great for taking the page for a test spin, but if you want to see your page on the web, you need to deploy it.

2.5 Deploying your web page

Deploying your page means uploading the HTML file to your web host. How you go about this depends on the host, so check out the host's support pages for the specific procedure. Here are the general steps that you follow on most web hosts:

1 Sign into your web hosting provider.
2 Navigate to the page where you upload your web page files.
3 Upload the subfolder you created in the previous section, including that folder's `index.html` file.

For this example, I'm going to deploy my Pun Generator to Cloudflare by following these steps (although refer to appendix B for more specific instructions):

4 In the Cloudflare dashboard's navigation sidebar, under Workers & Pages, click Overview.
5 Click the Create Application button, shown in figure 2.7. (If this is your first Cloudflare deployment, you won't have the Create Application button onscreen. In that case, skip this step.)

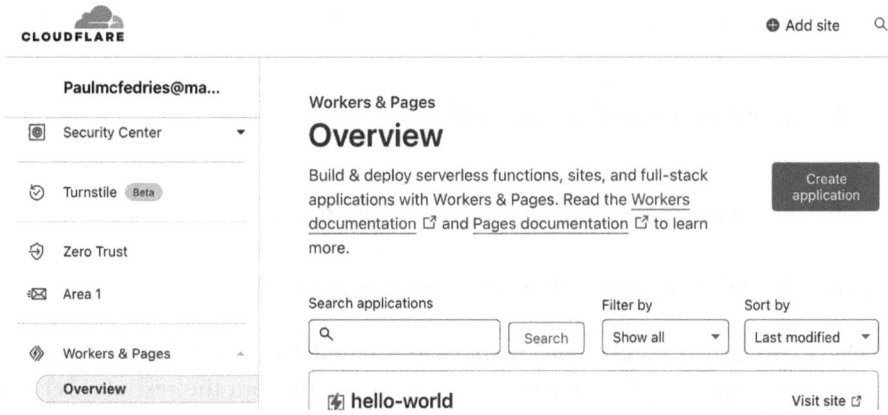

Figure 2.7   On the Overview page, click Create Application.

6   Click the Pages tab.

7   Scroll down to the Create Using Direct Upload section, and then click Upload Assets.

8   Type a name for your project, and then click Create Project, as shown in figure 2.8.

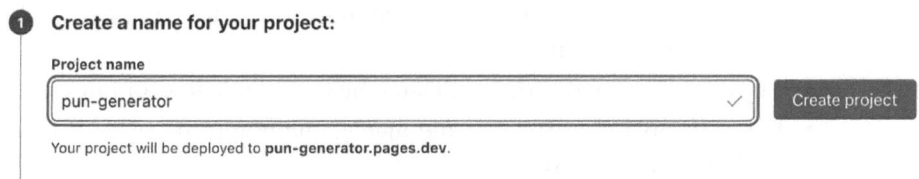

Figure 2.8   Type a project name, and then click Create Project.

9   Upload your site folder by using one of the following methods:
   a   Drag your website folder, and drop it in the upload area.
   b   Click Select from Computer, and then click Upload Folder. In the dialog that appears, navigate to the project folder, and then click Upload.

10 If your web browser asks you to confirm the operation, click Upload.

11 Click Deploy Site.

12 Click the link to view the deployed site in the web browser. Figure 2.9 shows my Pun Generator deployed to https://pun-generator.pages.dev.

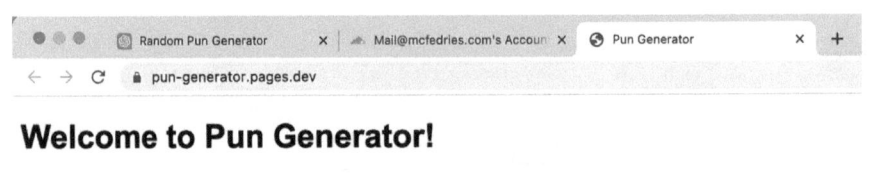

Welcome to Pun Generator!

Generate Pun

What do you call cheese that isn't yours? Nacho Cheese.

Figure 2.9   The Pun Generator website deployed to Cloudflare Pages.

There you have it: a web page created with ChatGPT's help and deployed to the web in just a few steps. Yes, the page you created was simple, but the rest of this book is dedicated to showing you how to get ChatGPT to help you build much more sophisticated and useful websites.

Summary

- The basic process for getting ChatGPT's help to build a web page is the prompt-copy-save-deploy cycle.
- When prompting ChatGPT, include a goal, what data you need, the action you want the page to perform, and the interface with which the user initiates the action.
- If ChatGPT doesn't give you everything you ask for, run a second prompt to request the missing information.
- Copy the generated code by clicking the Copy Code icon or button.
- Use your operating system's file management app to create a folder in which you'll store all your web projects.
- In your text editor, paste the copied code into a new text file, and then save that file as index.html in a new subfolder created for the project.
- Deploy the website by uploading the project data to your web hosting provider.

Working with fonts, colors, and headings

In chapter 2, I took you through the process of creating a functioning web page from scratch using a relatively simple ChatGPT prompt. The resulting page worked well, but it wasn't much to look at. That plain page was fine because I wanted to keep things simple, but if you're going to build some kind of presence on the web, you'll definitely want the resulting page to look good.

In this chapter, you take the first step in that direction by examining several page formatting options that can go a long way toward making any web page more attractive and more readable. These options include typefaces, type sizes, colors, and headings. Here, you'll learn why these are important and how you can get ChatGPT to help you make these design choices for your page. All this information then goes into a detailed prompt that you'll pass along to ChatGPT to produce the web page code for a personal home page that gives you a slice of the web that you can call your own. If you're curious, this chapter also explains the code generated by ChatGPT and shows you a few ways to customize the code without having to prompt ChatGPT all over again.

3.1   *Taking a peek at this chapter's project*

The project you're going to ask ChatGPT to help you with in this chapter is a simple personal home page that consists of some or all of the following components:

- A title (which could be just your name)
- A subtitle (a tagline that sums up the page—or you—for readers)
- A brief biography
- A brief description of what you do for a living
- A list of your hobbies and interests
- A list of your favorite books, movies, TV shows, bands, and so on

Figure 3.1 shows an example of the type of page you'll be creating with the help of ChatGPT.

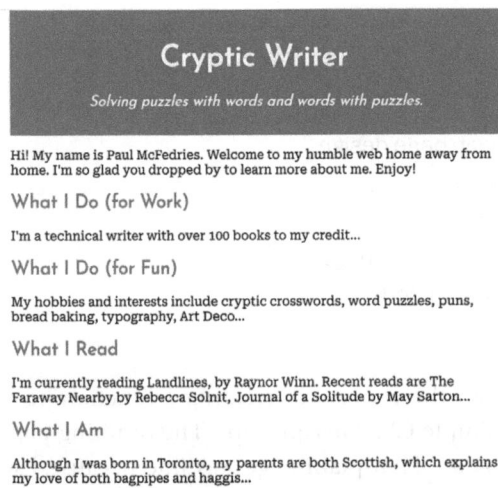

Figure 3.1   A personal home page generated by ChatGPT

It's your page, of course, so feel free to add anything else that you want the world to know about you. You can also modify this page slightly to turn it into an online résumé or curriculum vitae.

Before getting to the specifics of prompting ChatGPT to generate the code for your personal home page, you can use the model to generate some design suggestions, including the site title and subtitle, typefaces, and color scheme. You'll use these suggestions later when building your prompt.

3.2   Building the personal home page

To help you use ChatGPT to build your personal home page, the next few sections take you through each component of the page, from the title to the type to the colors. In each case, I give you some background, show you the relevant HTML and/or CSS, if any, and then show you how to ask ChatGPT to generate what you need.

3.2.1   Getting site title and subtitle suggestions

The most obvious title for your personal home page is your name. If that's not creative enough for you, put ChatGPT to work to suggest not only a site title but also a subtitle or tagline to appear below the title.

One useful way to prompt ChatGPT for a title and subtitle is to combine what you do for a living with one or more hobbies or interests and see what ChatGPT can come up with. Here's a generic prompt you can use:

```
You are a wordsmith that can generate catchy and creative titles and taglines
for personal home pages. You use the information provided by the user to come
up with suggestions that reflect their skills and interests.

I am X and my favorite hobby is Y.

First, think of some words or phrases that relate to X and Y.

Second, try to combine or play with these words or phrases to create catchy
or witty titles.

Third, add a tagline that explains or expands on the title.
```

In this prompt, replace *X* with your job title or description and replace *Y* with one or more interests or hobbies. Figure 3.2 shows my results (generated using Bing Copilot in Creative mode). If you find a title and subtitle you like (they don't have to come from the same suggestion), copy them somewhere so you can use them later when you prompt ChatGPT to create the code for your homepage.

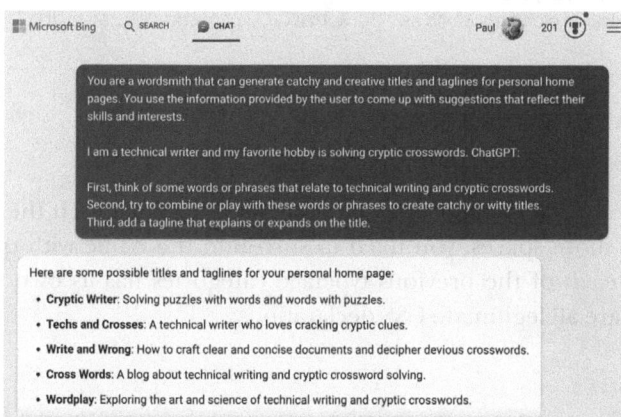

Figure 3.2   Prompting ChatGPT for a page title and tagline

The web page font is the styling of the page text. This is a huge topic, but for our purposes here, you can consider just three components: the typeface, the type size, and the type style.

3.2.2   *Styling the typeface*

The *typeface* is a distinctive design that's common to any related set of letters, numbers, and symbols. Wait a minute, I hear you say, isn't that a *font*? What's the difference? For all practical purposes, the two terms are interchangeable. Technically, though, a font is a particular implementation of a typeface, meaning the typeface is rendered with a specific size and style. Arial is a typeface; Arial 16-point bold is a font.

Here are the five typeface categories you'll come across most often:

Serif —A *serif* (rhymes with *sheriff*) typeface contains fine cross strokes (called *feet*) at the extremities of each character. These subtle appendages give the typeface a traditional, classy look, but they can get lost when displayed on a screen at small sizes.	ChatGPT: Magic or just math?
Sans serif —A *sans-serif* typeface doesn't contain cross strokes on the extremities of characters. These typefaces usually have a clean, modern look that's well suited to screen text, particularly at small sizes.	ChatGPT: Magic or just math?
Monospace —A *monospace* typeface (also called a *fixed-width* typeface) uses the same amount of space for each character, so skinny letters such as *i* and *I* take up as much space as wider letters such as *m* and *w*.	ChatGPT: Magic or just math?
Cursive —The *cursive* typefaces are designed to resemble handwritten pen or brush writing.	ChatGPT: Magic or just math?
Fantasy —*Fantasy* typefaces usually are fanciful designs that have some extreme elements (such as being extra-thick).	ChatGPT: Magic or just math?

In CSS code, the typeface is specified using the `font-family` property:

```
font-family: typeface;
```

You replace the `typeface` placeholder with the name of the typeface. (If the typeface name includes one or more spaces, you need to surround the name with quotation marks.) For example, each of the previous typeface categories has its own CSS keyword, so the following are all legitimate CSS declarations:

```
font-family: serif;
font-family: sans-serif;
font-family: monospace;
font-family: cursive;
font-family: fantasy;
```

These five keywords—serif, sans-serif, monospace, cursive, and fantasy—represent the so-called *generic* typefaces, which are available in every web browser. If you want to use one of these generic typefaces for a component of your web page, you can include the appropriate typeface keyword as part of your instruction to ChatGPT:

```
Style the web page tagline with the generic cursive typeface.
```

Note, too, that it's also possible to specify multiple typefaces in a single declaration, and the web browser uses the first typeface (reading left to right) that's installed on the user's device. This is important to remember because ChatGPT will almost always specify multiple typefaces in its generated CSS. Here's an example from the web page code we examine later in this chapter:

```
font-family: 'Roboto Serif', serif;
```

This declaration means the web browser will first try to load the Roboto Serif typeface. If it can't, for some reason, it will fall back to using the generic serif typeface instead.

The next major type component you'll work with is the type size.

3.2.3 Setting the type size

The *type size* is the relative size of each character. Type sizes are usually measured in pixels (shortened to px), and the default text size of regular page text is 16 pixels (written 16px in web page code).

In CSS code, the type size is specified using the font-size property:

```
font-size: size;
```

Here, replace size with the type size you want. For example, many people find the default text size of 16 px a bit too small for comfortable reading, so it's common to specify a larger type size, such as 20 px:

```
font-size: 20px;
```

Figure 3.3 demonstrates a few common type sizes.

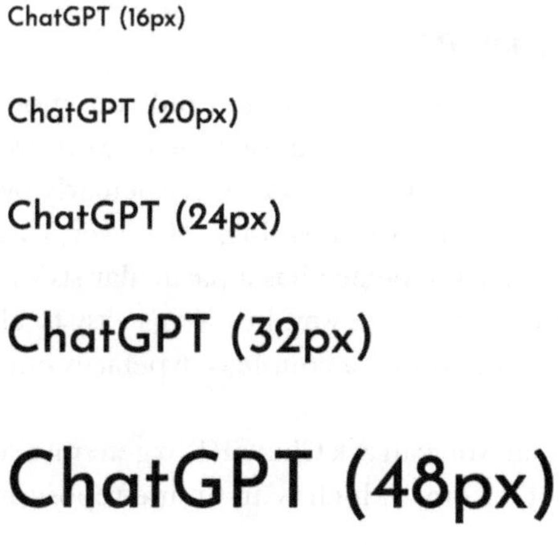

ChatGPT (16px)

ChatGPT (20px)

ChatGPT (24px)

ChatGPT (32px)

ChatGPT (48px)

Figure 3.3
Some common
type sizes

Here's an example instruction to ChatGPT to specify a type size for a page component:

```
Style the web page tagline with a font size of 24px.
```

3.2.4   Working with type styles

The *type style* is special styling applied to one or more characters or words. The two most common styles are **bold** and *italics*.

For bold text, CSS uses the `font-weight` property set to the `bold` keyword:

```
font-weight: bold;
```

Here's an example instruction to ChatGPT to make a page component bold:

```
Style the first paragraph with bold.
```

For italic, CSS uses the `font-style` property set to the `italic` keyword:

```
font-style: italic;
```

Here's an example instruction to ChatGPT to style a page component with italics:

```
Style the web page tagline with italics.
```

> **NOTE**   You can also mark up keywords, titles, and other special text with bold or italics using HTML tags. You learn how these tags work in chapter 12.

With just these three aspects of web typography—the typeface, the type size, and the type style—you can go a long way toward making your pages look great. When you're prompting ChatGPT, you can include separate instructions for the type to apply to a component, as just shown, or you can put everything in a single instruction, as in this example:

```
Style the web page tagline with the Arial typeface, 24px type size, and
italics.
```

If you're not sure what typeface to use in your project, ChatGPT can help, as I show in the next section.

3.2.5   Getting typeface suggestions from ChatGPT

The generic typefaces that I mentioned earlier are fine, but did you know there are hundreds of typefaces available? That's good news because it means your web projects can stand out from the crowd by using interesting typefaces, particularly by using different typefaces for the regular page text and the headings. However, you can't just choose two random typefaces. Because each typeface has a particular style, it's easy to choose two typefaces that are mismatched in some way, just as it's easy to choose mismatched colors. But how can you not only choose a couple of typefaces but also make sure those typefaces go well together?

ChatGPT is here to help. In particular, you can ask ChatGPT to generate suggestions from Google Fonts (https://fonts.google.com), which is an online repository of more than 1,500 free typefaces. Here's a generic prompt you can use to have ChatGPT suggest a couple of compatible typefaces (one for headings and one for text):

```
You are a font aficionado that can generate awesome font combinations for
personal home pages. Use the information provided by the user to come up with
suggestions that reflect the theme of the personal home page.

My personal home page is related to X.

First, using only fonts available at Google Fonts, suggest a Y font for the
page headings.

Second, using only fonts available at Google Fonts, suggest a compatible Z
font for the page text.

Third, please do not include Roboto or Open Sans in your suggestions. Be
creative and bold in your choices.
```

Replace *X* with a word or phrase related to your personal home page, and replace *Y* and *Z* with either `serif` or `sans serif`. Unfortunately, ChatGPT often suggests the Roboto and Open Sans typefaces. These are excellent and beautiful fonts, for sure, but if you want something more interesting, be sure to exclude those common fonts in your prompt, as I did.

In figure 3.4, you can see that ChatGPT suggested the Josefin Sans and Roboto Serif typefaces for my page (generated using Bing Copilot in Creative mode). These are great typefaces that should work well together.

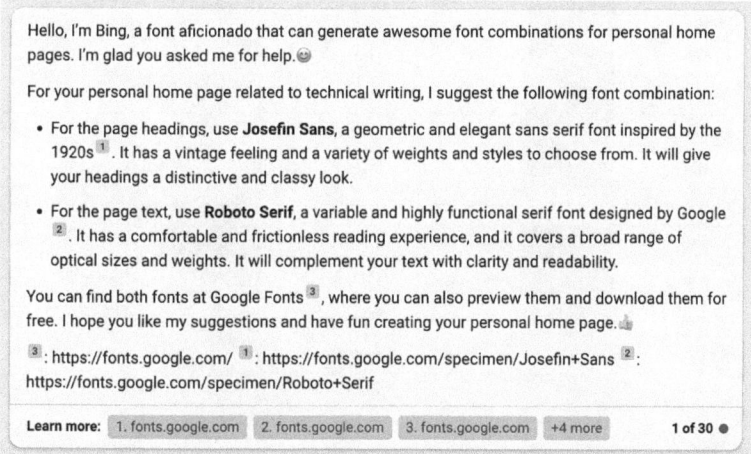

Figure 3.4   ChatGPT's typeface suggestions

If you're using Bing Copilot, the response may include some examples of the suggested typefaces. If not, follow the links to Google Fonts to examine the suggested typefaces to be sure you like what you see. If the suggested typefaces don't work for your design, ask ChatGPT to try again:

```
The suggested typefaces don't work for my personal home page design. Please
suggest two different typefaces.
```

Once you've got two typefaces you like, you don't need to do anything more than just write down or remember their names. You'll include the typeface names when you prompt ChatGPT to build your web page code.

3.2.6   *Generating a color scheme*

By default, web pages use black text on a white background. That color combination makes the text easy to read, but it's not going to win any design awards. You don't need to go crazy with color, but thinking outside the black-text-on-white box is an easy way to give your readers a bit of eye candy.

There are many ways to specify color on the web, but the easiest is to use one of the web's 140 predefined color names (or keywords). They run from aliceblue to yellow and include not only standard colors such as red, green, and blue but also decidedly nonstandard hues such as lemonchiffon, darkorchid, and wheat.

I've put the complete list of color keywords on my Web Design Playground site at wdpg.io/2/colorkeywords. Figure 3.5 shows a partial list.

Color	Keyword	RGB Value		Keyword	RGB Value		Keyword	RGB Value
	crimson	#dc143c		lightpink	#ffb6c1		pink	#ffc0cb
	hotpink	#ff69b4		lavenderblush	#fff0f5		palevioletred	#db7093
	orchid	#da70d6		deeppink	#ff1493		mediumvioletred	#c71585
	violet	#ee82ee		thistle	#d8bfd8		plum	#dda0dd
	darkmagenta	#8b008b		magenta	#ff00ff		fuchsia	#ff00ff
	mediumorchid	#ba55d3		purple	#800080		rebeccapurple	#663399
	indigo	#4b0082		darkviolet	#9400d3		darkorchid	#9932cc
	mediumslateblue	#7b68ee		blueviolet	#8a2be2		mediumpurple	#9370db
	lavender	#e6e6fa		slateblue	#6a5acd		darkslateblue	#483d8b
	mediumblue	#0000cd		ghostwhite	#f8f8ff		blue	#0000ff
	navy	#000080		midnightblue	#191970		darkblue	#00008b
	lightsteelblue	#b0c4de		royalblue	#4169e1		cornflowerblue	#6495ed
	dodgerblue	#1e90ff		lightslategray	#778899		slategray	#708090
	lightskyblue	#87cefa		aliceblue	#f0f8ff		steelblue	#4682b4
	lightblue	#add8e6		skyblue	#87ceeb		deepskyblue	#00bfff
	azure	#f0ffff		powderblue	#b0e0e6		cadetblue	#5f9ea0
				lightcyan	#e0ffff		paleturquoise	#afeeee

Figure 3.5   To see a complete list of the CSS color keywords on the Web Design Playground, surf to wdpg.io/2/ colorkeywords.

In the list shown in figure 3.5, you need only bother with the Color column and the Keyword column. You can safely ignore the weirdness in the RGB Value column.

CSS defines two color-related properties. The first property is `color`, which you use to apply a color to some text, and the second is `background-color` (sometimes shortened to just `background`), which you use to apply a color to an element's background:

```
color: keyword1;
background-color: keyword2;
```

You replace `keyword1` and `keyword2` with a color keyword, such as `darkblue` and `lavender`:

```
color: darkblue;
background-color: lavender;
```

> **WARNING**   When you're choosing colors for your web pages, you need to ensure that your text remains readable by selecting text and background colors that have sufficient contrast. Dark text on a light background or light text on a dark background is what you want to aim for.

Your home page doesn't require a complex color scheme, but you may want to eschew black-text-on-white for something more interesting. Here's a prompt you can use to get ChatGPT to help you generate a color scheme for your home page:

```
You are web designer and know how to create beautiful and compelling color
schemes. Use the information provided by the user to come up with suggestions
that reflect the theme of the personal home page.

My personal home page is related to X.

First, design a color scheme for my personal home page. I want the page to
be visually appealing and easy on the eyes. I'm thinking of using Y as the
dominant hue. Suggest two other colors that would go well with Y.

Second, show some examples of the suggested color scheme.

Third, when suggesting colors, please use the standard CSS color keywords,
such as aliceblue and papayawhip.
```

Replace *X* with a word or phrase related to your personal home page, and replace *Y* with the keyword for the color you want to use as the main hue on your site. I prompted ChatGPT for a color scheme with `dodgerblue` as the main hue, and figure 3.6 shows the result (generated using Bing Copilot in Creative mode).

For a technical writing website, you can use DodgerBlue as the dominant hue. It is a bright blue color that is easy on the eyes and can be used as a background color. You can pair it with **LightGray** or **WhiteSmoke** to create a clean and professional look [1].

Another option is to use **LightSlateGray** or **SlateGray** as the secondary color. These colors are darker than DodgerBlue and can be used for headings or other text elements [2].

I hope this helps! Let me know if you have any other questions.

Learn more: 1. colorhexa.com   2. alvarotrigo.com   3. html.am   4. w3schools.com   1 of 30 ●

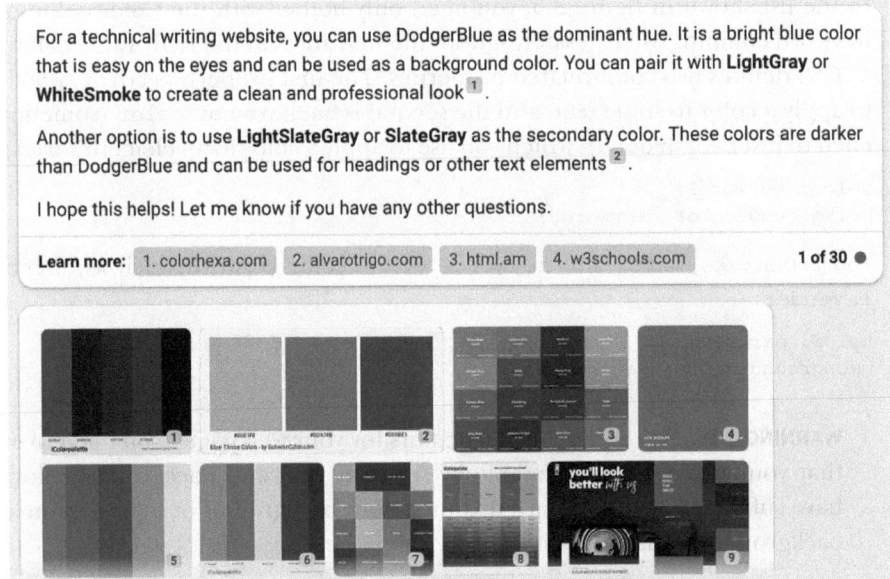

Figure 3.6   ChatGPT's color scheme suggestions

Note that the prompt asks ChatGPT to suggest colors using standard CSS color keywords. You'll use these keywords as part of your prompt when you ask ChatGPT to generate your web page code.

You're almost ready to build the home page prompt for ChatGPT. Your last bit of preparation is understanding how web page headings work, which is the topic of the next section.

3.2.7   *Understanding web page headings*

A web page *heading* is a bolded word or phrase that's set off vertically from the rest of the text and serves as a title for the page or a section of the page. For most web pages, only three types of headings are used:

- A single main heading, which is the page title
- One or more second-level headings, which act as the titles for each major article or section of the page
- Within each second-level heading, one or more third-level headings, which act as the subsection titles

Fortunately, you don't usually have to get too specific about all this because ChatGPT will almost always figure out the heading hierarchy for you automatically. However, you may want to control the font size of your headings to get the look you want. To give you an idea of what you're dealing with, here are some notes about font sizes for the first three heading levels:

- *First-level headings*—The default font size is 32 px. Depending on the title, its length, and the effect you want to achieve, first-level headings (designated in HTML using the `<h1>` tag) can be much larger, such as 48 px, 72 px, or even bigger.
- *Second-level headings*—The default font size is 24 px. However, it's not uncommon for second-level headings (designated in HTML using the `<h2>` tag) to be a bit larger, such as 28 px or 32 px.
- *Third-level headings*—The default font size is about 18.2 px. Since this default size is only a bit bigger than regular page text (16 px), you may prefer to style your third-level headings (which are designated in HTML using the `<h3>` tag) to be larger, such as 20 px or 24 px.

Again, you don't have to get too deep into the web code weeds here. For most web page prompts, you'll only need to tell ChatGPT what type size you want for each heading, assuming the default heading sizes don't fit your page design.

3.2.8 Crafting the prompt

You now have everything you need to prompt ChatGPT to provide you with the web code for your home page. Your prompt should begin as follows:

```
I want to build a personal homepage. I don't know how to code, so I need you
to provide the code for me.

First, write the HTML code for a simple web page that includes the following:
```

You then specify the content of your page, including the following (refer to figure 3.7):

- A header (refer to chapter 4) that includes your page title and subtitle.
- A main section that starts with an introductory paragraph (which may be something like a welcome message to the reader).
- One or more second-level headings followed by some text. For example, the heading "Movies I Like" could be followed by a list of your favorite films. For each item, you don't need to provide the complete text; just a few words or the first sentence is fine. You can complete the text later after ChatGPT has generated the code.

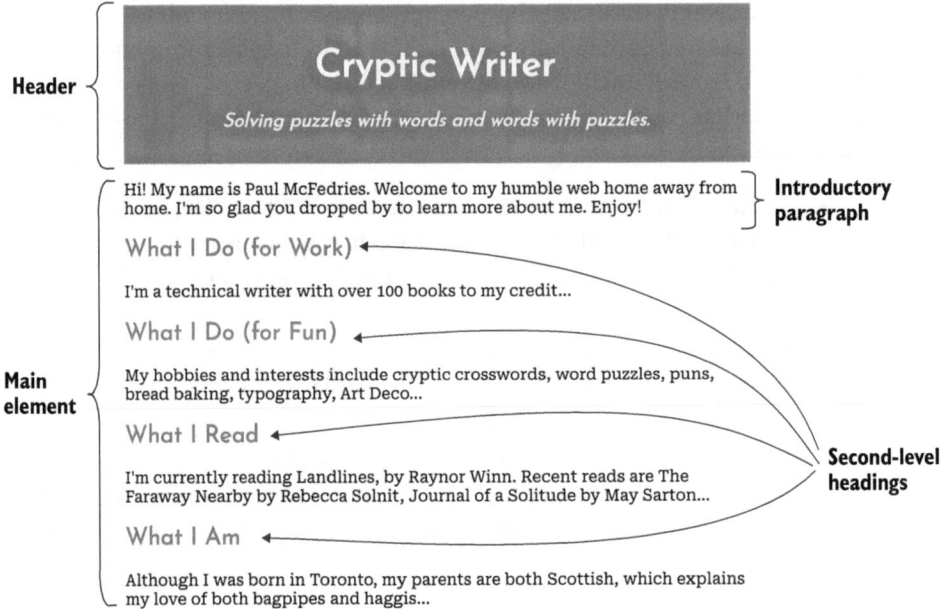

Figure 3.7   The sections of the personal home page

Next, you ask ChatGPT to generate the CSS for how you want your page formatted:

```
Second, in a separate file please write the CSS code for the following:
```

You then specify the formatting, including the following:

- The header background color (this should be the primary color from your color scheme).
- The type size and color you want to use for the page title and subtitle (the color should be the secondary color from your color scheme).
- The type size and color of the second-level headings (the color should be the primary color from your color scheme).
- The type size of the regular page text.
- The fonts to use for the headings and regular page text.
- A maximum width for the page. This prevents the lines of text from getting too long. A maximum length of 800 px is fine for most pages.

Here's an example prompt for my home page:

```
I want to build a personal homepage. I don't know how to code, so I need you
to provide the code for me.

First, write the HTML code for a simple web page that includes the following:
 * A header that includes the title "Cryptic Writer" and the subtitle
"Solving puzzles with words and words with puzzles."
```

* A main section where the first paragraph contains the text between the
triple quotation marks:
"""Hi! My name is Paul McFedries. Welcome to my humble web home away from
home. I'm so glad you dropped by to learn more about me. Enjoy!""".
 * The second-level heading "What I Do (for Work)" followed by a paragraph
that contains the text between the triple quotation marks:
"""I'm a technical writer with over 100 books to my credit..."""
* The second-level heading "What I Do (for Fun)" followed by a paragraph that
contains the text between the triple quotation marks:
"""My hobbies and interests include cryptic crosswords, word puzzles, puns,
bread baking, typography, Art Deco..."""
* The second-level heading "What I Read" followed by a paragraph that
contains the text between the triple quotation marks:
"""I'm currently reading Landlines, by Raynor Winn. Recent reads are The
Faraway Nearby by Rebecca Solnit, Journal of a Solitude by May Sarton..."""
* The second-level heading "What I Am" followed by a paragraph that contains
the text between the triple quotation marks:
"""Although I was born in Toronto, my parents are both Scottish, which
explains my love of both bagpipes and haggis..."""

Second, in a separate file please write the CSS code for the following:
* The header background color is dodgerblue with 20px padding all around.
Center the title and subtitle.
 * The title font size is 48px with color whitesmoke.
 * The subtitle font size is 24px with color whitesmoke and formatted as
italic.
 * The second-level heading font size is 32px with color dodgerblue.
 * The main section font size is 20px.
 * For the headings, use the Josefin Sans font from Google Fonts. For the
rest of the text, use the Roboto Serif font from Google Fonts.
 * The page is centered.
 * The page is responsive with a maximum width of 800px.

> **NOTE** I included the instruction to center the page because a page that doesn't
> take up the entire browser window (as this page won't in any window that's wider
> than 800 px) usually looks better when it's centered within the window.

ChatGPT should create the HTML code first, which you can copy and then paste and
save to a file named index.html. In that code, you should see a line near the top similar
to the following:

```
<link rel="stylesheet" type="text/css" href="styles.css">
```

This code tells the web browser to look for the CSS code in a file named styles.css,
so your next task is to copy the generated CSS code and then paste it and save it to
a file named styles.css (or whatever name you see in the <link> tag). Be sure to save
styles.css in the same folder as your index.html file. Refer to appendix A to learn more
about working HTML and CSS files. I submitted this prompt to Bing Copilot in Precise
mode, and the code it generated resulted in the page shown in figure 3.8.

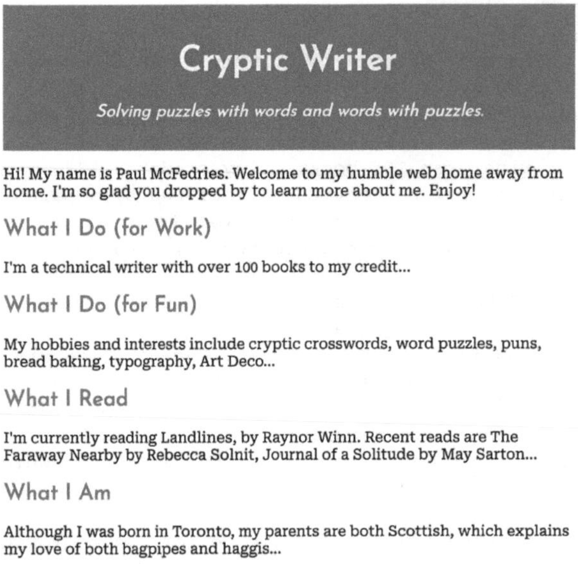

Cryptic Writer

Solving puzzles with words and words with puzzles.

Hi! My name is Paul McFedries. Welcome to my humble web home away from home. I'm so glad you dropped by to learn more about me. Enjoy!

What I Do (for Work)

I'm a technical writer with over 100 books to my credit...

What I Do (for Fun)

My hobbies and interests include cryptic crosswords, word puzzles, puns, bread baking, typography, Art Deco...

What I Read

I'm currently reading Landlines, by Raynor Winn. Recent reads are The Faraway Nearby by Rebecca Solnit, Journal of a Solitude by May Sarton...

What I Am

Although I was born in Toronto, my parents are both Scottish, which explains my love of both bagpipes and haggis...

Figure 3.8   My personal home page generated by ChatGPT

At this point, if you're happy with the personal home page that ChatGPT made for you, you can skip the rest of this chapter and deploy the code as I describe in appendix B. However, if you're curious to know a bit more about the code that ChatGPT generated, continue with the next section.

3.3   *Examining the personal home page code*

In this section, I'm going to give you a brief, nontechnical overview of the personal home page code that ChatGPT generated for me (and that produced the page shown in figure 3.8). The code that ChatGPT generates for you isn't likely to be the same, for two reasons:

- ChatGPT has a degree of randomness built in, so even identical prompts can often generate slightly different responses.
- The web page code generated by ChatGPT varies depending on the version of the model (GPT-3.5 versus GPT-4), the app used (OpenAI versus Copilot), and, for Copilot, the mode used (creative, balanced, or precise).

That said, your personal home page code will likely be very similar to mine, so the code annotations in the next two sections should be useful if you're curious about how the code is doing its work.

3.3.1   *Examining the HTML*

I'll start with the HTML code generated by ChatGPT for my personal home page, which is shown here:

```
<!DOCTYPE html>
<html>
  <head>
    <link href="https://fonts.googleapis.com/css?family=Josefin+Sans|Roboto+Serif"
rel="stylesheet">
    <link rel="stylesheet" type="text/css" href="styles.css">
    <title>Cryptic Writer</title>
  </head>
  <body>
    <header>
      <h1>Cryptic Writer</h1>
      <h2>Solving puzzles with words and words with puzzles.</h2>
    </header>
    <main>
      <p>Hi! My name is Paul McFedries. Welcome to my humble
         web home away from home. I'm so glad you dropped by
         to learn more about me. Enjoy!</p>
      <h2>What I Do (for Work)</h2>
      <p>I'm a technical writer with over 100 books to my credit...</p>
      <h2>What I Do (for Fun)</h2>
      <p>My hobbies and interests include cryptic crosswords,
         word puzzles, puns, bread baking, typography, Art Deco...</p>
      <h2>What I Read</h2>
      <p>I'm currently reading Landlines, by Raynor Winn. Recent
         reads are The Faraway Nearby by Rebecca Solnit, Journal
         of a Solitude by May Sarton...</p>
      <h2>What I Am</h2>
      <p>Although I was born in Toronto, my parents are both
         Scottish, which explains my love of both bagpipes and
         haggis...</p>
    </main>
  </body>
</html>
```

Loads the Josefin Sans and Roboto Serif fonts from Google Fonts

Tells the web browser where to find the CSS code

Page header

Page title

Page subtitle

Main section of the page

Paragraph of regular text

Second-level headings

Note, in particular, the code that tells the web browser where to find the CSS code, which I describe in the next section.

3.3.2   Examining the CSS

The CSS code that ChatGPT generated for my home page is shown here:

```
body {
  font-family: 'Roboto Serif', serif;
  max-width: 800px;
  margin: auto;
}

header {
  background-color: dodgerblue;
  padding: 20px;
  text-align: center;
}

header h1 {
```

Applies Roboto Serif to the page text

Sets the maximum page width to 800 px

Centers the page

Sets the header background to dodgerblue

Centers the text within the header

Adds 20 px of space around the header text

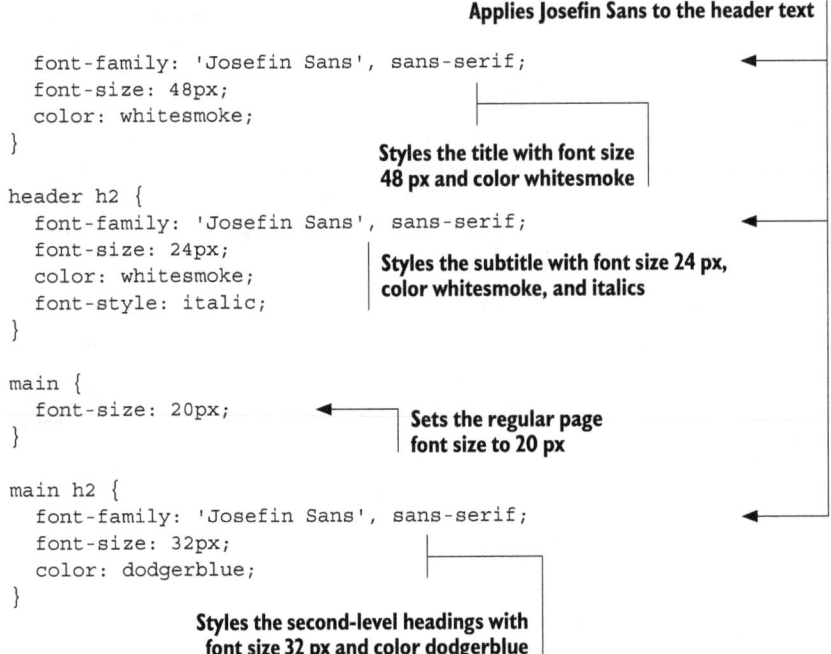

Applies Josefin Sans to the header text

```
    font-family: 'Josefin Sans', sans-serif;
    font-size: 48px;
    color: whitesmoke;
}
```

Styles the title with font size
48 px and color whitesmoke

```
header h2 {
    font-family: 'Josefin Sans', sans-serif;
    font-size: 24px;
    color: whitesmoke;
    font-style: italic;
}
```

Styles the subtitle with font size 24 px,
color whitesmoke, and italics

```
main {
    font-size: 20px;
}
```

Sets the regular page
font size to 20 px

```
main h2 {
    font-family: 'Josefin Sans', sans-serif;
    font-size: 32px;
    color: dodgerblue;
}
```

Styles the second-level headings with
font size 32 px and color dodgerblue

If you like, you can use these annotations to tweak your web page code, as I describe in the next section.

3.4   *Customizing the personal home page*

If the personal home page code that ChatGPT generated for you isn't what you wanted, you have two choices:

- If the resulting page isn't close to what you want, it's probably best to rewrite your prompt, start a new chat session, and try again.
- If the resulting page is pretty good but just needs a few adjustments, ask ChatGPT to make those adjustments for you. Be sure you submit this request in the same session as your original prompt.

For the second case, if the code produced by ChatGPT really does just need some small tweaks, consider modifying the code manually based on the annotations I provided in the previous section. Because you don't know web page code, it's best not to try to make any major changes. However, that still leaves quite a few ways you can alter the code to get the page you want.

First, here are some customization suggestions for the HTML code:

- In the header, you can edit the title or subtitle. Just be sure not to edit or delete the associated HTML tags: <h1> and </h1> for the title; <h2> and </h2> for the subtitle.

- In the main section of the HTML code, you can add, delete, or edit the text within each second-level heading (that is, the text between the `<h2>` and `</h2>` tags; be sure you don't edit or delete these tags).
- In the main section of the HTML code, you can add, delete, or edit the text within each paragraph (that is, the text between the `<p>` and `</p>` tags; be sure you don't edit or delete these tags).
- In the main section of the HTML code, you can add a new paragraph by typing a `<p>` tag, followed by your paragraph text, followed by the `</p>` tag.

Now here are a few customization ideas for the CSS code:

- If you want your home page to have a different maximum width, change the `max-width` value to something other than `800px`.
- For any color value, you can change the existing color to a different color keyword.
- For any font-size value, you can change the number to increase or decrease the font size. Just be sure you leave the `px` unit in place.
- To make your page code more accessible, consider converting all px measurements to rem measurements. 1 rem is, by default, equivalent to 16 px, so 20 px is 1.25 rem, 24 px is 1.5 rem, 32 px is 2 rem, 48 px is 3 rem, and so on. The rem unit is more accessible because it measures font sizes relative to the default font size the browser user has defined in their browser settings.

Summary

- By telling ChatGPT a little about your page content, you can prompt it to generate creative titles and subtitles.
- ChatGPT can help you with three key aspects of web typography: the typeface, the type size, and style.
- You can ask ChatGPT to create a color scheme using any of the 140 color keywords offered by CSS.
- Almost all web pages use headings: one first-level heading that acts as the page title, as well one or more second- and third-level headings.
- For best results, your page prompt should be as specific as possible, including colors, font sizes, and heading levels.
- Save the generated HTML to the index.html file and the generated CSS to the filename suggested by ChatGPT in the HTML code, usually styles.css.

Adding structure to a page

This chapter covers

- The role of the page header and footer
- Inserting an image into a web page
- Adding links to social media sites
- Prompting ChatGPT to build a book club page
- Examining and customizing the ChatGPT web page code

In chapter 3, you learned how to get ChatGPT to help you build a personal home page. One of the big takeaways from that process is that the more specific your prompt, the more the resulting code reflects your requirements, and the closer the resulting page will be to your original page vision.

Two aspects that might have surprised you about the process in chapter 3 were the length of the final prompt and the amount of detail it contained. However, long, detailed prompts are the only way to ensure that ChatGPT generates code that meets your design goals. In this chapter, you supply ChatGPT with a bit more detail by adding a couple of structural elements—the page header and the page footer—that are common to almost all web pages. You also learn how to include a couple of useful content elements: one or more images and one or more social media links. All this information then goes into a detailed prompt that you'll pass along to ChatGPT to produce the code for a book club page that gives you and other club members a home on the web.

This chapter also provides a high-level explanation of the code generated by ChatGPT. It even provides a few tips for customizing the code manually to get everything just the way you want.

4.1 Understanding this chapter's project

In this chapter, you're going to enlist ChatGPT to help you build a simple web page for a book club. The resulting page will include the following components:

- A header element that includes the following:
  - The book club logo
  - The book club name
  - A tagline that describes or otherwise sums up the club
- A main element that includes the following:
  - An introductory section that describes the book club
  - A "What We're Reading" section that displays information about the book club's current selection, including the front cover, title, and summary
  - A "Next Meetup" section that displays information about the next club meeting, including the date, time, location, and some book-related questions to consider
- A footer element that includes the following:
  - A copyright notice
  - Links to the club's social media accounts

Figure 4.1 shows an example of the type of page you'll be creating with the help of ChatGPT.

For your own page, you might want to discuss the page design with your group members to see if there's any content you're missing. You could also modify this page slightly to turn it into the home page for a reading group, discussion group, literary society, or any kind of meetup.

**Figure 4.1
A book club
page built
with ChatGPT-
generated code**

4.2 *Building the book club page*

The goal of this chapter is to use ChatGPT's help to construct a simple book club page that demonstrates the following fundamental elements of a web page: the header, the footer, and images. You also learn how to add links to one or more social media accounts. At the end of this section, you put all this together in a complete prompt to build the book club page.

4.2.1 *Introducing the page header*

The page header is a section that appears at the top of the page. In almost all cases, the header extends across the entire width of the page. However, it's worth pointing out here that this doesn't mean the header will necessarily extend across the entire width of the browser window. Why? Because, as you'll see in this chapter's project and most of this book's example pages, it's usually best to restrict the width of the web page so that the lines of text don't become too wide and therefore too difficult to read.

The header acts as a kind of introduction to the page, which means it usually includes one or more of the following elements:

- The page icon or logo
- The page title and an optional tagline or subtitle
- Links to social media accounts

It's common (although by no means necessary) to set off the header from the rest of the page by styling it with a different background color.

When prompting ChatGPT, you can specify a header and its contents by including an instruction along the following lines:

```
Add a header element that includes an image named logo.png, the title "Code &
Prose", and the tagline "Diving deep into the narrative side of code".
```

> **NOTE** All the prompts in this chapter are available on this book's website (www .manning.com/books/build-a-website-with-chatgpt) and in the book's GitHub repository (https://github.com/paulmcfe/websites-with-chatgpt).

Here's some example HTML code that ChatGPT might generate based on this instruction:

```
<header>
    <img src="logo.png" alt="Code & Prose logo">
    <h1>Code & Prose</h1>
    <p>Diving deep into the narrative side of code</p>
</header>
```

Note that the header is marked up using the header element, which means the header content appears between the <header> and </header> tags, as shown in this example. (I talk about the <img> tag a little later in this chapter; for the <h1> tag, refer to chapter 3; for the <p> tag, refer to chapter 5.) Figure 4.2 shows how this code can appear after some CSS has been applied to it. The header's bottom-of-the-page counterpart is the footer, which I discuss next.

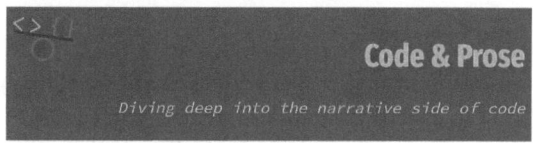

Figure 4.2 A page header

4.2.2 Introducing the page footer

The page footer is a section that appears at the bottom of the page. Like the header, the footer almost always extends the full width of the page, and the footer height depends on its content. Footers are usually fairly simple affairs that include one or both of the following:

- A copyright notice
- Links to social media accounts

Note that although it's possible for social media links to appear in either the header or the footer, they shouldn't appear in both. In this chapter's project, the social media links will appear in the footer.

Again, it's common to set off the footer from the rest of the page by styling it with a different background color. It's also common to populate the footer with links to other major site pages, a topic I cover in chapter 7.

As part of your ChatGPT prompt, you can specify a footer and its contents by including an instruction similar to the following:

```
Add a footer element that includes the text "Copyright" (spelled out, do not
include the Copyright symbol), followed by the current year, followed by
"Code & Prose".
```

ChatGPT might generate the following code based on this instruction:

```
<footer>
    <p>
        Copyright 2023 Code & Prose
    </p>
</footer>
```

Note that the footer is marked up using the `footer` element, which means the footer content appears between the `<footer>` and `</footer>` tags, as shown in this example. Figure 4.3 demonstrates how the browser renders this code after some CSS has been applied. Next, you learn a vital aspect of the elements you see on a web page: the box model.

Copyright 2023 Code & Prose

Figure 4.3   A page footer

4.2.3   *Introducing padding, borders, and margins*

An important HTML concept to bear in mind is that every element on the page is surrounded by an invisible box. Why is that such a big deal? Because you can get ChatGPT to generate code to control many aspects of that box, including its interior spacing, borders, and exterior spacing. To get there, you need to become acquainted with the various parts of the box.

Figure 4.4 gives you an abstract look at the basic box parts, and figure 4.5 shows how these same parts affect some actual page content. There are four parts to each element box:

- *Content*—This area is the inner rectangle of the box, consisting of the content—such as some text or an image—contained in the box.
- *Padding*—This area between the content and the border represents extra whitespace added outside the top, right, bottom, and left edges of the content area.
- *Border*—This part runs along the outer edges of the padding area and surrounds the content and padding with lines.

- *Margin*—This area is the outer rectangle of the box, representing extra whitespace added outside of the top, right, bottom, and left borders.

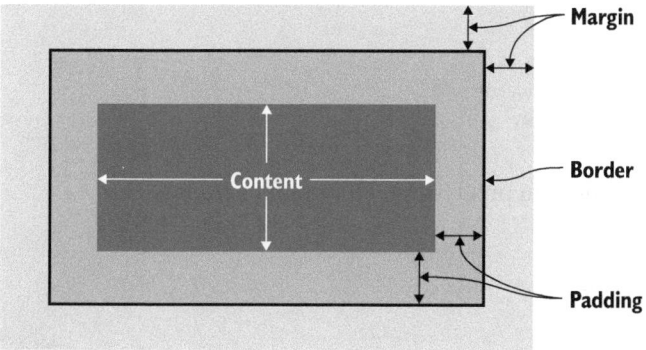

Figure 4.4   The main parts of an element box

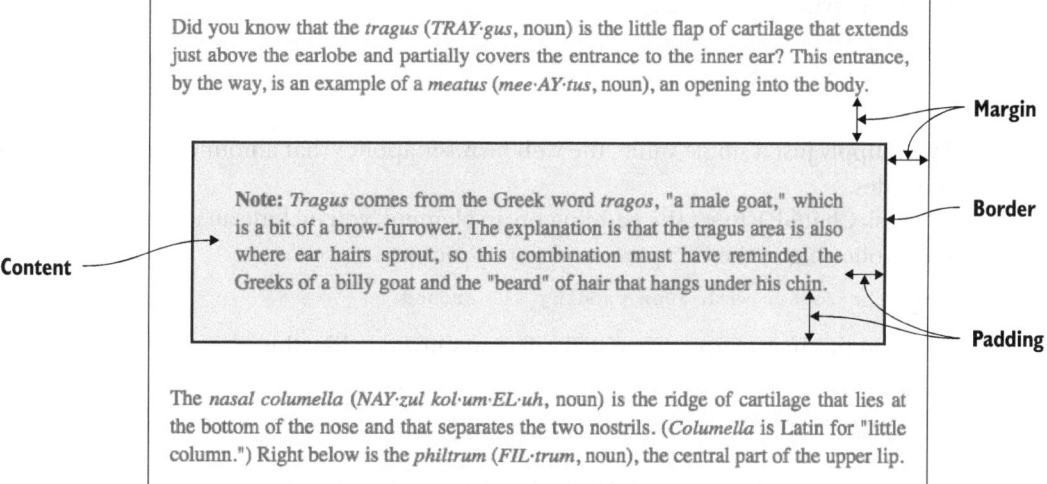

Figure 4.5   The element box parts as they appear with actual page content

The combination of the content area, padding, border, and margin is known in CSS circles as the *box model*. Keeping all this in mind the best you can, it's time to turn your attention to the useful and powerful CSS properties that enable you to manipulate any element box. First up is changing the box padding.

ADDING PADDING

In the element box, the padding is the whitespace added above, below, to the left, and to the right of the content. If you add a border to your element, as described in the next section, the padding is the space between your content and the border. The padding gives the element a bit of room to breathe in its box, ensuring that the content isn't crowded by its own border or by nearby elements.

You set the padding by applying a value to one or more of the four sides:

```
element {
    padding-top: top-value;
    padding-right: right-value;
    padding-bottom: bottom-value;
    padding-left: left-value;
}
```

Each value is a measurement in pixels (px). Here's an example:

```
header {
    padding-top: 16px;
    padding-right: 24px;
    padding-bottom: 12px;
    padding-left: 20px;
}
```

You can also use a `padding` shorthand property to set all the padding values with a single declaration. You can duplicate the rule in the preceding example by using the shorthand syntax as follows:

```
header {
    padding: 16px 24px 12px 20px;
}
```

If you supply just a single value, the web browser applies that amount of padding to all four sides.

To ask ChatGPT to set the padding on an element, you include an instruction similar to the following in the CSS portion of your prompt:

```
Style the footer with 10px padding all around.
```

Based on this instruction, ChatGPT will generate code like this:

```
header {
    padding: 10px;
}
```

The next part of the box model is the border.

SURROUNDING AN ELEMENT WITH A BORDER

In the element box, the border is the line that defines the outer edge of the padding on four sides: top, right, bottom, and left. In this way, the border comes between the element's padding and its margin. The border is optional, but it's often useful to provide the reader with a visual indicator that the enclosed content is separate from any nearby content. To create a basic border around an element, use the `border` property, as shown in figure 4.6.

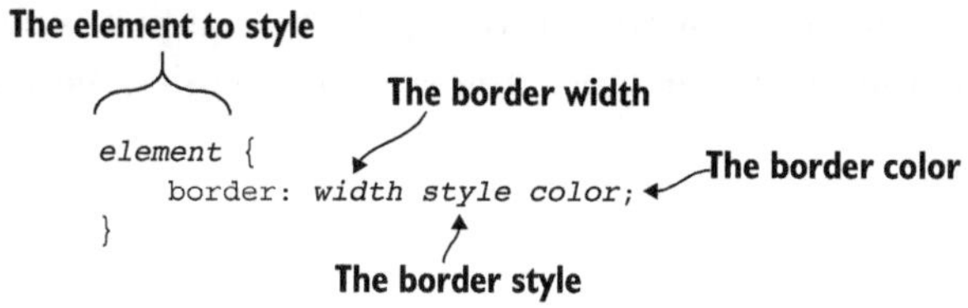

The element to style

Figure 4.6   **The syntax of the `border` property**

The `width` value is a measurement in px. You can also set the value to any of the following keywords: `thin`, `medium`, or `thick`. For the `style` value, you can use any of the following keywords: `dotted`, `dashed`, `solid`, `double`, `groove`, `ridge`, `inset`, `outset`, `hidden`, or `none`. For the `color` parameter, you can use any of the color names you learned about in chapter 3.

To ask ChatGPT to add a border around an element, you include an instruction similar to the following in the CSS portion of your prompt:

```
Style the nav element with a 1px, solid, black border.
```

Based on this instruction, ChatGPT will generate code like this:

```
nav {
    border: 1px solid black;
}
```

The final aspect of the box model I'll discuss here is the margin.

WORKING WITH MARGINS

In the element box, the margin is the whitespace added above, below, to the left, and to the right of the border. The margin lets you control the space between elements. Positive margin values, for example, prevent the page elements from bumping into one another or overlapping and also keep the elements from brushing against the edges of the browser viewport. On the other hand, if your design requires elements to overlap, you can achieve this effect by using negative margin values.

You apply the margin by setting a value to one or more of an element's four sides:

```
element {
    margin-top: top-value;
    margin-right: right-value;
    margin-bottom: bottom-value;
    margin-left: left-value;
}
```

Each margin value is a measurement in px. Here's an example:

```
footer {
    margin-top: 24px;
    margin-right: 40px;
    margin-bottom: 32px;
    margin-left: 48px;
}
```

As with padding, a margin shorthand property lets you apply the margins using a single declaration. You can rewrite the rule in the preceding example by using the shorthand syntax like so:

```
footer {
    margin: 24px 40px 32px 48px;
}
```

If you supply just a single value, the web browser applies that margin value to all four sides of the element.

To ask ChatGPT to set the margin on an element, you include an instruction similar to the following in the CSS portion of your prompt:

```
Style the body with 16px padding all around.
```

Based on this instruction, ChatGPT will generate code like this:

```
body {
    padding: 16px;
}
```

Earlier, you saw an example of a header that included an image. How to work with web page images is introduced in the next section.

4.2.4   *Working with images*

Although most web pages convey information (however loosely you define that term) using words, pages that are nothing but text are a little intimidating and, often, a lot boring! Sure, you can (and should) use typefaces, colors, and text styles to spruce up the page (as I described in chapter 3). However, a relatively easy way to enliven an otherwise dull wall of text is to give your readers some eye candy by inserting an image or two. That's not to say your web page images should be merely decorative. Images are a great way to supplement your page text, display information concisely, and help your readers retain what they read on your pages.

An image is a separate file you can tell ChatGPT to reference in your page's HTML code. (Refer to chapter 10 for a more detailed treatment of images and how they are inserted into a web page.) The web has standardized on four formats that account for almost all web imagery, as summarized in table 4.1.

My assumption in this chapter is that you already have the images you want to include in your page. For the book club project, you need two images:

- A logo for the book club; this image will go in the page header.
- The front cover of the book the club is currently reading; this image will go in the main section of the page.

You need to know the names of all the image files you want to include in your page because you'll be including those names in your prompt.

Table 4.1 Image file formats

Name	Extension	Description	Uses
GIF	.gif	This is the original web graphics format (the name is short for Graphics Interchange Format, which is pronounced "giff" or "jiff"). GIFs are limited to 256 colors, can have transparent backgrounds, and can be combined into short animations.	Use GIFs if you want to combine multiple images into a single animated image.
JPEG	.jpg, .jpeg	This format (which gets its name from Joint Photographic Experts Group and is pronounced "jay-peg") supports complex images that have many millions of colors. The main advantage of JPEG files is that they're compressed, so even digitized photographs and other high-quality images can be a reasonably small size for faster downloading. Note, however, that JPEG compression is lossy, which means it makes the image smaller by discarding redundant pixels. The higher the compression, the more pixels are discarded and the less sharp the image appears.	If you have a photo or similarly complex image, JPEG is almost always the best choice because it gives the smallest file size.
PNG	.png	This format (short for Portable Network Graphics and pronounced "p-n-g" or "ping") supports millions of colors. It's a compressed format, but unlike JPEGs, PNGs use lossless compression. Images retain sharpness, but the file sizes can be quite big. PNG also supports transparency.	If you have an illustration or icon that uses solid colors or a photo that contains large areas of near-solid color, PNG is best because it gives you a reasonably small file size while retaining excellent image quality. You can also use PNG if you need transparency effects.
SVG	.svg	This format (short for Scalable Vector Graphics) uses vectors rather than pixels to generate an image. These vectors are encoded as a set of instructions in XML format, meaning the image can be altered in a text editor and can be manipulated to produce animations.	If you have a logo or icon and have a graphics program that can save files as SVG (such as Adobe Illustrator or Inkscape), this format is a good choice because it produces small files that can be scaled to any size without distortion.

NOTE   One of the most fun aspects of working with generative AI models is getting them to create entirely new images from text prompts. I talk about generating new images from text using OpenAI's DALL-E model in chapter 5.

You may also want to obtain icons for each social media account associated with your book club, discussed next.

4.2.5   *Adding social media links*

In this modern age, no web page looks complete without at least a few links to social media sites. This chapter's project assumes you want to link to accounts on Facebook, X (Twitter), and Instagram. For each link, you'll need the following:

- The account username
- An icon for the social media site

For the latter, you don't need to download a separate image file from the web (unless you prefer to go that route). Instead, you'll ask ChatGPT to link to an icon toolkit named Font Awesome, which includes icons for all major social media sites. (The one exception, as I write this, is the Threads social media site, the icon for which hadn't yet been added to Font Awesome.)

4.2.6   Crafting the prompt

If you've gone through the ChatGPT prompts in the previous section, you now have what you need to prompt ChatGPT to generate the code for your book club page. Your prompt should begin like this:

```
I want to build a web page for a book club. I don't know how to code, so I
need you to provide the code for me.
```

```
First, write the HTML code for a web page that includes the following:
```

You then specify the content of your page, including the following (refer to figure 4.7):

- A header that includes your club logo, page title, and tagline
- A main element that starts with a section that introduces visitors to your book club
- A section that displays information about the book the club is currently reading, including the book cover, title, summary, and page count
- A section that displays information about the club's next meetup, including the date, time, location, and some questions for members to consider in advance
- A footer that includes a copyright notice and links to your club's social media accounts

Next, you ask ChatGPT to generate the CSS for how you want your page formatted:

```
Second, in a separate file please write the CSS code for the following:
```

You then specify the formatting, including the following:

- The header background color (this should be the primary color from your color scheme).
- The type size and color you want to use for the page title and tagline (the color should be the lightest color from your color scheme).
- The type size and color of the second-level headings (the color should be the primary color from your color scheme).
- The type size of the regular page text.
- The fonts to use for the headings and regular page text.
- A maximum width for the page. This prevents the lines of text from getting too long. A maximum length of 800 px is fine for most pages.

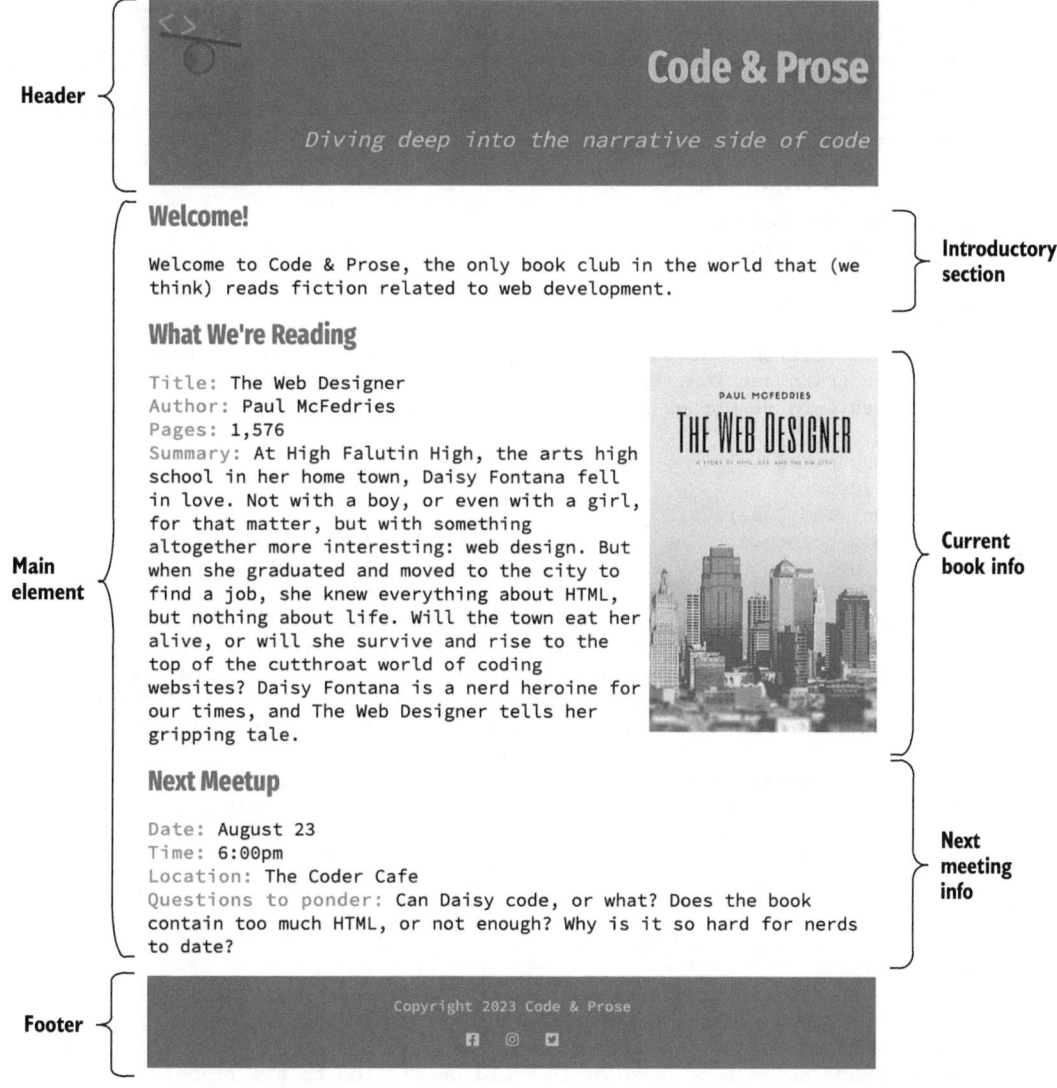

Figure 4.7 **The sections of the book club page**

Here's an example prompt for my own book club page:

I want to build a web page for a book club. I don't know how to code, so I need you to provide the code for me.

First, write the HTML code for a web page that includes the following:
 * A header element that includes an image named logo.png, the title "Code & Prose", and the tagline "Diving deep into the narrative side of code".
 * A main element that contains three sections.
 * The first section contains the second-level heading "Welcome!", followed by a paragraph that contains the text between the triple quotation marks:

"""Welcome to Code & Prose, the only book club in the world that (we think) reads fiction related to web development.""".
* A second section that begins with the second-level heading "What We're Reading".
* In the second section, include the image named book-cover.png, followed by the text between the triple quotation marks, where each word or phrase before a colon is bold:
"""
Title: The Web Designer
Author: Paul McFedries
Pages: 1,576
Summary: At High Falutin High, [etc.]
"""
* A third section that begins with the second-level heading "Next Meetup".
* In the third section, include the text between the triple quotation marks, where each word or phrase before a colon is bold:
"""
Date: August 23
Time: 6:00pm
Location: The Coder Cafe
Questions to ponder: Can Daisy code, or what? Does the book contain too much HTML, or not enough? Why is it so hard for nerds to date?
"""
* A footer element that includes the text "Copyright" (spelled out, do not include the Copyright symbol), followed by the current year, followed by "Code & Prose". In a separate paragraph, the footer also includes three links to social media accounts: one for Facebook (username: CodeAndProse), Instagram (username: codeandprose), and Twitter (username: codenprose).

Second, in a separate file write the CSS code for the following:
* The header background color is darkorchid with 10px padding all around. Float the logo to the left and right-align the title and tagline.
* The title font size is 48px with color lightsteelblue.
* The tagline font size is 24px with color lightsteelblue and formatted as italic.
* The second-level heading font size is 30px with color darkorchid and a top margin of 15px.
* The main element font size is 20px.
* In the second and third sections, the bold text should use the color mediumseagreen.
* The image named book-cover.png should be floated to the right.
* For the title and headings, use the Fira Sans Extra Condensed Bold font from Google Fonts. For the rest of the text, use the Source Code Pro font from Google Fonts.
* The footer background color is darkorchid with 5px padding all around and a 10px top margin. The text color is lightsteelblue. Center the text and social media links.
* For the social media links, use the corresponding Font Awesome icons.
* The entire page is centered in the browser window.
* The page is responsive with a maximum width of 800px.

NOTE   Given the length of this prompt, if you use Bing Copilot or Microsoft Copilot, be sure to use Precise mode, which has a 4,000-character prompt limit.

ChatGPT should create the HTML code first, which you can copy and then paste and save to a file named index.html. In that code, you should see a line near the top similar to the following:

```
<link rel="stylesheet" type="text/css" href="styles.css">
```

This code tells the web browser to look for the CSS code in a file named styles.css, so your next task is to copy the generated CSS code, then paste it and save it to a file named styles.css (or whatever name you see in the `<link>` tag). Be sure to save styles.css in the same folder as your index.html file. You also need to copy your image files into the same folder. Refer to appendix A to learn more about working with web page files. I submitted this prompt to GPT-4 using OpenAI's ChatGPT app, and the code it generated resulted in the page shown in figure 4.8.

If you're satisfied with the book club page that ChatGPT generated for you, you can skip the rest of this chapter and deploy the code as I describe in appendix B. However, if you'd like to know a bit more about the code that ChatGPT generated, the next section gives you a closer look.

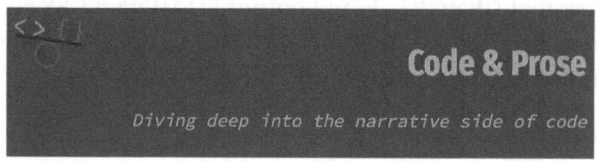

Welcome!

Welcome to Code & Prose, the only book club in the world that (we think) reads fiction related to web development.

What We're Reading

Title: The Web Designer
Author: Paul McFedries
Pages: 1,576
Summary: At High Falutin High, the arts high school in her home town, Daisy Fontana fell in love. Not with a boy, or even with a girl, for that matter, but with something altogether more interesting: web design. But when she graduated and moved to the city to find a job, she knew everything about HTML, but nothing about life. Will the town eat her alive, or will she survive and rise to the top of the cutthroat world of coding websites? Daisy Fontana is a nerd heroine for our times, and The Web Designer tells her gripping tale.

Next Meetup

Date: August 23
Time: 6:00pm
Location: The Coder Cafe
Questions to ponder: Can Daisy code, or what? Does the book contain too much HTML, or not enough? Why is it so hard for nerds to date?

Figure 4.8   My book club page generated by ChatGPT

4.3   *Examining the code*

I'm going to give you a short and reasonably nontechnical overview of the book club page code that ChatGPT generated based on my prompt from the previous section (that page is shown in figure 4.8). Your ChatGPT-generated code will be different from mine not only because your text and images will be different but also because

- ChatGPT's algorithms include some built-in randomness, so the same prompt will often generate slightly different code each time you run it.
- ChatGPT's output varies depending on the model (GPT-3.5 versus GPT-4) and the app (OpenAI versus Bing Copilot). For Bing Copilot, the output also depends on the conversation style (creative, balanced, or precise).

NOTE   The generated HTML and CSS code for my book club are available on the book's website (www.manning.com/books/build-a-website-with-chatgpt) and in the GitHub repository (https://github.com/paulmcfe/websites-with-chatgpt).

However, every version of ChatGPT should output HTML and CSS code that's at least similar to what's displayed in the next two sections, so my code annotations should help you understand what's happening under the hood.

4.3.1   *Examining the HTML*

The HTML code that ChatGPT generated for my book club is shown here:

```
<!DOCTYPE html>
<html>
<head>                                    Tells the web browser
    <title>Code & Prose</title>           where to find the CSS code      Loads the
    <link rel="stylesheet" href="styles.css">        ◄──────              page fonts
    <link rel="preconnect" href="https://fonts.gstatic.com">    ◄──       from Google
    <link href="https://fonts.googleapis.com/css2                         Fonts
           ?family=  Fira+Sans+Extra+Condensed:wght@700
           &family=Source+Code+Pro&display=swap"
           rel="stylesheet">                        ◄──
    <link rel="stylesheet"
           href="https://cdnjs.cloudflare.com/ajax/libs/font-awesome/6.5.2
           /css/all.min.css">
</head>                                                          Page header
<body>                                                                ◄──
    <header>
        <img src="logo.png" alt="Code & Prose logo" id="logo">  ◄── Page logo
        <h1>Code & Prose</h1>                                   ◄── Page title
        <p>Diving deep into the narrative side of code</p>      ◄── Page tagline
    </header>
    <main>
        <section>                              ◄────── First section of the page
            <h2>Welcome!</h2>
            <p>Welcome to Code & Prose, the only book
               club in the world that (we think)
               reads fiction related to web
```

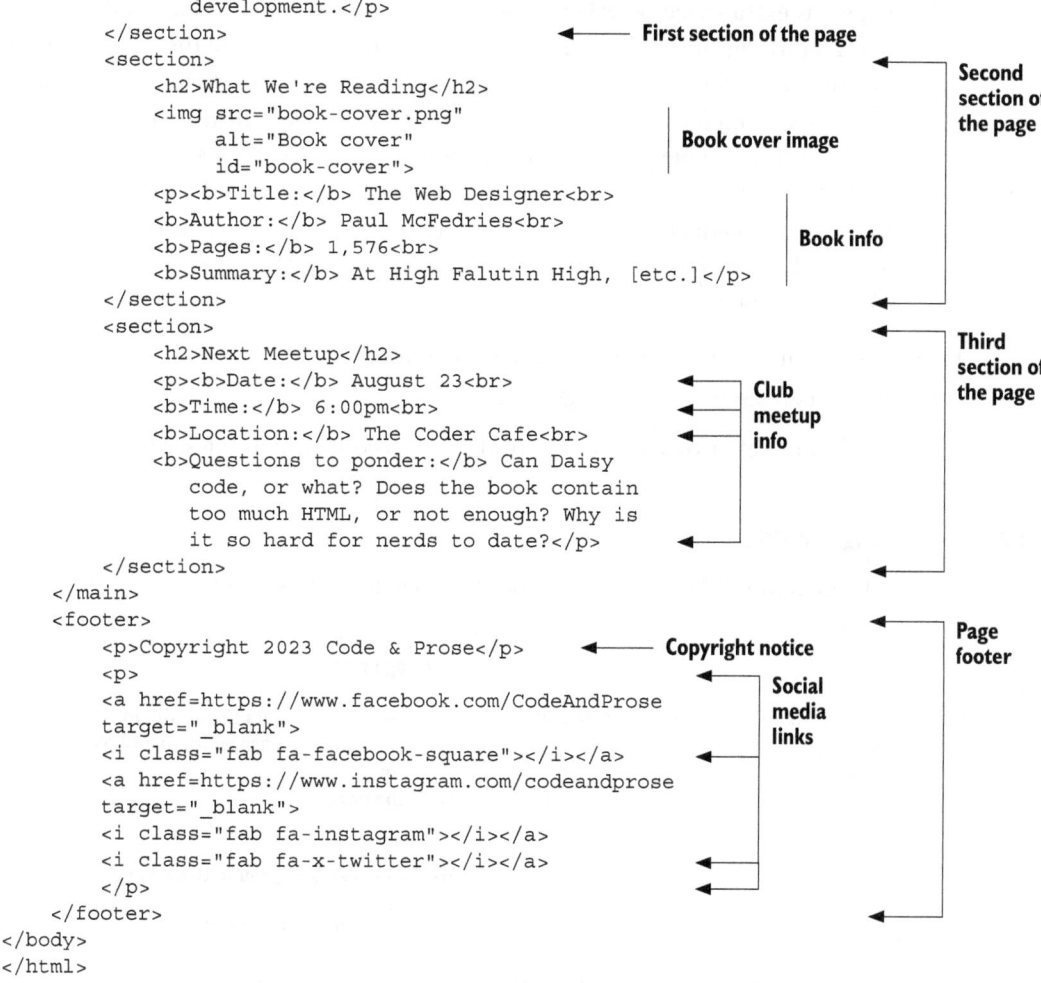

```
            development.</p>
        </section>                          ◄──── First section of the page
        <section>                                                            Second
            <h2>What We're Reading</h2>                                       section of
            <img src="book-cover.png"                                        the page
                alt="Book cover"            Book cover image
                id="book-cover">
            <p><b>Title:</b> The Web Designer<br>
            <b>Author:</b> Paul McFedries<br>
            <b>Pages:</b> 1,576<br>         Book info
            <b>Summary:</b> At High Falutin High, [etc.]</p>
        </section>
        <section>                                                            Third
            <h2>Next Meetup</h2>                                              section of
            <p><b>Date:</b> August 23<br>        Club                         the page
            <b>Time:</b> 6:00pm<br>              meetup
            <b>Location:</b> The Coder Cafe<br>  info
            <b>Questions to ponder:</b> Can Daisy
                code, or what? Does the book contain
                too much HTML, or not enough? Why is
                it so hard for nerds to date?</p>
        </section>
    </main>
    <footer>                                                                 Page
        <p>Copyright 2023 Code & Prose</p>   ◄──── Copyright notice           footer
        <p>                                      Social
        <a href=https://www.facebook.com/CodeAndProse  media
        target="_blank">                         links
        <i class="fab fa-facebook-square"></i></a>
        <a href=https://www.instagram.com/codeandprose
        target="_blank">
        <i class="fab fa-instagram"></i></a>
        <i class="fab fa-x-twitter"></i></a>
        </p>
    </footer>
</body>
</html>
```

NOTE In my own experiments, ChatGPT occasionally produced code that added unusual characters to the page. If you see unusual characters, you can almost always fix the problem by adding the code `<meta charset="utf-8">` immediately after the `<head>` tag in the HTML file. This tag tells the web browser how to handle certain characters, such as curly quotation marks (" and ").

Here are a few notes to bear in mind when reading the HTML code:

- The page's two images are referenced using the `<img>` tag, where the `src` value is the name of the image file. If you change the name of your image file, be sure to change the corresponding `src` value, as well.

- In the book info and the meetup info, the `<br>` tag tells the web browser to start the next item on the next line, with no extra space between the two lines. If your page has extra space between these lines, it means ChatGPT has used <p> (for paragraph) tags instead of
 (for line break) tags. Delete the <p> tag at the beginning of each line and replace the </p> tag at the end of each line with <br>.

- In the social media links, the target="_blank" code tells the web browser to open the link in a new tab. To open the link in the same tab, instead (which is the preferred method), you can delete the target="_blank" code from each link.
- In the social media links, the class values reference a particular Font Awesome icon to display as the link text. For example, class="fab fa-instagram" displays the Instagram icon.

Finally, note that the HTML code includes the following line:

```
<link rel="stylesheet" href="styles.css">
```

This tag tells the web browser where to find the CSS code, which I describe in the next section.

4.3.2   *Examining the CSS*

ChatGPT's generated CSS code for my book club page is shown here:

```
body {
    font-family: 'Source Code Pro', monospace;
    color: black;
    max-width: 800px;
    margin: auto;
}
header {
    background-color: darkorchid;
    padding: 10px;
}
header img {
    float: left;
}
header h1 {
    font-family: 'Fira Sans Extra Condensed', sans-serif;
    font-size: 48px;
    color: lightsteelblue;
    text-align: right;
}
header p {
    font-size: 24px;
    color: lightsteelblue;
    font-style: italic;
    text-align: right;
    clear: right;
}
main {
    font-size: 20px;
```

Applies Source Code Pro to the page text

Sets the maximum page width to 800 px

Centers the page

Sets the header background to darkorchid

Adds 10 px of space around the header text

Floats the logo to the left

Applies Fira Sans Extra Condensed to the title

Styles the title: font size 48 px, color lightsteelblue, right-aligned

Styles the tagline: font size 24 px, color lightsteelblue, italics, right-aligned

Sets the regular page font size to 20 px

```
}
h2 {
    font-family: 'Fira Sans Extra Condensed', sans-serif;
    font-size: 30px;
    color: darkorchid;
    margin-top: 15px;
}
section:nth-child(2) img {
    float: right;
}
section:nth-child(2) p b,
section:nth-child(3) p b {
    color: mediumseagreen;
}
footer {
    background-color: darkorchid;
    color: lightsteelblue;
    padding: 5px;
    margin-top: 10px;
    text-align: center;
}
footer a {
    margin: 0 10px;
    color: lightsteelblue;
    text-decoration: none;
}
```

Styles the second-level headings: Fira Sans Extra Condensed font, font size 30 px, color darkorchid, top margin 15 px

◄——— **Floats the book cover to the right**

◄——— **Applies the color mediumseagreen to the bold text**

Styles the footer: background color darkorchid, text color lightsteelblue, padding 5 px, top margin 10 px, and text centered

Styles the footer links: left and right margins 10 px, text color lightsteelblue, no underline

If you like, you can use these annotations to tweak your web page code, as I describe in the next section.

4.4   Customizing the page

If ChatGPT's book club page code isn't right for some reason, you have two ways to fix things:

- If the page is far from what you want, rewrite your prompt, start a new chat session, and try again.
- If the page is close to what you want, ask ChatGPT to make the necessary adjustments. Be sure you submit this request in the same session as your original prompt.

For the second case, if the code produced by ChatGPT really does just need some small tweaks, consider modifying the code manually based on the annotations I provided in the previous section. Because you don't know web page code, it's best not to try to make any major changes. However, that still leaves quite a few ways you can alter the code to get the page you want.

First, here are some customization suggestions for the HTML code:

- In the header, you can edit the title or tagline. Just be sure not to edit or delete the associated HTML tags: `<h1>` and `</h1>` for the title; `<p>` and `</p>` for the tagline.

- In the main section of the HTML code, you can add, delete, or edit the text in each second-level heading (that is, the text between the `<h2>` and `</h2>` tags; be sure you don't edit or delete these tags).

- In the main section of the HTML code, you can add, delete, or edit the text in each paragraph (that is, the text between the `<p>` and `</p>` tags; be sure you don't edit or delete these tags).

- In the main section of the HTML code, you can add a new section by typing a `<section>` tag followed by the `</section>` tag. Between these tags, you can add a heading (some text between the `<h2>` and `</h2>` tags) and a paragraph (some text between the `<p>` and `</p>` tags).

Now, here are a few customization ideas for the CSS code:

- If you want your page to have a different maximum width, change the `max-width` value to something other than `800px`. For example, if you increase the font size (as I describe in a moment), you may want to increase the page width; decreasing the font size means you can decrease the page width. Try out different widths (usually within the range of 600 px on the low side and 1,000 px on the high side) until you find one that suits your page.

- For any color value, you can change the existing color to a different color keyword. Note, however, that changing a single color can throw off your page color scheme. If you don't like your page colors, pick a new primary color and then prompt ChatGPT again to create a color scheme from that hue.

- For any font size value, you can change the number to increase or decrease the font size. For example, if your text feels cramped and hard to read, try bumping up the font size value by a pixel or two. Just make sure you leave the px unit in place.

- For any padding or margin value, you can change the number to increase or decrease the padding or margins. For example, if your page content seems crowded, you can open things up by increasing the padding and/or the margins. Similarly, if your page items seem disconnected from each other, try decreasing the margins. In each case, be sure to leave the px unit in place.

- To make your page code more accessible, consider converting all px measurements to rem measurements. 1 rem is, by default, equivalent to 16 px, so 20 px is 1.25 rem; 24 px is 1.5 rem; 32 px is 2 rem; 48 px is 3 rem; and so on. The rem unit is more accessible because it measures font sizes relative to the default font size the browser user has defined in their browser settings.

Summary

- Almost all web pages start with a header that includes at least a logo, the page title, and the page tagline or subtitle.

- Most web pages finish with a footer that includes at least a copyright notice and a few social media links.

- Each element on the page is surrounded by an invisible box that consists of four parts: the content, which is the text or image contained in the box; the padding, which is the whitespace between the content and the border; the border, which runs along the outer edges of the padding area and surrounds the content and padding with lines; and the margin, which is the extra whitespace added outside of the top, right, bottom, and left borders.

- To include an image in your page, you need to know the name of the image file, and you need to store the image file in the same folder as your web page code files.

- To include social media links in your page, you need to know the username for each social media account.

- For best results, your page prompt should be as specific as possible, including colors, font sizes, and heading levels.

- Save the generated HTML to the index.html file and the generated CSS to the filename suggested by ChatGPT in the HTML code, usually styles.css.

Publishing page posts

This chapter covers

- Collaborating with ChatGPT to publish posts as accordions
- Generating new images using DALL-E
- Prompting ChatGPT to build an online journal page
- Examining and customizing the ChatGPT web page code

Although many people dislike writing, lots of us truly enjoy the act of putting pen to paper, or fingers to keyboard. Many of us love to write so much that, besides our more "serious" writing, we keep up a regular writing habit in the form of a frequently updated diary or journal. And a surprising number of those folks have a hankering to post these musings online. In fact, whenever I talk to people about building web pages, by far the most common question is, "How do I start an online journal/diary/blog?"

Fortunately, if you have some stuff already written, it's straightforward to get ChatGPT to help you create a web page where you can publish your prose for all the world to read. You can also use AI to generate new images for things like site logos, icons, and page illustrations. This chapter also shows you how to use the combination of ChatGPT and OpenAI's DALL-E image-creation model to generate whatever images you need for your page.

All this information goes into a detailed prompt that you'll pass along to ChatGPT to produce the code for an online journal page where you can post whatever writing you want to share. This chapter also provides a high-level explanation of the code generated by ChatGPT and even gives a few tips for customizing the code manually to get everything just the way you want.

5.1 Understanding this chapter's project

In this chapter, you're going to enlist ChatGPT to help you build a simple web page for an online journal. The final page will include the following components:

- A header element that includes the following:
  - The journal logo (generated by Dall-E)
  - The journal title
  - The journal tagline
- A main element where the journal entries appear. Each entry shows only its title at first but, when clicked, shows the entry content.
- A footer element that includes a copyright notice.

Figure 5.1 shows an example of the type of page you'll build with ChatGPT's help in this chapter. The simplicity of this page means you can easily modify it to store entries for a blog or travel diary, essays, book or movie reviews, fan fiction stories, or really any kind of periodic writing.

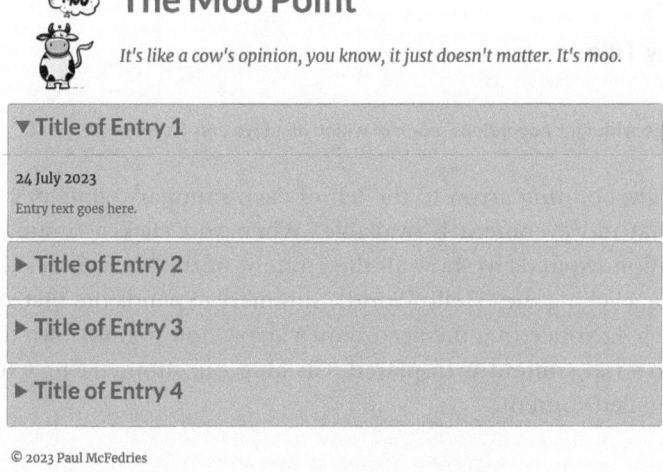

Figure 5.1 An online journal page generated by ChatGPT

5.2   *Building the online journal page*

Before crafting the prompt that will generate the code for your online journal page, you need a bit of background about a web page element called an accordion as well as how to get AI to create new images from text prompts. The next couple of sections provide the details.

5.2.1   *Working with accordions*

The only new web page technology that you learn about in this chapter is the *accordion*, which is an interactive HTML element that enables users to toggle between showing just an item's title and the item's title and content. An accordion consists of two elements:

- *Summary*—An element that acts as a title or description for the accordion
- *Details*—An element that contains the entirety of the accordion content, including the summary element and any other content you provide (such as one or more articles, headings, paragraphs, images, and so on)

The idea behind an accordion is that, by default, all you see at first is the summary element. For example, figure 5.2 shows part of a web page with four accordions. Each is currently showing only its summary element, such as "Hello World!" at the top, which is the summary text for the first accordion.

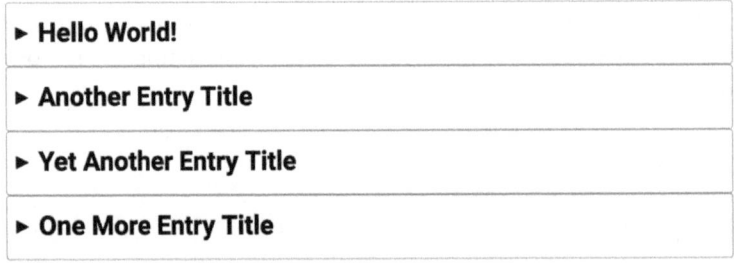

Figure 5.2   A web page with four accordions, each of which displays only its summary text

Notice, too, the right-pointing arrow to the left of each summary element's text. This arrow indicates that more content is available. When you click a summary (or its arrow), the accordion expands to show all the content in the accordion's details element. For example, clicking the "Hello World!" summary expands the first accordion, as shown in figure 5.3. Notice that the accordion's arrow now points down to indicate that the accordion's full content is displayed. Clicking the summary text (or arrow) again hides the detailed content.

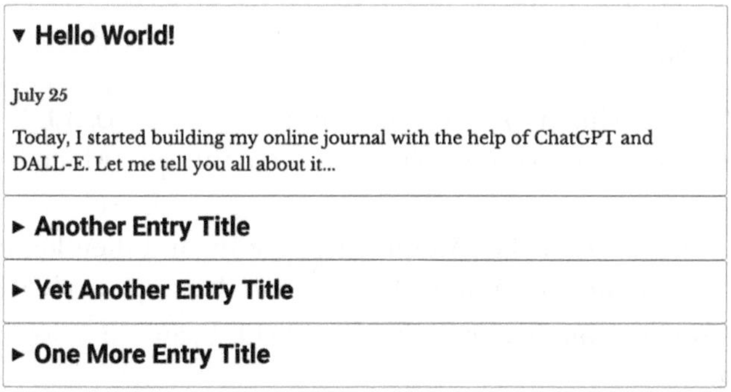

> ▼ **Hello World!**
>
> July 25
>
> Today, I started building my online journal with the help of ChatGPT and
> DALL-E. Let me tell you all about it...
>
> ▶ **Another Entry Title**
>
> ▶ **Yet Another Entry Title**
>
> ▶ **One More Entry Title**

Figure 5.3 Clicking the first summary element opens the accordion to display its full content.

To prompt ChatGPT to use accordions on your page, you can include an instruction
similar to the following:

```
Include a main section where each entry is an accordion using the HTML
summary and details elements. For each entry, the summary text is the entry
title and the details include the entry date, followed by the entry text.
Please provide four sample entries going back four days from today.
```

The point of using accordions is that you can fit quite a few posts on your page without
overwhelming visitors with a ton of content. The best news? Just tell ChatGPT that you
want to use accordions on your page, and it will handle all the HTML and CSS details
for you.

5.2.2 Generating images with GPT-4 and DALL-E

It's delightfully amazing that GPT-4 can generate essays, poems, emails, and, of course,
web page code from relatively simple prompts. However, if there's one feature that
makes GPT-4 "indistinguishable from magic" (in Arthur C. Clarke's words), it's the
model's ability to convert natural language into images. That is, given a text prompt
that describes something (a scene, an object, a person, and so on), GPT-4 can use that
description to generate an image to match.

The tool behind this seemingly magical feat is DALL-E (a blend of the *WALL-E* movie
title and the last name of the artist Salvador Dali), an OpenAI model optimized for converting natural language text descriptions into images.

> **WARNING** As you learn in the sections that follow, DALL-E is pretty good at turn-
> ing text into images, but it's *only* pretty good. It will only rarely generate images
> that you can use directly. You'll either have to tweak the images yourself in a
> graphics program or enlist the help of a graphics pro to modify a DALL-E image
> or use a generated image as a prototype for the final design.

ACCESSING DALL-E

You have two ways to access DALL-E:

- *OpenAI DALL-E app*—This app gives you direct access to DALL-E via your OpenAI account. There are a couple of ways to get to the app (which is shown in figure 5.4):
  - Go to https://openai.com, click Menu, click Log In, and then log in to your OpenAI account. In the selection of OpenAI tools that appear, click DALL-E.
  - Go to https://openai.com/dall-e-2, click Try DALL-E, and then log in to your OpenAI account.

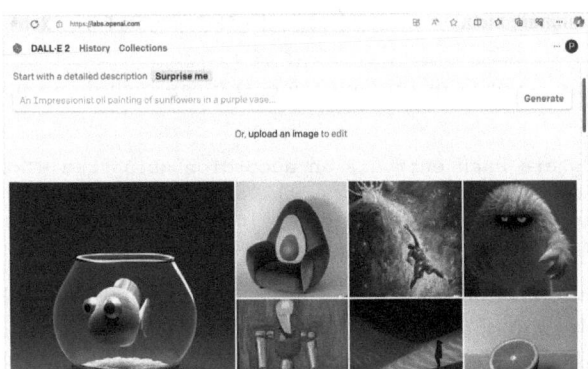

Figure 5.4   The OpenAI DALL-E app

- *Copilot Image Creator*—Using Microsoft Edge, go to https://www.bing.com/images/create (refer to figure 5.5) or https://copilot.microsoft.com/images/create; or, in Copilot, direct your prompt to Image Creator (for example, `Ask Image Creator for an image of a dog running on the moon`).

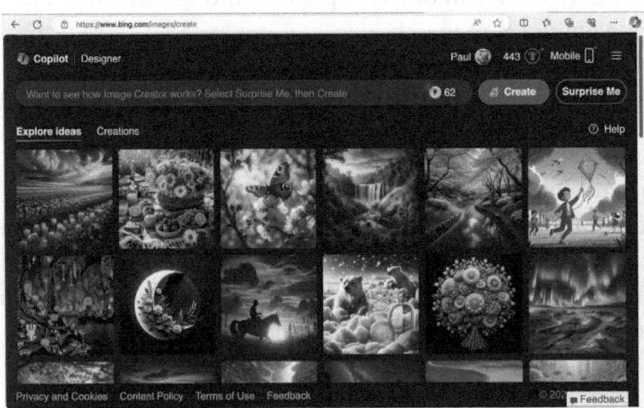

Figure 5.5   Copilot Image Creator

NOTE   Using DALL-E via the Open AI app isn't free. To use it, you need to pur-chase credits, where one credit is good for a single DALL-E request. As I write this, you can buy 115 credits for US $15 through your OpenAI account. Note that using DALL-E via Microsoft Copilot is free.

PROMPTING DALL-E

Getting DALL-E to produce satisfying images is a bit of an art in itself. The biggest mis-take that DALL-E rookies make is treating the app like a chatbot and providing it with instructions for what you want it to do. Instead, assume that your image already exists and that what you're writing is a detailed description for a person who is blind or has some other visual impairment that prevents them from seeing the image.

In your description, include not only the elements you want to see in the image but also one or more (more is usually better) keywords that specify the exact style of the image. Here are some ideas:

- *The mood*—Use keywords that evoke a positive mood (*bright, light, vibrant, peaceful*) or a negative mood (*gloomy, dark, muted, melancholic, stormy*).
- *The overall aesthetic*—For example, *Gothic, steampunk, cyberpunk, post-apocalyptic, Afro-futurism.*
- *The medium*—For example, *photograph, illustration, painting, cartoon.*
- *The specifics of the medium*—Some examples:
  - *Photograph*—Film type (*color, black and white*), context (*indoors, outdoors*), light-ing, angle (*long, medium, close-up*), depth of field (*shallow, deep*).
  - *Illustration*—Medium (*pencil, ink, charcoal, stencil, crayon,* and so on) and style (*digital art, collage, anime, Art Deco, Bauhaus,* and so on).
  - *Painting*—Medium (*watercolor, oil,* and so on) and style (*Impressionist, Manner-ist, Symbolist, Art Nouveau,* and so on).

NOTE The latest version of DALL-E (DALL-E 3) should be generally available by the time you read this. That's good news because, unlike previous versions of DALL-E, this latest version is much better at rendering text. If your image requires text, go ahead and include it in your description. However, check the resulting image text carefully because DALL-E 3 often either omits a letter or adds an extra letter.

To give you a sense of how prompting DALL-E works, it helps to go through a few examples. For my online journal page, I prompted Copilot as follows:

```
Please ask image creator to create a cartoon of a cow standing on two legs
with a text bubble over the cow's head that says "Moo".
```

Figure 5.6 shows the images I received. The one in the top left is pretty good!

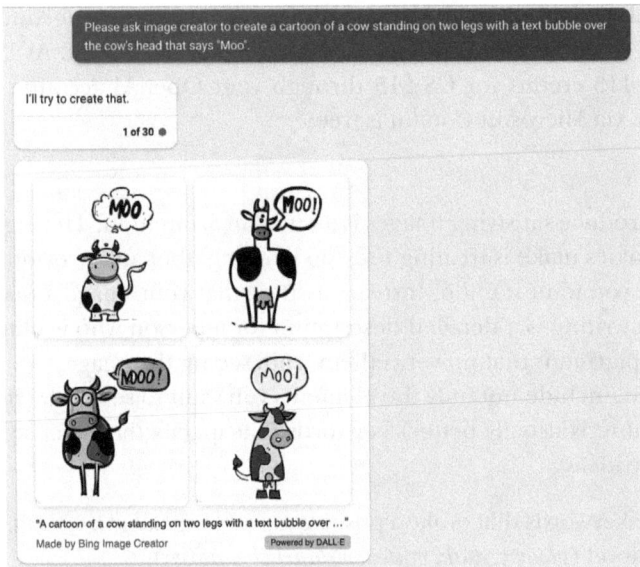

Figure 5.6   Cartoons generated by Image Creator based on my prompt

Here's an example prompt for a photograph that includes the keywords `medium shot` and `fluorescent lighting`:

```
A photograph of a golden retriever browsing in a library, medium shot,
fluorescent lighting.
```

Figure 5.7 shows an image that DALL-E generated from this prompt.

Figure 5.7   A photographic image generated by DALL-E

Here's a prompt for a digital art illustration that uses the keywords `post-apocalyptic` and `desolate`:

```
A digital art illustration of an old-fashioned diner in a post-apocalyptic,
desolate street scene.
```

Figure 5.8 shows an example DALL-E image generated from this prompt.

Figure 5.8   An illustration generated by DALL-E

Here's a prompt for an illuminated manuscript page that uses the keywords `bright` and `lavish`:

```
A bright, lavish, illuminated manuscript page that includes "Lorem ipsum"
text and drawings of cats in the margins.
```

Figure 5.9 shows an image that DALL-E created from this prompt.

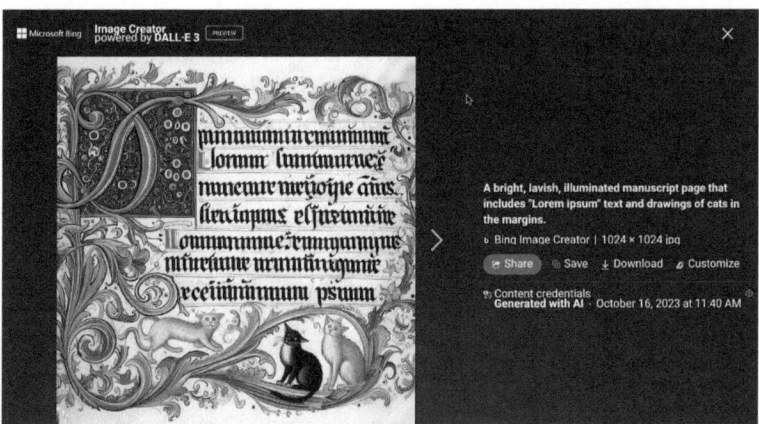

Figure 5.9   A DALL-E-generated illuminated manuscript page with cats

If DALL-E generates an image that you want to use (either to edit or to serve as a prototype), your next step is to save that image to your computer.

SAVING A GENERATED IMAGE

Once you have an image you want to use on your web page, you need to save the image to your computer:

- *OpenAI DALL-E app*—Click the image, click the three-dot (...) button that appears in the upper-right corner of the image, and then click Download.
- *Copilot Image Creator*—Click the image, and then click Download.

Either way, the image lands in your computer's Downloads folder. Move the image file to the same folder that holds your HTML and CSS files (which you'll create in the next section), and then rename the image with your preferred filename.

Now that you know how to get ChatGPT to help you write and edit text and generate images, you're ready to build the prompt that generates the web page code for an online journal.

5.2.3   *Crafting the prompt*

This chapter's project is an online journal page. Before proceeding, you should have the following at hand:

- A page logo, title, and tagline
- The names of the typefaces you want to use for the page headings and page text
- The names of the colors you want to apply to the page backgrounds and text

Refer to chapter 3 to learn more about these design elements and how to prompt ChatGPT for title, typeface, and color suggestions.

Even if you haven't got some writing to publish, you can still go through the process of prompting ChatGPT for your online journal HTML and CSS because the code will include placeholders for your text. You want to let ChatGPT know right away both that you want it to help you build a web page and that you don't know how to code so it will have to generate the code for you. That's all done by starting your prompt like this:

```
I want to build a web page for an online journal. I don't know how to code,
so I need you to provide the code for me.

First, write the HTML code for a web page that includes the following:
```

You then specify the content of your page, including the following (refer to figure 5.10):

- A header that includes your logo, page title, and tagline.
- A main element where each entry is an accordion using the HTML summary and details elements.
- For each entry, the summary text is the entry title, and the details element includes the entry date followed by the entry text.
- A footer that includes a copyright notice.

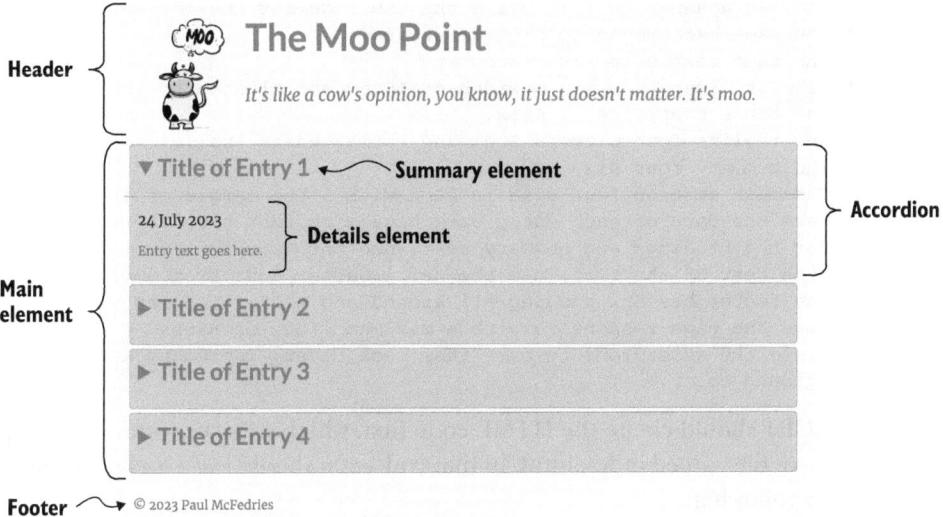

Figure 5.10 The sections of the online journal page

Next, you ask ChatGPT to generate the CSS for how you want your page formatted:

```
Second, in a separate file please write the CSS code for the following:
```

You then specify the formatting, including the following:

- The page background color and text color.
- The type sizes you want to use for the page title and tagline.
- The type size of the summary elements.
- The fonts to use for the headings, summaries, and regular page text.
- A maximum width for the page. This prevents the lines of text from getting too long. A maximum length of 850 px is fine for most pages.

Here's an example prompt for my own online journal page:

```
I want to build a web page for an online journal. I don't know how to code,
so I need you to provide the code for me.

First, write the HTML code for a web page that includes the following:
 * A header element that includes an image named logo.png, the title "The Moo
Point", and the tagline "It's like a cow's opinion, you know, it just doesn't
matter. It's moo."
 * A main section where each entry is an accordion using the HTML summary and
details elements.
 * For each entry, the summary text is the entry title and the details
include the entry date, followed by the entry text.
 * Please provide four sample entries going back four days from today.
 * A footer element that includes the Copyright symbol, followed by the
current year, followed by "Paul McFedries".
 * In the page head section, include the tag <meta charset="utf-8">.
```

```
Second, in a separate file write the CSS code for the following:
 * The page background color is mintcream.
 * The page text color is slategray.
 * Make the image a maximum width of 150px and floated to the left.
 * The title font size is 48px.
 * The tagline font size is 22px and formatted as italic.
 * The summary font size is 30px.
 * The main section font size is 20px with a top margin of 48px.
 * Make the date of each entry dark blue with font size 18px.
 * For the headings and summary text, use the Lato font from Google Fonts.
For the rest of the text, use the Merriweather font from Google Fonts.
 * The footer has 5px padding all around and a 10px top margin.
 * Make the page responsive with a maximum width of 850px.
 * Style the accordions to make them look nicer, including a powderblue
background color.
```

ChatGPT should create the HTML code first, which you can copy and then paste and save to a file named index.html. In that code, you should see a line near the top similar to the following:

```
<link rel="stylesheet" type="text/css" href="styles.css">
```

This code tells the web browser to look for the CSS code in a file named styles.css, so your next task is to copy the generated CSS code, paste it into a file, and save it as styles.css (or whatever name you see in the `<link>` tag). Be sure to save styles.css in the same folder as your index.html file. You also need to copy your image file into the same folder. Refer to appendix A to learn more about working web page files.

I submitted this prompt to GPT-4 using OpenAI's ChatGPT app. The code it generated resulted in the page shown in figure 5.11.

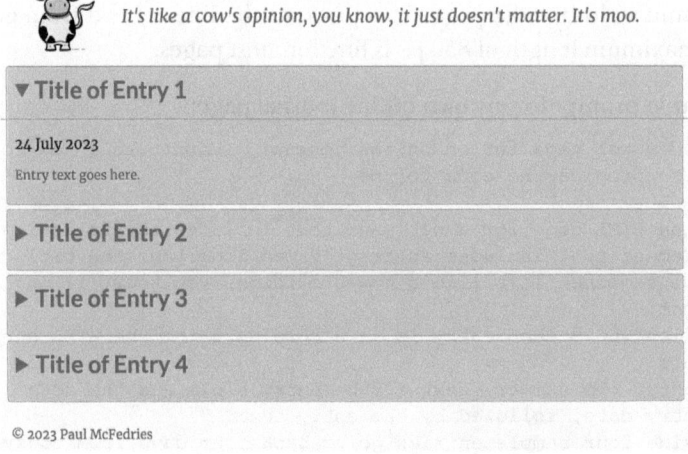

Figure 5.11   My online journal page generated by ChatGPT

NOTE To get the page shown in figure 5.11, I had to correct a mistake that ChatGPT made in the CSS code. I talk about this error in the next section.

If you like the online journal that ChatGPT made for you, you can skip the rest of this chapter and deploy the code as I describe in appendix B. However, if you'd like to know more about the code ChatGPT generated, the next section gives you a closer look.

5.3 Examining the code

If you're curious about the code that ChatGPT generates, in this section, I'm going to provide you with a brief and not-too-technical overview of the online journal code that resulted from my prompt from the previous section (that journal page is shown in figure 5.11). Your ChatGPT-generated code will be different from mine not only because your text and images will be different but also because

- ChatGPT's algorithms include some built-in randomness, so the same prompt will often generate slightly different code each time you run it.
- ChatGPT's output varies depending on the model (GPT-3.5 versus GPT-4) and the app (OpenAI versus Copilot). For Copilot, the output also depends on the conversation style (creative, balanced, or precise).

NOTE The generated HTML and CSS code for my online journal page are available on this book's website (www.manning.com/books/build-a-website-with-chatgpt) and in the book's GitHub repository: https://github.com/paulmcfe/websites-with-chatgpt.

However, every version of ChatGPT should output HTML and CSS code that's at least similar to what's displayed in the next two sections, so my code annotations should help you understand what's happening under the hood.

5.3.1 Examining the HTML

The HTML code that ChatGPT generated for my online journal page is shown here:

```
<!DOCTYPE html>
<html>
    <head>
        <meta charset="utf-8">          ◄─── Specifies the page character set
        <title>The Moo Point</title>
        <link rel="stylesheet"          ◄─── Tells the web browser
            href="styles.css">                where to find the CSS code
        <link rel="preconnect"
            href="https://fonts.googleapis.com">
        <link rel="preconnect"
            href=https://fonts.gstatic.com
            crossorigin>                              Loads the
        <link href="https://fonts.googleapis.com/css2?    page fonts
        family=Lato:wght@400;700&family=Merriweather:     from Google
        ital,wght@0,400;0,700;1,400&                      Fonts
        display=swap" rel="stylesheet">
```

```
    </head>
    <body>
        <header>
            <img src="logo.png" alt="Logo">                    Page logo
            <h1 class="title">The Moo Point</h1>               Page title
            <p class="tagline">
                It's like a cow's opinion, you know, it
                just doesn't matter. It's moo.                 Page
            </p>                                               tagline
        </header>

        <main>                              Entry summary (title)
            <details>
                <summary class="entry-title">
                    Title of Entry 1
                </summary>                              Entry date
                <p class="entry-date">24 July 2023</p>
                <p class="entry-text">Entry text goes here.</p>
            </details>
                                                        Entry text

            <details>
                <summary class="entry-title">Title of Entry 2</summary>
                <p class="entry-date">25 July 2023</p>
                <p class="entry-text">Entry text goes here.</p>
            </details>

            <details>
                <summary class="entry-title">Title of Entry 3</summary>
                <p class="entry-date">26 July 2023</p>
                <p class="entry-text">Entry text goes here.</p>
            </details>

            <details>
                <summary class="entry-title">Title of Entry 4</summary>
                <p class="entry-date">27 July 2023</p>
                <p class="entry-text">Entry text goes here.</p>
            </details>
        </main>

        <footer>
            <p>&copy; 2023 Paul McFedries</p>                  Page footer
        </footer>
    </body>
</html>
```

Page header · *Details element* (margin labels)

Here are a few notes to bear in mind when reading the HTML code:

- The code <meta charset="utf-8"> immediately after the <head> tag in the HTML file tells the browser the character set used in the page. You don't need to know what this means, only that this tag is required to make the copyright symbol display properly. It will also help characters such as em dashes (—) and curly quotation marks (" and ") display properly if you use those and similar characters in your journal entries.

- This code uses placeholder text for the entries, so you'd need to add your own title, date, and text for each entry.
- If the page tagline sounds familiar, it's a line borrowed from the character Joey of the old TV show *Friends*.

Finally, note that the HTML code includes the following line:

```
<link rel="stylesheet" href="styles.css">
```

This tag tells the web browser where to find the CSS code, which I describe in the next section.

5.3.2 Examining the CSS

ChatGPT's generated CSS code for my online journal page is shown here:

```
body {
    background-color: mintcream;
    color: slategray;
    font-family: 'Merriweather', serif;
    max-width: 850px;
    margin: 0 auto;
}
img {
    max-width: 150px;
    float: left;
}
h1 {
    font-size: 48px;
    font-family: 'Lato', sans-serif;
}
p.tagline {
    font-size: 22px;
    font-style: italic;
}
main {
    margin-top: 48px;
}
.summary, .entry-title {
    font-size: 30px;
    font-family: 'Lato', sans-serif;
}
.date {
    color: darkblue;
    font-size: 18px;
}
footer {
    padding: 5px;
    margin-top: 10px;
}
details {
    background: powderblue;
    margin: 5px 0;
    border: 1px solid #aaa;
    border-radius: 4px;
```

Sets the page background color, text color, and font

Centers the page

Sets the maximum page width to 850 px

Sets a maximum logo width, and floats it to the left

Sets the page title font size to 48 px, and applies the Lato font

Styles the tagline with font size 22 px and italics

Styles the entry titles with font size 30 px and the Lato font

Styles the entry date with color darkblue and font size 18 px

Applies special styles to the accordions

```
        padding: .625em .625em .625em .625em;
        width: 100%;
}
summary {
        font-weight: bold;
        margin: -.625em -.625em 0;
        padding: .625em;
}
details[open] {
        padding: .625em;
        border: 1px solid #aaa;
}
details[open] summary {
        border-bottom: 1px solid #aaa;
        margin-bottom: .625em;
}     #I
```

Fortunately, ChatGPT rarely makes mistakes when generating HTML and CSS code, but in this case, it did. To see the error, first look back at the following line from the HTML code (there are similar lines for each entry):

```
<p class="entry-date">24 July 2023</p>
```

In this `<p>` tag, the `class` attribute refers to a set of CSS styles applied to the paragraph. In this example, the class name is `entry-date`. In the CSS code, class styles are designated by appending a period (`.`) before the class name. However, you can scour the CSS code all day long, and you won't find any CSS rule that begins with `.entry-date`. The closest is `.date`, which means ChatGPT made a mistake. (How would you know? In this case, you'd know by looking at the page and noticing that the entry dates aren't formatted with the `darkblue` color as specified in the prompt.) In the CSS, you fix the problem by changing `.date` to `.entry-date`.

If you like, you can use the annotations from earlier in this section to tweak your web page code, as I describe next.

5.4   *Customizing the page*

If you're not happy with the page that ChatGPT generated for you, one possible fix is to modify your prompt and then resubmit it. However, for relatively small customizations, it's often easiest to edit the code manually.

First, here are some customization suggestions for the HTML code:

- In the header, you can edit the title or tagline. Just be sure not to edit or delete the associated HTML tags: `<h1>` and `</h1>` for the title, and `<p>` and `</p>` for the tagline.
- To add a new entry (that is, a new accordion), follow these steps:
  a   Open the HTML file in a text editor.
  b   Select an existing entry. That is, select everything between and including a single pair of `<details>` and `</details>` tags, as shown in figure 5.12.

```
11   <body>
12       <header>
13           <img src="logo.png" alt="Logo">
14           <h1 class="title">The Moo Point</h1>
15           <p class="tagline">It's like a cow's opinion, you know, it just doesn't matter. It's
             moo.</p>
16       </header>
17
18       <main>
19           <details>
20               <summary class="entry-title">Title of Entry 1</summary>
21               <p class="entry-date">24 July 2023</p>
22               <p class="entry-text">Entry text goes here.</p>
23           </details>
24
25           <details>
26               <summary class="entry-title">Title of Entry 2</summary>
27               <p class="entry-date">25 July 2023</p>
28               <p class="entry-text">Entry text goes here.</p>
29           </details>
30
31           <details>
32               <summary class="entry-title">Title of Entry 3</summary>
33               <p class="entry-date">26 July 2023</p>
34               <p class="entry-text">Entry text goes here.</p>
35           </details>
```

Select an existing entry.

Ln 19, Col 1 (182)   HTML ◇   Tabs (4 sp) ⌄

Figure 5.12   Select an existing accordion entry.

c   Copy the entry (for example, by pressing either Ctrl-C or Cmd-C).

d   Create a new line at the point where you want the new entry to appear. For example, if you want the new entry to appear above the existing entries, position the cursor immediately before the first <details> tag and then press Enter or Return.

e   Position the cursor on the new line you just created, as shown in figure 5.13.

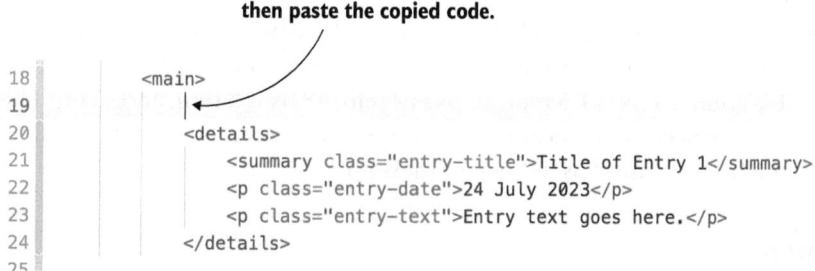

Position the cursor here and then paste the copied code.

```
18   <main>
19   
20       <details>
21           <summary class="entry-title">Title of Entry 1</summary>
22           <p class="entry-date">24 July 2023</p>
23           <p class="entry-text">Entry text goes here.</p>
24       </details>
25
```

Figure 5.13   Position the cursor where you want to paste the code you copied.

f   Paste the copied code (for example, by pressing either Ctrl-C or Cmd-C).

g   Edit the entry title, date, and text.

- If your entry text includes multiple paragraphs, you can ensure that each paragraph renders properly by surrounding it with a `<p class="entry-text">` tag at the beginning and a `</p>` tag at the end:

```
<main>
    <details>
        <summary class="entry-title">Title of Entry 1</summary>
        <p class="entry-date">24 July 2023</p>
        <p class="entry-text">Entry text goes here.</p>
        <p class="entry-text">Another paragraph goes here.</p>
        <p class="entry-text">You can keep going if you want.</p>
    </details>
```

- In the footer section of the HTML code, you can add links to your social media accounts, as I describe in chapter 4.

Now, here are a few customization ideas for the CSS code:

- To format the text of each entry, add `.entry-text { }` to the bottom of your CSS code and populate it with the formatting you want. For example, the following code adjusts the entry font size:

```
.entry-text {
    font-size: 20px;
}
```

- If you want your page to have a different maximum width, change the `max-width` value to something other than `850px`.
- For any color value, you can change the existing color to a different color keyword.
- For any font size value, you can change the number to increase or decrease the font size. Just make sure you leave the `px` unit in place.
- For any padding or margin value, you can change the number to increase or decrease the padding or margins. In each case, be sure to leave the `px` unit in place.
- To make your page code more accessible, consider converting all px measurements to rem measurements. 1 rem is by default equivalent to 16 px, so 20 px is 1.25 rem, 24 px is 1.5 rem, 32 px is 2 rem, 48 px is 3 rem, and so on. The rem unit is more accessible because it measures font sizes relative to the default font size the browser user has defined in their browser settings.

Summary

- An accordion is a special HTML feature that consists of a summary (the title or description of the accordion) and details (the entirety of the accordion content).
- Clicking the accordion summary toggles the full accordion content between hidden and displayed.

- To get AI to generate an image from a text prompt, use either OpenAI's DALL-E app or Copilot's Image Creator.
- When prompting for an image, use keywords to evoke the overall mood and aesthetic, the medium, and the specifics of the medium.
- For best results, your page prompt should be as specific as possible, including colors, font sizes, and heading levels.
- Save the generated HTML to the index.html file and the generated CSS to the filename suggested by ChatGPT in the HTML code, usually styles.css.

Adding links and navigation

This chapter covers

- Creating links to other sites and pages
- Creating a navigation bar for your site
- Asking ChatGPT to help you design your pages
- Prompting ChatGPT to build an information website for an organization
- Examining and customizing ChatGPT's web page code

In each of the web projects you've seen so far in this book, you've cajoled ChatGPT into providing you with the code for a single web page. One-page websites are legion on the web, but it's more common for a site to have two or more pages. Once you add that second page, however, questions quickly arise: How do you get a site visitor from your home page to the other page? And once someone gets to that other page, how do you get them back to the home page? How do you figure all this out with a site that has three, four, or even more pages?

Answering these and similar questions is the topic of this chapter. In the pages that follow, you learn how to enable a visitor to your site to jump from one page to another by asking ChatGPT to craft some web page code that creates a clickable link to another page. You also learn how to ask ChatGPT to create a special web page element called a navigation bar that brings links to all your site pages into a single, handy location for easy access.

All this information then goes into a detailed prompt that you'll pass along to ChatGPT to produce the code for a very common project pattern: a website that provides information about an organization. This chapter also provides a high-level explanation of the code generated by ChatGPT and pointers for customizing the code manually to get everything just the way you want.

6.1 Understanding this chapter's project

In this chapter, you're going to enlist ChatGPT to help you build a simple information website for an organization. The final page will include the following components:

- A header element that includes the site title and tagline
- A navigation element with links to the site's other pages
- A main element that includes an introduction to the site as well as some engaging content for the reader
- A footer element that includes a copyright notice

Figure 6.1 shows an example of an information website home page created from code generated by ChatGPT. This kind of website can be easily modified to act as an information site for a community, charity, event, team, or band, or even a favorite movie or TV show.

Figure 6.1 An information website home page generated by ChatGPT

6.2   *Building the information site home page*

An information website contains multiple web pages, so it's a good idea to build the site in stages. My recommended process is summarized here:

1 Prompt ChatGPT to generate the HTML code for the website's home page.
2 Prompt ChatGPT to generate the CSS code for the website's styling. Note that it's best to combine these first two steps into a single prompt.
3 For each of your other site pages, prompt ChatGPT to generate the HTML code for that page. In particular, the prompt for each of the other site pages should include the following:

   – An instruction to use the same CSS file in which you saved the CSS generated in step 2.
   – An instruction to not generate any extra styles, particularly inline styles (that is, CSS code inserted directly into HTML tags). ChatGPT always wants to include CSS styling with its HTML output, so without this instruction, ChatGPT will almost certainly add extra styles, which could conflict with or override the styles in the CSS file.

Before you get to all that, take a minute to familiarize yourself with the new web page technology introduced in this chapter.

6.2.1   *Creating links*

One of the signal traits of HTML (in fact, it's the *H* in *HTML*) is *hypertext*, which is just a fancy word for links that take you to other pages, whether those pages exist elsewhere on your website or anywhere on the web. A link is usually a word or phrase configured so that when someone clicks that text, the web browser navigates to whatever web page is specified by the link's configuration.

If you're linking to a page on your site in the same directory as the current HTML file, you can ask ChatGPT for a link to that filename. Here's some code that asks for a link to a page named about.html:

```
Provide the HTML code for a link to a web page named about.html.
```

Figure 6.2 shows the output from the ChatGPT app. Here's the HTML code returned by ChatGPT:

```
<a href="about.html">About</a>
```

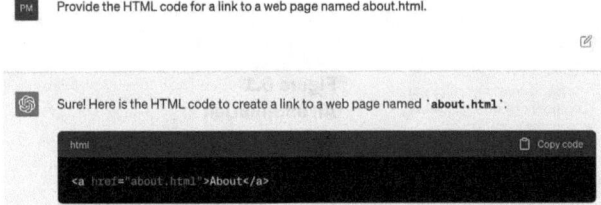

**Figure 6.2
ChatGPT's code
for a link to the
about.html page**

As the code shows, the HTML tags you use to create a link are <a> and its corresponding </a> closing tag. In the a element, you use the href attribute to insert the address—often called the *URL* (short for *uniform resource locator*)—of your link. Figure 6.3 shows how this element works.

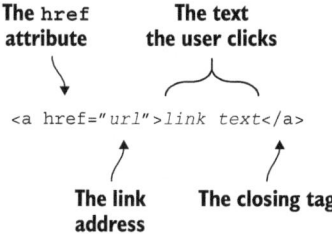

Figure 6.3   The syntax to use for the <a> **tag**

If the file on your site that you want to link to resides in a different directory, you need to include that directory name in your prompt:

```
Provide the HTML code for a link to a web page named index.html in the /faq
directory.
```

Figure 6.4 shows the output from the ChatGPT app. Here's the HTML code returned by ChatGPT:

```
<a href="/faq/index.html">FAQ</a>
```

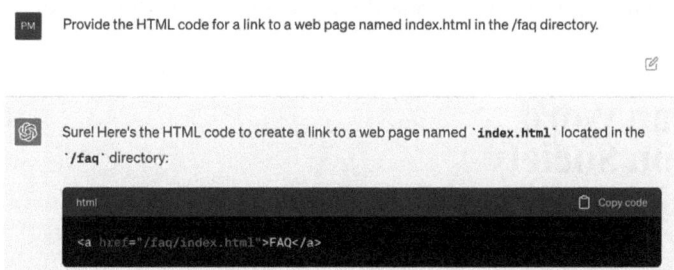

Figure 6.4   ChatGPT's code for a link to the index.html page in the /faq directory

Notice that I preceded the directory name with a slash (/), which tells the AI that the specified directory runs off my site's root directory. If, instead, the location is a subdirectory of the directory where your HTML file resides, leave off the slash in the prompt.

For an external web page, it's usually easiest to create an empty link (that is, <a href="">link text</a>, surf to the page, copy the address, and then paste that address between the quotation marks of the href attribute value. However, if the page is describable—for example, you know the site's name and can describe the page content uniquely in a few words—why not get your AI assistant to do the dirty work for you? Here's an example:

```
Provide the HTML code for a link to the Wikipedia page on rutabagas.
```

Figure 6.5 shows the output from the ChatGPT app. Here's the HTML code returned by ChatGPT:

```
<a href="https://en.wikipedia.org/wiki/Rutabaga">Rutabaga</a>
```

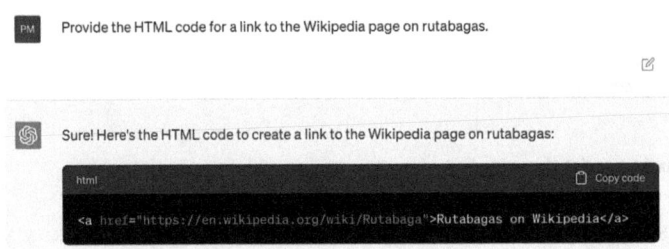

Figure 6.5   ChatGPT's code for a link to the rutabagas page on Wikipedia

6.2.2   Creating the navigation bar

One very common website pattern is the *navigation bar*, which is a collection of links to the other pages on the website (or, if the site is large, to the site's most important pages). The navigation bar can be horizontal or vertical, but the most common config- uration is a horizontal strip that runs across the page, just below the header. Figure 6.6 shows an example.

Figure 6.6   An example of a navigation bar

In HTML, you create a navigation bar using the `<nav>` and `</nav>` tags. Between these tags, you add the links to each site page. You can ask ChatGPT to generate a similar navigation bar by including the following instruction in your prompt:

```
Create a navigation element that includes five links:
* The text "Home" that links to the file "index.html".
* The text "Blog" that links to the file "blog.html".
* The text "FAQ" that links to the file "faq.html".
* The text "About" that links to the file "about.html".
* The text "Contact" that links to the file "contact.html".
```

Based on this instruction, ChatGPT will generate HTML code similar to the following (which is the code that created the navigation bar shown in figure 6.6):

```
<nav>
    <a href="index.html">Home</a>
    <a href="blog.html">Blog</a>
    <a href="faq.html">FAQ</a>
    <a href="about.html">About</a>
    <a href="contact.html">Contact</a>
</nav>
```

You may notice two strange things about how the browser renders the list in figure 6.6:

- The list runs horizontally instead of vertically.
- The list items are spaced evenly across the page.

The browser renders the navigation bar that way because of the following CSS code, which applies a few properties to the nav element:

```
nav {
    border-top: 1px solid midnightblue;
    border-bottom: 1px solid midnightblue;
    display: flex;
    justify-content: space-between;
    margin: 20px 0;
    padding: 10px 0;
}
```

Adds a border above and below the nav element

Turns the nav element into a Flexbox container

Styles the nav element's margins and padding

Tells the browser to space the items evenly

The main thing to note here is the `display: flex` declaration, which converts the `nav` element into a Flexbox container. By default, it displays its items horizontally rather than vertically. (You'll learn more about Flexbox in chapter 10.)

> **NOTE** Depending on the number of items in your navigation bar, that element may be too wide to render well on small screens, particularly smartphone screens in portrait mode. The usual solution is to convert the navigation element to an icon that displays a menu when clicked or tapped. To learn how to prompt ChatGPT to generate the code for a menu like this, see chapter 12.

Now you have everything you need to know to create your home page prompt for ChatGPT.

6.2.3 *Crafting the home page prompt*

This chapter's project is an information website. Before moving on to the prompting portion of the show, make sure you already have these items:

- Some or all of the following: a page logo, title, and tagline
- The names of the typefaces you want to use for the page headings and the page text
- The keywords of the colors you want to apply to the page backgrounds and text

Refer to chapter 3 to learn more about these design elements and how to prompt ChatGPT for title, typeface, and color suggestions.

You're now ready to enlist ChatGPT to help you generate the code for your information website's home page. Your prompt should begin like this:

```
I want to build a web page for an information website. I don't know how to
code, so I need you to provide the code for me.
```

```
First, write the HTML code for a web page that includes the following:
```

You then specify the content of your page, including the following (refer to figure 6.7):

- A header that includes your site title and tagline
- A navigation element that includes links to the other site pages (or the site's main pages)
- A main element with a lead paragraph that welcomes visitors to the site
- One or more section elements that display engaging content to the reader
- A footer that includes a copyright notice

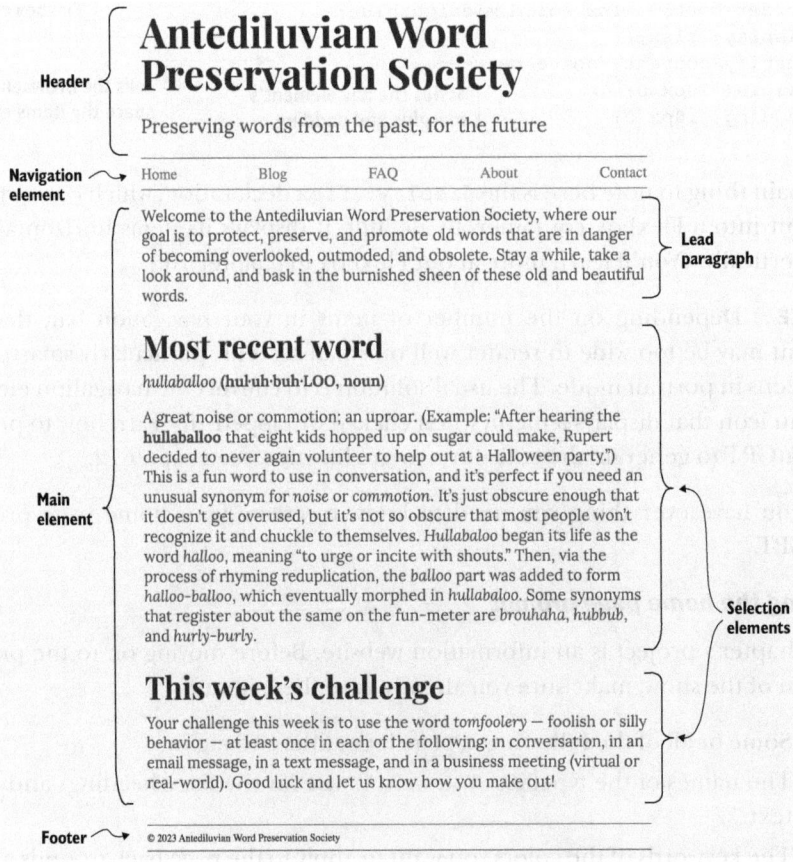

Figure 6.7 The elements of the information website home page

Next, you ask ChatGPT to generate the CSS for how you want your page formatted:

```
Second, in a separate file please write the CSS code for the following:
```

You then specify the formatting, including the following:

- The page background color and text color
- The type sizes you want to use for the page title and tagline
- The type size of the headers and page text
- The fonts to use for the headings and regular page text
- A maximum width for the page. This prevents the lines of text from getting too long. A maximum length of 800 px is fine for this type of site.

Here's an example prompt for my own information page:

```
I want to build a home page for an information website. I don't know how to code, so
I need you to provide the code for me.

First, write the HTML code for a web page that includes the following:
 * The page title is "Antediluvian Word Preservation Society".
 * A header that includes the title "Antediluvian Word Preservation Society" and the
tagline "Preserving words from the past, for the future".
 * After the header, a navigation element that includes five links:
   * The text "Home" that links to the file "index.html".
   * The text "Blog" that links to the file "blog.html".
   * The text "FAQ" that links to the file "faq.html".
   * The text "About" that links to the file "about.html".
   * The text "Contact" that links to the file "contact.html".
 * A main element that includes the following:
   * An introductory paragraph that includes the text "Welcome to the Antediluvian
Word Preservation Society, where our goal is to protect, preserve, and promote old
words that are in danger of becoming overlooked, outmoded, and obsolete. Stay a
while, take a look around, and bask in the burnished sheen of these old and beautiful
words."
   * A section element with the second-level heading "Most recent word", followed by a
third-level heading with the text "*hullaballoo* (hul·uh·buh·LOO, noun)", followed by
a paragraph that includes the text "A great noise or commotion; an uproar. (Example:
"After hearing the **hullaballoo** that eight kids hopped up on sugar could make,
Rupert decided to never again volunteer to help out at a Halloween party.") [etc.]."
   * Another section element with the second-level heading "This week's challenge"
followed by a paragraph that includes the text "Your challenge this week is to use
the word *tomfoolery* — foolish or silly behavior — at least once in each of the
following: in conversation, in an email message, in a text message, and in a business
meeting (virtual or real-world). Good luck and let us know how you make out!"
   * In the above text, make each word that's surrounded by double asterisks bold, and
make each word that's surrounded by single asterisks italic.
 * A footer element that includes the Copyright symbol, followed by the current year,
followed by "Antediluvian Word Preservation Society".
 * In the page head section, include the tag <meta charset="utf-8">.

Second, in a separate file write the CSS code for the following:
 * The body element has 25px padding and a background color of oldlace.
 * Make the title 64px, line height 1, color midnightblue, 20px bottom margin, and
the Playfair Display typeface from Google Fonts.
```

```
* Make the tagline font size 30px.
* The navigation element has a top and bottom border colored midnightblue.
* The navigation element has 20px top and bottom border and 10px top and bottom
padding.
* Style the navigation links with font size 24px;
* Space the navigation links so that they span the entire width of the body.
* Style the second-level headings with size 48px, 30px top margin, 10px bottom
margin, the color midnightblue, and the Playfair Display typeface from Google Fonts.
* Style the rest of the page text with size 24px, the color darkslategray, and the
Lora typeface from Google Fonts.
* Style the links with the color steelblue and no underline.
* The footer has 10px top and bottom padding, a 50px top margin, and a top and
bottom border colored midnightblue.
* The page has a maximum width of 800px and is centered within the browser window.
```

ChatGPT should create the HTML code first, which you can copy and then paste and save to a file named index.html. In that code, you should see a line near the top similar to the following:

```
<link rel="stylesheet" type="text/css" href="styles.css">
```

This code tells the web browser to look for the CSS code in a file named styles.css, so your next task is to copy the generated CSS code, paste it into a file, and save it as styles.css (or whatever name you see in the `<link>` tag). Be sure to save styles.css in the same folder as your index.html file. You also need to copy your image file into the same folder. Refer to appendix A to learn more about working with web page files.

I submitted this prompt to GPT-4 using OpenAI's ChatGPT app. The code it generated resulted in the page shown in figure 6.8.

Figure 6.8
My information website home page generated by ChatGPT

If you like the information website that ChatGPT made for you, you can skip the rest of this chapter and deploy the code as I describe in appendix B. However, if you'd like to know more about the code ChatGPT generated, the next section gives you a closer look.

6.3 Examining the home page code

If you're curious about the code that ChatGPT generates, in this section, I'm going to provide you with a brief and not-too-technical overview of the information website code that resulted from my prompt from the previous section (the information website home page is shown in figure 6.8).

> **NOTE** The generated HTML and CSS code for my information website home page are available on this book's website (www.manning.com/books/build-a -website-with-chatgpt) and in the book's GitHub repository: https://github .com/paulmcfe/websites-with-chatgpt.

Every version of ChatGPT should output HTML and CSS code that's at least similar to what's displayed in the next two sections, so my code annotations should help you understand what's happening under the hood.

6.3.1 Examining the HTML

The HTML code that ChatGPT generated for my information site's home page is shown here:

```
<!DOCTYPE html>
<html>                              Specifies the page character set
<head>
  <title>Antediluvian Word Preservation Society</title>
  <meta charset="utf-8">
  <link href="https://fonts.googleapis.com/css2?
  family= Playfair+Display:wght@400;700&display=swap"      Loads the page fonts
  rel="stylesheet">                                        from Google Fonts
  <link href="https://fonts.googleapis.com/css2?
  family=Lora:ital,wght@0,400;0,700;1,400&display=swap"    Tells the web
  rel="stylesheet">                                        browser where to
  <link rel="stylesheet" href="styles.css">               find the CSS code
</head>
<body>
  <header>                                                        Page
    <h1>Antediluvian Word Preservation Society</h1>              title      Page
    <p>Preserving words from the past, for the future</p>                  header
  </header>                                                      Page
  <nav>                                                          tagline
    <a href="index.html">Home</a>
    <a href="blog.html">Blog</a>
    <a href="faq.html">FAQ</a>                          Navigation element
    <a href="about.html">About</a>
    <a href="contact.html">Contact</a>
  </nav>
```

```
<main>
  <p>Welcome to the Antediluvian Word Preservation Society,
     where our goal is to protect, preserve, and promote old
     words that are in danger of becoming overlooked, outmoded,
     and obsolete. Stay a while, take a look around, and bask
     in the burnished sheen of these old and beautiful words.</p>
  <section>
    <h2>Most recent word</h2>
    <h3><em>hullaballoo</em> (hul·uh·buh·LOO, noun)</h3>
    <p>A great noise or commotion; an uproar. (Example: "After hearing
       the <strong>hullaballoo</strong> that eight kids hopped up on
       sugar could make, Rupert decided to never again volunteer to help
       out at a Halloween party.") This is a fun word to use in
       conversation, and it's perfect if you need an unusual synonym for
       <em>noise</em> or <em>commotion</em>. It's just obscure enough
       that it doesn't get overused, but it's not so obscure that most
       people won't recognize it and chuckle to themselves.
       <em>Hullabaloo</em> began its life as the word <em>halloo</em>,
       meaning "to urge or incite with shouts." Then, via the process of
       rhyming reduplication, the <em>balloo</em> part was added to form
       <em>halloo-balloo</em>, which eventually morphed in
       <em>hullabaloo</em>. Some synonyms that register about the same on
       the fun-meter are <em>brouhaha</em>, <em>hubbub</em>, and
       <em>hurly-burly</em>.</p>
  </section>
  <section>
    <h2>This week's challenge</h2>
      <p>Your challenge this week is to use the word <em>tomfoolery</em>
      -- foolish or silly behavior -- at least once in each of the
      following: in conversation, in an email message, in a text
      message, and in a business meeting (virtual or real-world).
      Good luck and let us know how you make out!</p>
  </section>
</main>
<footer>
  &copy; 2023 Antediluvian Word Preservation Society
</footer>
</body>
</html>
```

(margin annotations: "Main element" pointing to the `<main>` element; "Page footer" pointing to the `<footer>` element)

Here are a few notes to bear in mind when reading the HTML code:

- The code `<meta charset="utf-8">` in the `<head>` tag in the HTML file tells the browser the character set used in the page. You don't need to know what this means, only that this tag is required to make the copyright symbol display properly. It will also help characters such as em dashes (—) and curly quotation marks (" and ") display properly if you use those and similar characters in your page text.

- For some reason, ChatGPT referenced the two Google Fonts typefaces using two separate `<link>` tags. No idea why, but it works, so I just went with it.

- In the prompt, I asked ChatGPT to look for words surrounded by double asterisks (for example, `**hullaballoo**`) and make those words bold. In the HTML, ChatGPT replaced the double asterisks with the `<strong>` and `</strong>` tags, which make the text between them bold.
- Similarly, I asked ChatGPT to look for words surrounded by single asterisks (for example, `*noise*`) and make those words italic. In the HTML, ChatGPT replaced the asterisks with the `<em>` and `</em>` tags, which make the text between them italic.

Note that the HTML code includes the following line:

```
<link rel="stylesheet" href="styles.css">
```

This tag tells the web browser where to find the CSS code, which I describe in the next section.

6.3.2 Examining the CSS

ChatGPT's generated CSS code for my information website home page is shown here:

```
body {
  background-color: oldlace;    ← Sets the page background color
  max-width: 800px;             ← Sets the maximum page width to 800 px
  margin: 0 auto;               ← Centers the page
  padding: 25px;
}
header h1 {
  font-size: 64px;
  line-height: 1;
  color: midnightblue;          Styles the page title font size to
  font-family: 'Playfair Display', serif;    64 px, with color midnightblue
  margin-bottom: 20px;          and the Playfair Display font
}
header p {
  font-size: 30px;              ← Styles the tagline with font size 30 px
}
nav {
  border-top: 1px solid midnightblue;
  border-bottom: 1px solid midnightblue;
  margin: 20px 0;               Styles the nav element (as
  padding: 10px 0;              described earlier)
  display: flex;
  justify-content: space-between;
}
nav a {
    font-size: 24px;            ← Sizes the nav links to 24 px
}
a {
  color: steelblue;             Styles the page links with color
  text-decoration: none;        steelblue and no underline
}
h2 {
```

```
   font-size: 48px;
   color: midnightblue;
   font-family: 'Playfair Display', serif;
   margin: 30px 0 0;
}
h3, p, main p {
   font-size: 24px;
   color: darkslategray;
   font-family: 'Lora', serif;
   margin-top: 8px;
}
footer {
   border-top: 1px solid midnightblue;
   border-bottom: 1px solid midnightblue;
   padding: 10px 0;
   margin-top: 50px;
}
```

Styles the second-level headings with font size 48 px, color midnightblue, and the Playfair Display font

Styles the regular page text with font size 24 px, color darkslategray, and the Lora font

Styles the footer

If you like, you can use these annotations to tweak your web page code, as I describe in the next section.

6.4   *Customizing the home page*

If ChatGPT's information website code is off for some reason, you have two ways to fix things:

- If the page is far from what you want, rewrite your prompt, start a new chat session, and try again.
- If the page is close to what you want, ask ChatGPT to make the necessary adjustments for you. Be sure you submit this request in the same session as your original prompt.

For the second case, if the code produced by ChatGPT really just needs some small tweaks, consider modifying the code manually based on the annotations I provided in the previous section. Because you don't know web page code, it's best not to try to make any major changes. However, that leaves quite a few ways you can alter the code to get the page you want.

First, here are some customization suggestions for the HTML code:

- In the header, you can edit the title or tagline. Just be sure not to edit or delete the associated HTML tags: `<h1>` and `</h1>` for the title, and `<p>` and `</p>` for the tagline.
- Edit the `section` elements as you need, adjusting the heading and text.
- To add a new section, follow these steps:
   a   Open the HTML file in a text editor.
   b   Select an existing section. That is, select everything between and including a single pair of `<section>` and `</section>` tags, as shown in figure 6.9.

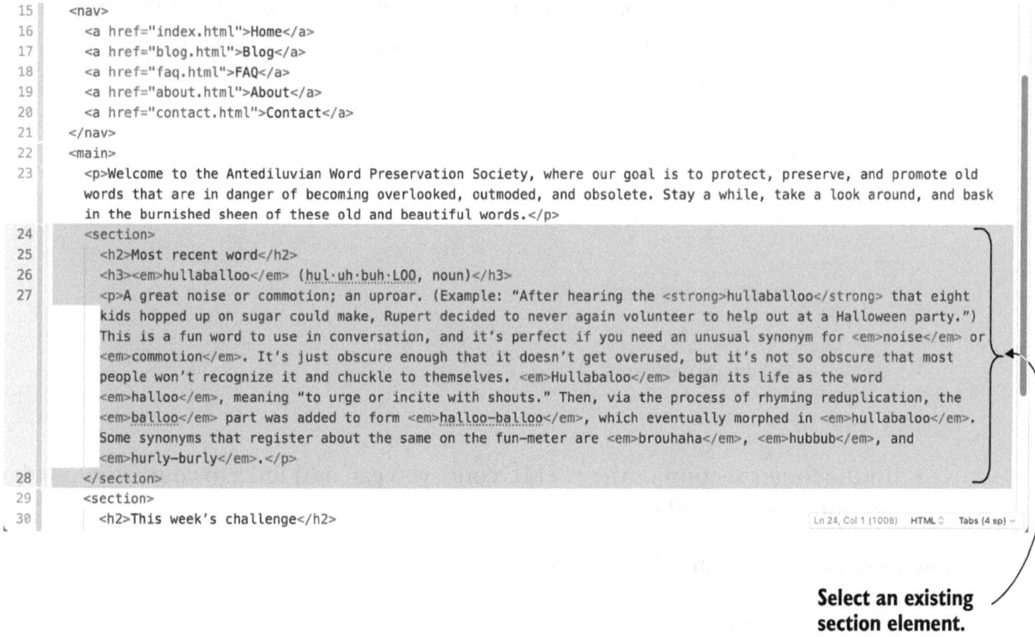

```
15    <nav>
16      <a href="index.html">Home</a>
17      <a href="blog.html">Blog</a>
18      <a href="faq.html">FAQ</a>
19      <a href="about.html">About</a>
20      <a href="contact.html">Contact</a>
21    </nav>
22    <main>
23      <p>Welcome to the Antediluvian Word Preservation Society, where our goal is to protect, preserve, and promote old
        words that are in danger of becoming overlooked, outmoded, and obsolete. Stay a while, take a look around, and bask
        in the burnished sheen of these old and beautiful words.</p>
24      <section>
25        <h2>Most recent word</h2>
26        <h3><em>hullaballoo</em> (hul·uh·buh·LOO, noun)</h3>
27        <p>A great noise or commotion; an uproar. (Example: "After hearing the <strong>hullaballoo</strong> that eight
          kids hopped up on sugar could make, Rupert decided to never again volunteer to help out at a Halloween party.")
          This is a fun word to use in conversation, and it's perfect if you need an unusual synonym for <em>noise</em> or
          <em>commotion</em>. It's just obscure enough that it doesn't get overused, but it's not so obscure that most
          people won't recognize it and chuckle to themselves. <em>Hullaballoo</em> began its life as the word
          <em>halloo</em>, meaning "to urge or incite with shouts." Then, via the process of rhyming reduplication, the
          <em>balloo</em> part was added to form <em>halloo-balloo</em>, which eventually morphed in <em>hullabaloo</em>.
          Some synonyms that register about the same on the fun-meter are <em>brouhaha</em>, <em>hubbub</em>, and
          <em>hurly-burly</em>.</p>
28      </section>
29      <section>
30        <h2>This week's challenge</h2>
```

Ln 24, Col 1 (1008)   HTML ◇   Tabs (4 sp) ⌄

Select an existing
section element.

Figure 6.9   Select an existing section element.

a Copy the entry (for example, by pressing either Ctrl-C or Cmd-C).

b Create a new line at the point where you want the new section to appear. For example, if you want the new section to appear above the page's first section, position the cursor immediately before the first `<section>` tag, and then press Enter or Return.

c Position the cursor on the new line you just created, as shown in figure 6.10.

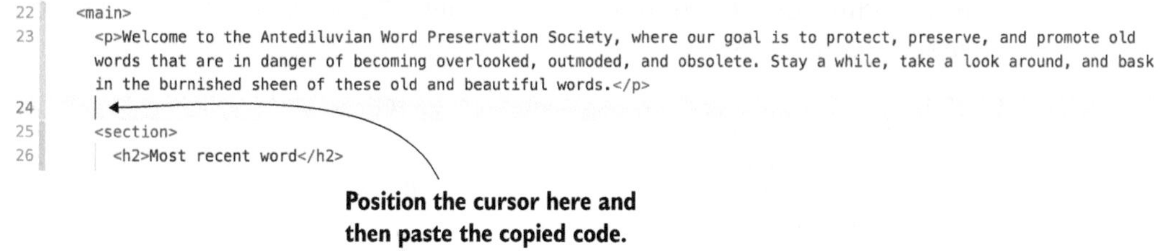

```
22    <main>
23      <p>Welcome to the Antediluvian Word Preservation Society, where our goal is to protect, preserve, and promote old
        words that are in danger of becoming overlooked, outmoded, and obsolete. Stay a while, take a look around, and bask
        in the burnished sheen of these old and beautiful words.</p>
24      |  ◀
25      <section>
26        <h2>Most recent word</h2>
```

Position the cursor here and
then paste the copied code.

Figure 6.10   Position the cursor where you want to paste the code you copied.

d Paste the copied code (for example, by pressing either Ctrl-C or Cmd-C).

e Edit the section title and text.

- If your entry text includes multiple paragraphs, you can ensure that each paragraph renders properly by surrounding it with a `<p>` tag at the beginning and a `</p>` tag at the end:

```
<section>
    <h2>Section heading</h2>
    <p>
        First paragraph
    </p>
    <p>
        Second paragraph
    </p>
    <p>
        Third paragraph
    </p>
</section>
```

- In the footer section of the HTML code, you can add links to your social media accounts, as I describe in chapter 4.

Now, here are a few customization ideas for the CSS code:

- If you want your page to have a different maximum width, change the `max-width` value to something other than `800px`.
- For any color value, you can change the existing color to a different color keyword.
- For any font size value, you can change the number to increase or decrease the font size. Just make sure you leave the `px` unit in place.
- For any padding or margin value, you can change the number to increase or decrease the padding or margins. In each case, be sure to leave the `px` unit in place.
- To give your text more breathing room, create some extra space between each line by adding the declaration `line-height: 1.5;` somewhere in the CSS code's `body` rule:

```
body {
    background-color: oldlace;
    max-width: 800px;
    margin: 0 auto;
    padding: 25px;
    line-height: 1.5;
}
```

- To make your page code more accessible, consider converting all px measurements to rem measurements. 1 rem is by default equivalent to 16 px, so 20 px is 1.25 rem, 24 px is 1.5 rem, 32 px is 2 rem, 48 px is 3 rem, and so on. The rem unit is more accessible because it measures font sizes relative to the default font size the browser user has defined in their browser settings.

6.5 Building prompts for the other site pages

Although some information websites consist of just a single page, the majority have several pages, and many have quite a few. If that's the case for your site, your next task is to prompt ChatGPT for the code to create your other pages.

Fortunately, these other pages will have a structure very similar to your home page, with the only difference being that the `main` element will store each page's headings and text. All this means your prompt for each subtopic page will be very similar to the prompt for your home page. Note, too, that you don't need any new CSS for these subtopic pages, so you can skip the CSS part of the prompt.

Here's a generic prompt you can use:

```
I want to build a page for an information website. I don't know how to code,
so I need you to provide the code for me.

Write the HTML code for a web page that includes the following:
 * The page title is "[page title]".
 * A header element that includes the title "[site title]" and the tagline
"[site tagline]".
 * After the header, a navigation element that includes the following links:
[Copy your navigation links here]
 * A main element that includes the text between triple quotation marks.
 """
[page content goes here]
 """
 * A footer element that includes the Copyright symbol followed by the
current year, followed by "[site title]".
 * In the page head section, include the tag <meta charset="utf-8">.
 * In the page head section, include a reference to a stylesheet file named
"styles.css".
 * In the page head section, include a reference to the Google fonts X and Y.
 * Do not add any inline styles.
```

Note the final instruction to ChatGPT to not add inline styles, which refers to CSS code added directly to an HTML tag. In the absence of any CSS-related instructions, ChatGPT has a tendency to insert a few formatting suggestions in the form of inline styles. Because all the styling you need is already in your styles.css file, you have to tell ChatGPT to hold off adding any new styling that may mess up your pages. Figure 6.11 shows an example page generated by ChatGPT for my information site.

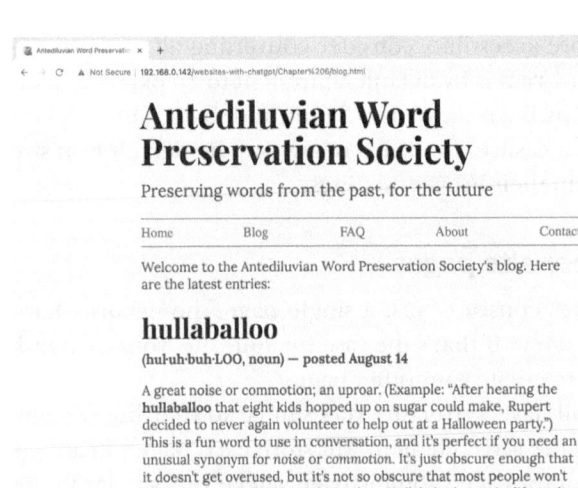

Figure 6.11   Another information site page generated by ChatGPT

Whatever type of entity you want to highlight—be it an organization, community, event, charity, team, or project—an information website is a great way to tell the world about it and help people learn more. Now, with ChatGPT as your coding partner, you can get an entire website up and running with just a few prompts.

Summary

- A link is a special HTML tag that, when clicked, takes the user to a specified web page.
- A navigation bar is a collection of links to the other pages on the website (or, if the site is large, to the site's most important pages).
- For best results, your page prompt should be as specific as possible, including colors, font sizes, and heading levels.
- Save the generated HTML to the index.html file and the generated CSS to the filename suggested by ChatGPT in the HTML code, usually styles.css.

Creating site content

7

This chapter covers

- Collaborating with ChatGPT to create and edit content
- Getting ChatGPT to write in your own style
- Getting AI help to edit your writing
- Adding a hero image
- Prompting ChatGPT to build a page for an interest or hobby
- Examining and customizing the ChatGPT web page code

As I explained in chapter 1, the *G* in GPT stands for *generative*, and it means you can use ChatGPT not only to have conversations but also to create new things. As you've seen so far in this book, that generated content can be ideas for the page title and tagline, suggestions for typefaces that match your page topic, color scheme recommendations, links, navigation bars, and, of course, the HTML and CSS code to build the final web page.

However, your generative content ambitions don't have to be restricted to small snippets of text and code. If you have an itch to put your true self on the web for all to see, one of the best ways to do that is to write about an interest or hobby that fascinates or engages you. If you're not sure what to write or you're having trouble getting started, this chapter shows you how to bring in ChatGPT as a collaborator to help you get going. You learn how to get AI-generated content ideas and writing suggestions, use AI for research, and even use ChatGPT to write in your voice.

You also learn how to craft a detailed prompt that you'll pass along to ChatGPT to produce the code for a page devoted to an interest or hobby, where you can post whatever content you and ChatGPT have created together. This chapter also provides a high-level explanation of the code generated by ChatGPT and even provides a few tips for customizing the code manually to get everything just the way you want.

7.1   *Understanding this chapter's project*

In this chapter, you create a simple website devoted to an interest or hobby. You're going to hire ChatGPT as your writing assistant to help you brainstorm ideas, do research, and create first drafts for the site content. The home page will include the following components:

- A header element that includes the following:
  - An image that takes up the full width and height of the browser window
  - The website title
  - The website tagline
  - A navigation element with links to other site pages
- A main element with some introductory text and links to the other site pages
- A footer element that includes a copyright notice

Figure 7.1 shows an example of an interest website's home page built with code generated by ChatGPT.

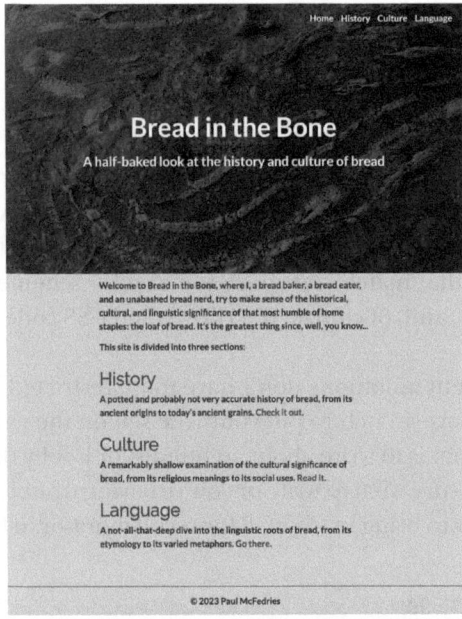

Figure 7.1
An interest
website
home page
generated by
ChatGPT

The other site pages will use a similar structure:

- A header element that includes the following:
  - A hero image
  - The page title
  - The page subtitle
  - A navigation element with links to other site pages
- A main element with the page text
- A footer element with a copyright notice

Figure 7.2 shows an example of such a page. The simplicity of these pages means you can easily customize them for use with any interest, hobby, or obsession you want to share with the world.

Figure 7.2   A subtopic page

7.2 Generating and editing text with ChatGPT

If you have a hankering not only to write but also to share that writing with others by posting it to the web, you may be more than a little leery about using ChatGPT as a writing assistant or even as a kind of ghost(in the machine)writer. If writing is important to you, it's also important that it's *your* writing, not something manufactured by AI.

However, none of that means you can't use ChatGPT for some of the grunt work associated with writing. Need some ideas for content? ChatGPT can help. Need to do some research for a post? That's right up ChatGPT's alley. Stuck facing a blank screen? Get ChatGPT to generate something, anything, and maybe a sentence or even a phrase of that text will be enough to spark your imagination. Not happy with something you wrote? Ask ChatGPT to take a look at it and suggest improvements.

There's really no end to the ways ChatGPT can act as your personal writing assistant. And, of course, if you want, you can even get ChatGPT to write everything for you. If you can do that and still sleep well at night, well, I'm not going to try to persuade you otherwise.

7.2.1 Getting ChatGPT to suggest writing ideas

ChatGPT excels at many tasks, but one of its strongest talents is suggesting ideas for writing on just about any topic, no matter how obscure or arcane. That is, if you have a general sense of the theme you want to pursue in your writing, ChatGPT can come up with content ideas from multiple angles.

You should begin your prompt by assigning ChatGPT a role:

```
You are an expert in [topic] and can generate interesting and creative ideas
about [topic] based on the following question.
```

Replace [topic] with a word or phrase that describes the theme or subject you want to write about.

Now add a question that will get ChatGPT to generate some ideas for a post. Here are a few examples to get you started:

```
What are the pros and cons of [topic]?
What are the top ten features of [topic]?
What are five things everyone needs to know about [topic]?
What are some common myths about [topic]?
How does a beginner get started with [topic]?
What are half a dozen tips and tricks to get the most out of [topic]?
```

Again, in each case, you replace [topic] with a word or phrase that describes the theme or subject you want to write about. For example, figure 7.3 shows the ideas that Copilot (in Creative mode) generated for me based on the following prompt:

```
You are an expert in bread baking and can generate interesting and creative
ideas about bread baking based on the following question.

How does a beginner get started with bread baking?
```

Bread baking is a wonderful hobby that can bring joy, satisfaction, and deliciousness to your life. It can also be intimidating for beginners who may not know where to start or what to do. Here are some tips and ideas to help you get started with bread baking:

- Start with simple recipes. There are many types of breads you can make, but some are easier than others. For example, you can try making a basic white bread, a no-knead bread, or a soda bread. These breads do not require a lot of ingredients, time, or skill, but they still taste great and give you a sense of accomplishment. You can find some easy bread recipes here and here.

- Learn the basics of bread making. Bread making is both an art and a science, and it helps to understand some of the principles behind it. For example, you should know the role of yeast, gluten, salt, sugar, and water in bread dough, how to knead, proof, shape, and bake your bread, and how to troubleshoot common problems like sticky dough, dense crumb, or burnt crust. You can learn more about the basics of bread making here and here.

- Experiment with different flours, grains, seeds, nuts, fruits, herbs, spices, and cheeses. Once you master the basic recipes, you can start to add some variety and flavor to your breads by incorporating different ingredients. For example, you can make whole wheat bread, rye bread, oatmeal bread, multigrain bread, sourdough bread, cinnamon raisin bread, cheese bread, garlic bread, or rosemary bread. The possibilities are endless and you can have fun creating your own combinations. You can find some inspiration for different bread flavors here and here.

- Have fun and be creative. Bread baking is not only a skill but also a form of expression. You can make your breads unique and personal by shaping them into different forms, decorating them with patterns or designs, or giving them funny names. You can also share your breads with your friends and family and enjoy their reactions and feedback. Bread baking is a rewarding and enjoyable hobby that can enrich your life in many ways.

I hope these tips and ideas will help you get started with bread baking. I'm sure you will love it as much as I do. Happy baking! 😊

1 of 30 ●

Figure 7.3 ChatGPT's ideas for getting started with bread baking

These are excellent suggestions and would serve nicely as a starting point for a post to interest beginners in baking bread. Note that it's important to consider ChatGPT's content ideas as just the beginning. It's up to you to flesh out the details to create an awesome post.

7.2.2 *Generating ideas for how to write about a topic*

In the previous section, you learned how to use ChatGPT to generate writing ideas. A similar use for ChatGPT is to ask it how to write about either a particular topic or a particular approach to a topic.

As usual, begin your prompt by assigning ChatGPT a role:

```
You are a writing coach and an expert on [topic] and can generate practical
and creative advice on how to write about [topic] based on the following
question.
```

Replace [topic] with a word or phrase that describes the theme or subject you want to explore through writing.

Next you add a question that will prompt ChatGPT to come up with ideas for how to write about your theme. Here are some examples:

```
What are the best ways to introduce a beginner to [topic]?
Once someone has learned the basics of [topic], what should I teach them next?
How do I get someone who knows nothing about [topic] excited about the subject?
What are some ways to write engagingly about [topic]?
What types of posts are most suited to writing about [topic]?
```

Again, replace [topic] in each example with text that describes the theme or subject of your writing. For example, figure 7.4 shows the writing ideas that Copilot (in Creative mode) generated from the following prompt:

```
You are a writing coach and an expert on bread baking and can generate
practical and creative advice on how to write about bread baking based on the
following question.

What are some ways to write engagingly about bread baking?
```

These are great suggestions not only for writing about bread baking but also for writing about almost anything else!

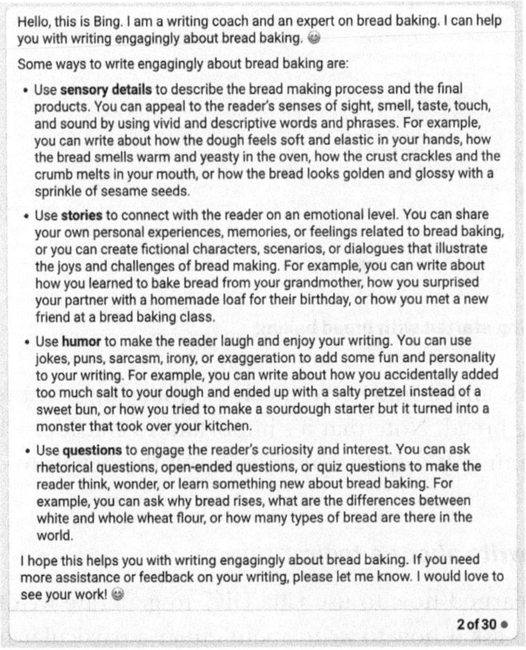

> Hello, this is Bing. I am a writing coach and an expert on bread baking. I can help you with writing engagingly about bread baking. 😊
>
> Some ways to write engagingly about bread baking are:
>
> • Use **sensory details** to describe the bread making process and the final products. You can appeal to the reader's senses of sight, smell, taste, touch, and sound by using vivid and descriptive words and phrases. For example, you can write about how the dough feels soft and elastic in your hands, how the bread smells warm and yeasty in the oven, how the crust crackles and the crumb melts in your mouth, or how the bread looks golden and glossy with a sprinkle of sesame seeds.
>
> • Use **stories** to connect with the reader on an emotional level. You can share your own personal experiences, memories, or feelings related to bread baking, or you can create fictional characters, scenarios, or dialogues that illustrate the joys and challenges of bread making. For example, you can write about how you learned to bake bread from your grandmother, how you surprised your partner with a homemade loaf for their birthday, or how you met a new friend at a bread baking class.
>
> • Use **humor** to make the reader laugh and enjoy your writing. You can use jokes, puns, sarcasm, irony, or exaggeration to add some fun and personality to your writing. For example, you can write about how you accidentally added too much salt to your dough and ended up with a salty pretzel instead of a sweet bun, or how you tried to make a sourdough starter but it turned into a monster that took over your kitchen.
>
> • Use **questions** to engage the reader's curiosity and interest. You can ask rhetorical questions, open-ended questions, or quiz questions to make the reader think, wonder, or learn something new about bread baking. For example, you can ask why bread rises, what are the differences between white and whole wheat flour, or how many types of bread are there in the world.
>
> I hope this helps you with writing engagingly about bread baking. If you need more assistance or feedback on your writing, please let me know. I would love to see your work! 😊
>
> 2 of 30 •

Figure 7.4   ChatGPT's advice for writing engagingly about bread baking

7.2.3   Getting ChatGPT help for researching a topic

The GPT models that underlie ChatGPT were trained on an impossible-to-imagine amount of data, which means they know quite a bit about almost any topic you care to name. That makes ChatGPT the perfect research assistant because you can ask it for help exploring whatever topic you want to write about, and you'll get back lots of helpful pointers.

Here's a prompt you can use to ask ChatGPT for research assistance:

```
Help me research [topic] for a general audience. I'm interested in A, B,
and C. Please provide X, Y, and Z. Also, include any interesting trivia or
anecdotes that might be engaging for readers. The goal is to provide a depth
```

of information that is accurate and detailed but also easily understood by a broad audience. Please provide links to your sources.

As usual, [topic] is a short description of the subject you want to research. Here's what the other placeholders represent:

- A, B, and C—General themes related to the overall topic.
- X, Y, and Z—Specific aspects of the overall topic.

> **TIP** The final sentence in the prompt assumes you're using a version of ChatGPT that's connected to the web. I highly recommend a web-connected version for this because the generated links enable you to fact-check ChatGPT's results and also give you more fodder for your research.

Here's an example:

```
Help me research the history of coffee for a general audience. I'm interested
in the discovery of coffee, its spread across the globe, and its cultural
impact in different societies. Please provide key historical figures and
events, notable varieties of coffee, and the evolution of coffee-drinking
habits over time. Also, include any interesting trivia or anecdotes that
might be engaging for readers. The goal is to provide a depth of information
that is accurate and detailed but also easily understood by a broad audience.
Please provide links to your sources.
```

Figure 7.5 shows the last part of an exceptionally long response to the previous prompt from Copilot (in Creative mode). The prompt assumes you're writing for a general audience, but of course, you should modify that depending on your intended reader.

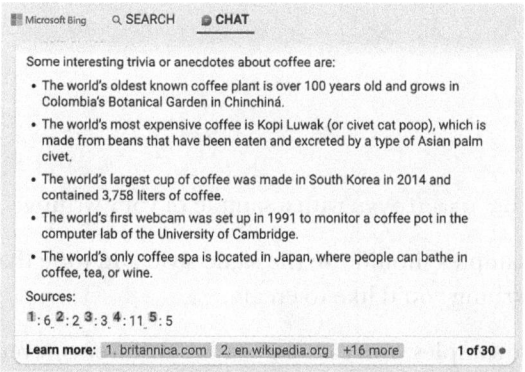

Figure 7.5   The last part of ChatGPT's response to a prompt for help researching the history of coffee

7.2.4   *Getting ChatGPT to write in your own voice*

An elusive goal of ChatGPT-generated writing is getting the model to output prose that sounds like you. Sure, ChatGPT can readily (and, often, amusingly) generate prose in the style of famous writers such as James Joyce, Emily Dickinson, and Dr. Seuss. That's because ChatGPT was (almost certainly) trained on large samples of those authors' writings. However, it's unlikely that ChatGPT has an inkling of how *you* write.

That's not a problem, however, because you can "train" ChatGPT to write like you. How? By giving ChatGPT several samples of your writing, asking it to analyze the tone and style of those samples, and then asking it to write something new in the same voice.

Here's the prompt:

```
You are an experienced ghostwriter. Given several examples of an author's
writing, you are skilled at detecting the tone and style of the writing and
emulating that writer's voice to generate new writing.

Below are several writing samples, with each sample between sets of triple
quotation marks.

Examine the samples to determine the writer's unique voice.

Emulate the writer's voice to generate X.

"""
Writing sample #1
"""

"""
Writing sample #2
"""

"""
Writing sample #3
"""

"""
Writing sample #4
"""

"""
Writing sample #5
"""
```

Replace each instance of `Writing sample #n` with a sample of your writing.

> **NOTE**   Ideally, your writing samples should use the same style and tone that you want to use for the piece of writing you'd like to create.

You don't have to include all five samples. You can use just two or three or even a single long sample, but remember that the more text you provide, the more accurate the analysis provided by ChatGPT and the more successful the prompt.

> **TIP**   If you have a favorite author whose writing style you admire and would like to emulate to a certain extent, include that in your prompt. For example, to ask ChatGPT to include a smidgen of the style and tone of Eudora Welty, add this to your prompt: `Please also include about 10 percent of the tone and style of Eudora Welty.`

In the prompt, replace *x* with a brief description of the writing you want ChatGPT to generate. Here's an example:

```
You are an experienced ghostwriter. Given several examples of an author's
writing, you are skilled at detecting the tone and style of the writing and
emulating that writer's voice to generate new writing.

Below are several writing samples, with each sample between sets of triple
quotation marks.

Examine the samples to determine the writer's unique voice.

Emulate the writer's voice to generate a satirical news story based on the
multiple pronunciations of the letters "ough".

"""
Researchers from Aalborg University announced today that they have finally
discovered the long sought-after Soup-Nuts Continuum. Scientists around the
world have been searching for this elusive item ever since Albert Einstein's
mother-in-law proposed its existence in 1922. "Today is an incredible day for
the physics community and for humanity as a whole," said senior researcher
Lars Grüntwerk. "Today, for the first time in history, we are on the verge of
knowing everything from soup to, well, you know, nuts."
"""

"""
SCHECHENECTADY, NY--After a long and tempestuous marriage, the two senses of
the word "oversight" have petitioned for a divorce. Citing irreconcilable
differences, the "responsible" sense of the word ("Watchful care or
management") and the "irresponsible" sense ("An omission or error") have
separated. "It just got to be too much after a while," said responsible
oversight. "The other oversight can't be trusted with even the smallest task.
It's 'Oops!' this and 'Sorry!' that. I believe in being careful and in making
sure that things get done right, so I just can't stand to live with such
neglect."
"""

"""
AIEA, Hawaii--Former United Nations Secretary General Boutros-Boutros Ghali
and current United Nations Undersecretary for Alphabet Mobilization Yada-
Yada Yada announced today the formation of the United Nations International
Vowel Assistance Committee. UNIVAC's mandate is "to help the vowel-deprived
wherever they may live and to fund vowel relief efforts in the hardest hit
areas." "We have a good stockpile of a's, e's, and o's," said Ng Ng, UNIVAC's
Letter Distribution Officer. "We hope to have an adequate supply of i's and
u's over the next six months. In the meantime, we can use our extra y's in a
pinch."
"""

"""
KALAMAZOO, Michigan--A group of disgruntled grammarians calling themselves
"Mad, We Are, As Hell" has filed a number of civil lawsuits over the past few
weeks. The targets of these suits are writers, raconteurs, and professional
man-in-the-street interviewees who, they claim, are inveterate violators
of the rules of grammar. The group's spokesperson, Millicent Peevish, Head
```

Shusher at the Kalamazoo District Library, said the grammarians could no
longer sit back and allow "the splitting of blameless infinitives and the
ending of sentences with evil, evil prepositions." A previous campaign --
called Shock and Appalled -- that focused on writing testy letters to the
editors of various local publications, had no discernible effect.
"""

"""
In a scathing report released today, communications experts have declared
that the instant messages teenagers exchange with each other are in reality
nothing but gibberish. U.S. Chatmaster General Todd Dood, with technical help
from the National Security Agency, examined thousands of instant messages.
It has long been thought that teen instant messages contained abbreviations
(such as LOL for "laughing out loud" and MAIBARP for "my acne is becoming a
real problem"), short forms (such as L8R for "later" and R2D2 for "R2D2"),
and slang (such as whassup for "what's up" and yo for "Hello, I am pleased to
meet your acquaintance. Do you wish to have a conversation?").
"""

Figure 7.6 shows the story that GPT-4 (Copilot in Creative mode) generated based on
my writing samples.

Based on the writing samples, I can determine that the writer's unique voice is:

- Humorous and witty, using wordplay, irony, and exaggeration to create satire.
- Informal and conversational, using colloquialisms, contractions, and direct address to the reader.
- Creative and inventive, using fictional names, places, and scenarios to illustrate absurd situations.
- Structured and coherent, using clear transitions, topic sentences, and conclusions to organize the text.

To emulate the writer's voice, I have generated a satirical news story based on the multiple pronunciations of the letters "ough". Here it is:

WASHINGTON, D.C.—In a landmark decision today, the Supreme Court ruled that the letters "ough" are unconstitutional. The justices unanimously agreed that the letters violate the First Amendment by creating confusion and ambiguity in the English language. "The letters 'ough' have no consistent pronunciation," said Chief Justice John Roberts. "They can sound like 'off', 'ow', 'oo', 'uff', 'oh', or 'aw'. This is an affront to the freedom of speech and expression of all Americans." The ruling was applauded by linguists, educators, and spelling bee champions, who have long campaigned for the elimination of "ough". "This is a victory for clarity and simplicity," said Professor Hugh Plough of Harvard University. "The letters 'ough' have caused enough trouble for enough people for enough time. It's time to get rid of them once and for all." The ruling will take effect immediately, requiring all written and spoken communication to replace "ough" with more phonetic alternatives. For example, "tough" will become "tuff", "though" will become "tho", and "doughnut" will become "donut". The ruling will also affect proper names, such as "Pittsburgh", which will become "Pittsberg", and "Loughborough", which will become "Lufbra". Some critics have argued that the ruling will have negative consequences for the cultural and historical heritage of the English language. They have also pointed out that some words will still have multiple pronunciations even after replacing "ough", such as "bouquet", "gourmet", and "croquet". However, the Supreme Court dismissed these concerns as irrelevant and insignificant. "We are not here to preserve the past, but to shape the future," said Justice Sonia Sotomayor. "The letters 'ough' are outdated and obsolete. They belong in the dustbin of history, along with other relics of linguistic chaos, such as silent letters, irregular verbs, and the Oxford comma."

1 of 30 ●

Figure 7.6   The story generated by Copilot in Creative mode

This is a pretty good first attempt: it matches the tone and style of the writing samples, it's a decent story idea, and it has some genuine humor. However, it's far from perfect:

- It contains some errors, such as including "Pittsburgh" as an example of a word that uses the letters "ough."
- Some of the writing is clunky and will require substantial rewriting to bring it up to snuff.
- The use of real names (such as Justice Sonia Sotomayer) in a satirical piece such as this is a bad choice. A better way to go would be to use made-up names that play on the letters "ough."

These sorts of problems are common with AI-generated writing, so you should always carefully proofread anything created by ChatGPT and be prepared to do quite a bit of rewriting.

7.2.5 *Rewriting post text*

After you've written some text, you may wonder if your prose could be improved in some way so it's funnier, more succinct, more verbose, easier to understand, more academic, and so on. Happily, as long as your text is either online or otherwise in a form that you can load into a web browser (such as an HTML file, a text file, or a PDF file), ChatGPT—specifically, the Microsoft Copilot app—is happy to help. Here's how:

1 In the Microsoft Edge browser, open the Copilot sidebar.
2 Navigate to the page or open the file that contains the text you want to rewrite.
3 Select the text you want to rewrite.
4 In the sidebar, you see the message `Send selected or copied text to chat?`, as shown in figure 7.7.

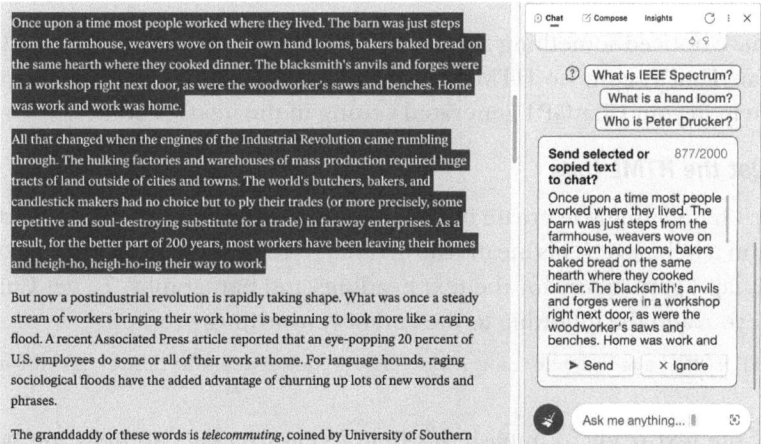

Figure 7.7   Select some text in the current page, and Copilot asks if you want to send it to the AI.

5   Click Send. Copilot asks what you want to do with the text.

6   Type your instruction. Here are some examples:

- Make it funnier

- Make it more succinct

- Make it easier to understand

- Make it more academic

- Rewrite it for a 10-year-old

7   Press Enter or Return. Copilot revises the selected text according to the instruction you provided in step 6.

Figure 7.8 shows the result when I asked Copilot to rewrite the selected text shown in figure 7.7 for a 10-year-old.

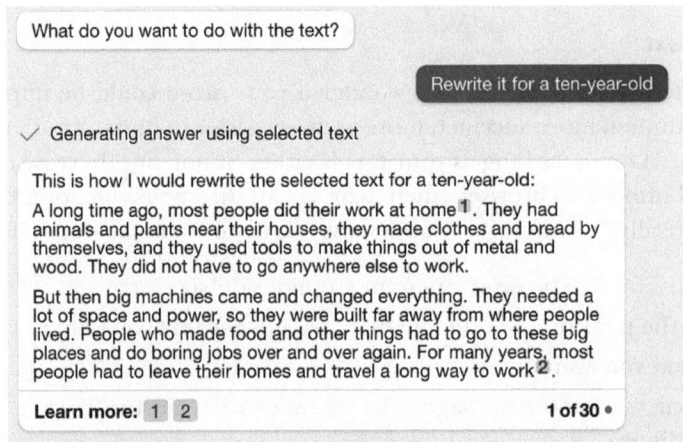

Figure 7.8   **The selected text from figure 7.7, rewritten for a 10-year-old**

You may have noticed something about all the writing samples I've had ChatGPT generate so far. That's right: no HTML tags! Those are important, so you learn how to include them in your ChatGPT-generated writing in the next section.

7.2.6   *Don't forget the HTML tags*

No matter what writing you create in collaboration with ChatGPT, in the end the text will reside in a web page. This means the text needs to be structured with the appropriate HTML tags, particularly for the text headings and paragraphs. To get ChatGPT to do this for you, add the following to the end of your writing prompt:

```
Please add HTML tags to the text, but don't generate the code for an entire
web page.
```

With your site text ready to publish, it's time to get ChatGPT to help you build your home page. You learn how in the next section.

7.3   *Building the home page*

Because this project is a multipage website, it's best to build the site's components in stages. The basic process is summarized here:

1   Prompt ChatGPT to generate the HTML code for the website's home page.
2   Prompt ChatGPT to generate the CSS code for the website's styling. Note that it's best to combine these first two steps into a single prompt.
3   For each of your other site pages, prompt ChatGPT to generate the HTML code for that page. In particular, the prompt for each of the other site pages should include the following:

  – An instruction to use the same CSS file in which you saved the CSS generated by step 2
  – An instruction to not generate any extra styles, particularly inline styles (that is, CSS code inserted directly into HTML tags)

Before you get to all that, take a minute to familiarize yourself with the new web page technology introduced in this chapter.

7.3.1   *Working with hero images*

The only new web page technology you learn about in this chapter is the *hero image*: an eye-catching photo or illustration that takes up the entire width (and usually the entire height) of the browser window when you first land on a page. Figure 7.9 shows an example web page that includes a hero image.

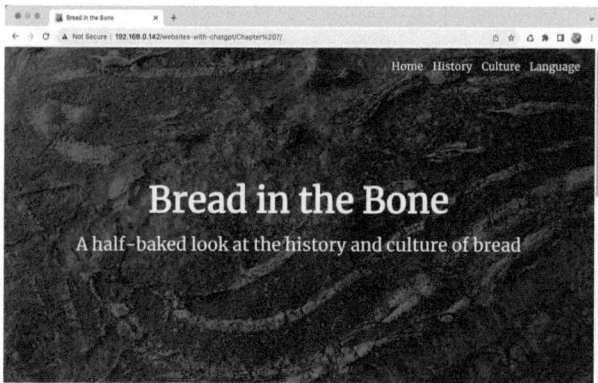

Figure 7.9   A web page with a hero image

Here are some pointers to bear in mind when using a hero image:

- The image subject should be relevant to your page topic.
- The image should be dramatic or eye-catching in some way.

- Use an image that's high-quality and free of distortions such as pixelation. If you're using a photo, it should be well-composed and well-lit.
- Don't use an image file that's too small, or it will get distorted when the browser expands it to fit the window. An image that's 1,200 pixels wide with an aspect ratio (that is, the ratio of width to height) of 16:9 is the ideal size for most larger screens (and for smaller device screens in landscape mode).
- Use an image that's not so busy that your text will get lost or be unreadable.
- As you see a bit later, you can tell ChatGPT to darken the image a little, so don't worry if your image appears too light for your text.
- If you don't have a suitable image, you can ask DALL-E or Copilot's Image Creator to generate one for you (as I described in chapter 5).

To get ChatGPT to add a hero image to a page, your prompt should include an instruction similar to the following:

```
Include a header that uses the file hero.jpg as a hero image.
```

Interestingly, when you examine the HTML code, you won't see a reference to the image file. For example, here's the HTML code that creates the header shown in figure 7.9:

```
<header>
    <nav>
        <ul>
            <li><a href="index.html">Home</a></li>
            <li><a href="history.html">History</a></li>
            <li><a href="culture.html">Culture</a></li>
            <li><a href="language.html">Language</a></li>
        </ul>
    </nav>
    <h1>Bread in the Bone</h1>
    <p>A half-baked look at the history and culture of bread</p>
</header>
```

The hero image is embedded into the `header` element in the CSS, as shown by this partial listing of the `header` rule used for the `header` element in figure 7.9:

```
header {
    background: url('hero.jpg') no-repeat center center fixed;
    background-size: cover;
}
```

This code tells the web browser to display the image file hero.jpg as the background of the `header` element and that the image should cover the entire element. Using a hero image is a great way to grab a visitor's attention right off the bat, which is why this has been one of the most popular web design trends for the past few years.

7.3.2 Crafting the home page prompt

This chapter's project is a website devoted to an interest or hobby. You're almost ready to construct the home page prompt for ChatGPT, but first you need to make sure you already have these items:

- Some or all of the following: a page logo, title, and tagline
- The names of the typefaces you want to use for the page headings and the page text
- The keywords of the colors you want to apply to the page backgrounds and text

Refer to chapter 3 to learn more about these design elements and how to prompt ChatGPT for title, typeface, and color suggestions.

The starting point for your interest or hobby website is the home page, which you can enlist ChatGPT to help you build. Your prompt should begin like this:

```
I want to build a web page for a website home page. I don't know how to code,
so I need you to provide the code for me.

First, write the HTML code for a web page that includes the following:
```

Then specify the content of your page, including the following (refer to figure 7.10):

- A header that includes your hero image, page title, and tagline and a navigation bar with links to your other site pages
- A main element that begins with an introductory paragraph welcoming visitors to your site
- For each of your site's subtopics, a section element that includes a header with the subtopic title, a description of the subtopic, and a link to the subtopic
- A footer that includes a copyright notice

Next, ask ChatGPT to generate the CSS for how you want your page formatted:

```
Second, in a separate file please write the CSS code for the following:
```

Specify the formatting, including the following:

- The page background color and text color.
- The type sizes and color you want to use for the page title, tagline, and navigation links.
- The fonts to use for the headings and regular page text.
- A maximum width for the main element. This prevents the lines of text from getting too long. A maximum length of 800 px is fine for most pages.

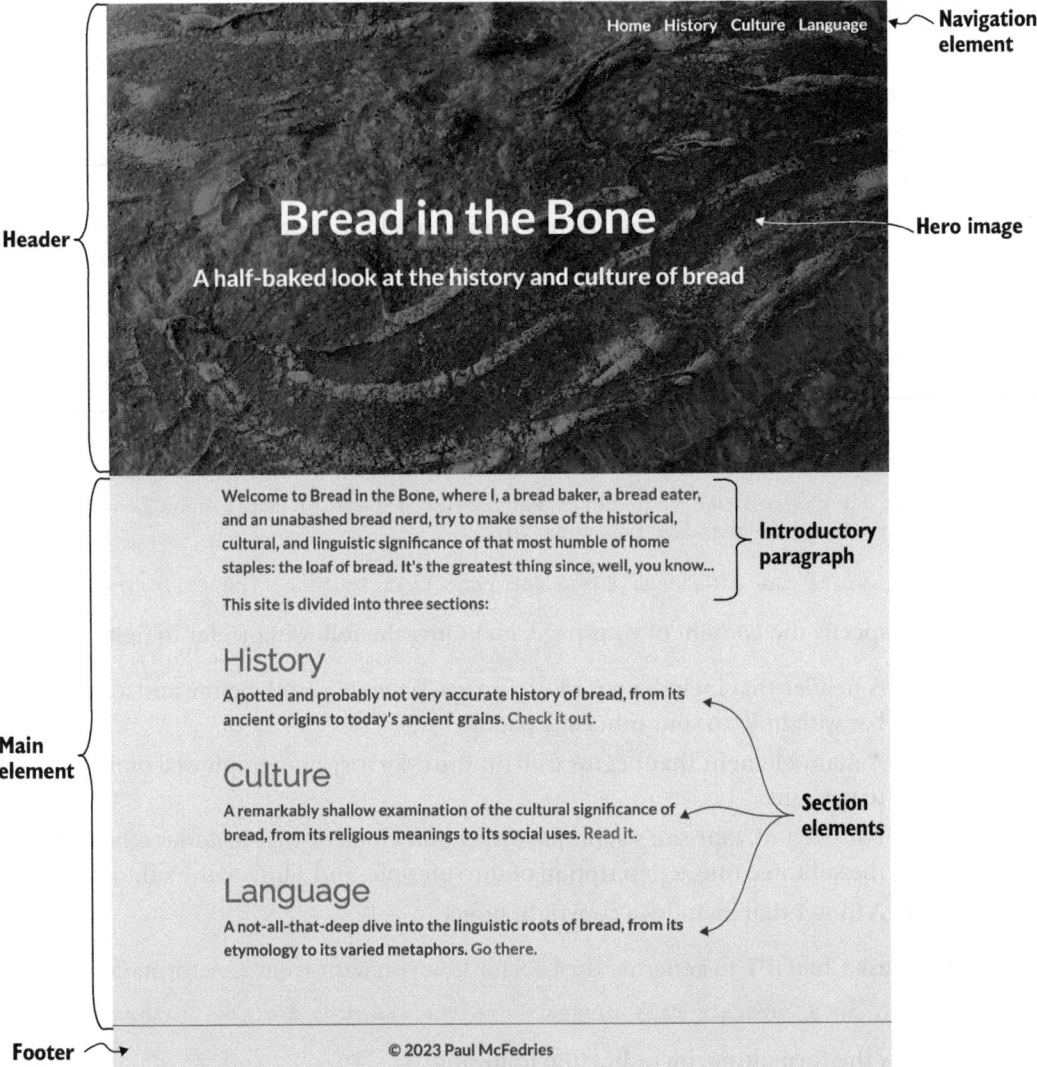

Figure 7.10   The sections of the interest site's home page

Here's an example prompt for my own home page:

```
I want to build a website home page. I don't know how to code, so I need you
to provide the code for me.

First, write the HTML code for a web page that includes the following:
 * A header that uses the file hero.jpg as a hero image.
 * The header also includes the title "Bread in the Bone" and the tagline "A
half-baked look at the history and culture of bread".
 * The header should also include four links in the upper-right corner:
   * The text "Home" that links to the file "index.html".
```

```
* The text "History" that links to the file "history.html".
* The text "Culture" that links to the file "culture.html".
* The text "Language" that links to the file "language.html".
* A main element that includes the following five elements:
* An introductory paragraph that includes the text "Welcome to Bread in
the Bone, where I, a bread baker, a bread eater, and an unabashed bread nerd,
try to make sense of the historical, cultural, and linguistic significance of
that most humble of home staples: the loaf of bread. It's the greatest thing
since, well, you know..."
* A second paragraph that consists of the text "This site is divided into
three sections:"
* The second-level heading "History" followed by a paragraph that includes
the text "A potted and probably not very accurate history of bread, from its
ancient origins to today's ancient grains." Then the text "Check it out." as
a link to "history.html".
* The second-level heading "Culture" followed by a paragraph that includes
the text "A remarkably shallow examination of the cultural significance of
bread, from its religious meanings to its social uses." Then the text "Read
it." as a link to "culture.html".
* The second-level heading "Language" followed by a paragraph that includes
the text "A not-all-that-deep dive into the linguistic roots and uses of the
word bread, from its etymology to its varied metaphors." Put the word "bread"
in italics. Then add the text "Go there." as a link to "language.html".
* A footer element that includes the Copyright symbol, followed by the
current year, followed by "Paul McFedries".
* In the page head section, include the tag <meta charset="utf-8">.

Second, in a separate file write the CSS code for the following:
* The page background color is wheat.
* The hero image covers the entire browser window.
* Add a linear gradient to the header background to darken the hero image
slightly.
* Make all the header text white.
* Make the title and tagline centered both horizontally and vertically.
* Make the title 72px.
* Make the tagline 36px.
* Make the header links 24px.
* Style the headings with size 48px, no bottom margin, the color
saddlebrown, and the Raleway typeface from Google Fonts.
* Style the rest of the page text with size 24px, a 20px bottom margin, and
the Lato typeface from Google Fonts.
* Style the main element's links with the color saddlebrown.
* The main section has 25px padding all around and a maximum width of 800px.
* The footer has a top border.
```

ChatGPT should create the HTML code first, which you can copy and then paste and save to a file named index.html. In that code, you should see a line near the top similar to the following:

```
<link rel="stylesheet" type="text/css" href="styles.css">
```

This code tells the web browser to look for the CSS code in a file named styles.css, so your next task is to copy the generated CSS code, paste it into a file, and save it as styles. css (or whatever name you see in the <link> tag). Be sure to save styles.css in the same folder as your index.html file. You also need to copy your hero image file into the same folder. Refer to appendix A to learn more about working web page files.

I submitted this prompt to GPT-4 using OpenAI's ChatGPT app. The code it generated resulted in the page shown in figure 7.11.

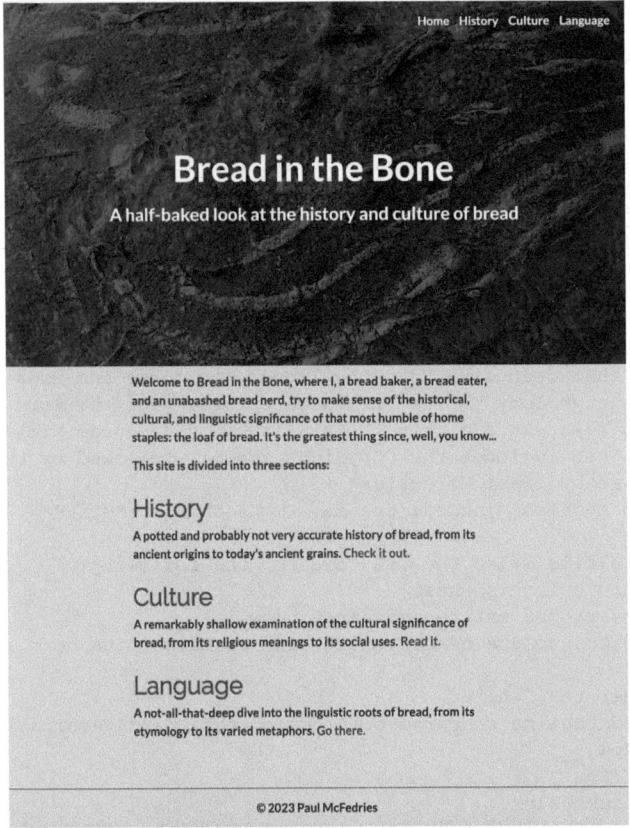

Figure 7.11   The home page generated by ChatGPT

If you like the home page that ChatGPT made for you, you can skip the rest of this section and move on to the other pages (refer to "Building prompts for the other site pages"). However, if you'd like to know a bit more about the code that ChatGPT generated, the next section gives you a closer look.

7.4   *Examining the home page code*

I'm going to give you a short and not-too-technical overview of the home page code that resulted from my prompt from the previous section (that home page is shown in figure 7.11).

NOTE The generated HTML and CSS code for my online journal page are available on this book's website (www.manning.com/books/build-a-website-with-chatgpt) and in the book's GitHub repository: https://github.com/paulmcfe/websites-with-chatgpt.

Every version of ChatGPT should output HTML and CSS code that's at least similar to what's displayed in the next two sections, so my code annotations should help you understand what's happening under the hood.

7.4.1 Examining the HTML

The HTML code that ChatGPT generated for my interest website home page is shown here:

```
<!DOCTYPE html>
<html lang="en">
<head>
    <meta charset="utf-8">                          Specifies the page character set
    <title>Bread in the Bone</title>
    <link href="https://fonts.googleapis.com/css2?    Loads the page fonts from Google Fonts
        family=Lato:wght@700&family=Raleway:wght@400&
        display=swap"rel="stylesheet">               Tells the web browser where to find the CSS code
    <link rel="stylesheet" href="styles.css">
</head>
<body>
    <header>
        <nav>
            <ul>
                <li><a href="index.html">Home</a></li>
                <li><a href="history.html">History</a></li>      Navigation element    Page header
                <li><a href="culture.html">Culture</a></li>
                <li><a href="language.html">Language</a></li>
            </ul>
        </nav>
        <h1>Bread in the Bone</h1>                    Page title
        <p>
            A half-baked look at the history
            and culture of bread                     Page tagline
        </p>
    </header>                                                               Page header

    <main>
        <p>
            Welcome to Bread in the Bone, where I, a bread baker, a
            bread eater, and an unabashed bread nerd, try to make
            sense of the historical, cultural, and linguistic       Page introduction    Main element
            significance of that most humble of home staples: the loaf
            of bread. It's the greatest thing since, well, you know...
        </p>
        <p>This site is divided into three sections:</p>
```

```
<section>
    <h2>History</h2>
    <p>
        A potted and probably not very accurate history of
        bread, from its ancient origins to today's ancient
        grains. <a href="history.html">Check it out.</a>
    </p>
</section>

<section>
    <h2>Culture</h2>
    <p>
        A remarkably shallow examination of the cultural
        significance of bread, from its religious meanings
        to its social uses. <a href="culture.html">Read it.</a>
    </p>
</section>

<section>
    <h2>Language</h2>
    <p>
        A not-all-that-deep dive into the linguistic roots
        of bread, from its etymology to its varied metaphors.
        <a href="language.html">Go there.</a>
    </p>
</section>
</main>

<footer>
    &copy; 2023 Paul McFedries
</footer>
</body>
</html>
```

Each section element has a heading, description, and link.

Main element

Page footer

Note that the HTML code includes the following line:

```
<link rel="stylesheet" href="styles.css">
```

This tag tells the web browser where to find the CSS code, which I describe in the next section.

7.4.2   *Examining the CSS*

ChatGPT's generated CSS code for my interest website home page is shown here:

```
* {
    margin: 0;
    padding: 0;
    box-sizing: border-box;
}
body {
    background: wheat;
    font-family: 'Lato', serif;
    font-size: 24px;
    color: #333;
}
```

Resets some styles

Styles the page background color, font, font size, and text color

```
header {
    background: url('hero.jpg') no-repeat center center fixed;      │ Sets up the hero image to
    background-size: cover;                                         │ fill the browser window
    color: white;
    display: flex;
    flex-direction: column;
    justify-content: center;                                        Centers the header text
    align-items: center;
    height: 100vh;
    position: relative;
    background-image:
        linear-gradient(rgba(0, 0, 0, 0.5),                         Darkens the hero image to
        rgba(0, 0, 0, 0.5)),                                        make the text easier to read
        url('hero.jpg');
}
nav ul {
    list-style-type: none;
    display: flex;
    gap: 20px;
    position: absolute;                                             Styles the navigation element
    top: 20px;
    right: 30px;
}
nav a {
    color: white;
    font-size: 24px;                                                Styles the navigation links
    text-decoration: none;
}
nav a:hover {
    text-decoration: underline;                                     Adds an underline to each nav
}                                                                   link when hovered over
.title-container {
    text-align: center;
}
h1 {
    font-size: 72px;                                                Sets the page title font size to 72 px, and
    font-family: 'Raleway', sans-serif;                             applies the Raleway font
    margin-bottom: 10px;
}
header p {
    font-size: 36px;              ◄──── Styles the tagline with font size 36 px
}
h2 {
    color: saddlebrown;                                             Styles the page headings with
    font-size: 48px;                                                color saddlebrown, font size 48 px,
    font-family: 'Raleway', sans-serif;                             and the Raleway font
    margin-top: 30px;
}
main p {
    margin-bottom: 20px;          ◄──── Adds a 20 px margin below each main element paragraph
}
main {
    padding: 25px;                                                  Styles the main element with 25 px
    max-width: 800px;                                               padding, 800 px maximum
    margin: 0 auto;                                                 width, and centered
```

```
}
a {
    color: saddlebrown;                          Styles the page links with color
    text-decoration: none;                       saddlebrown and no underline
}
a:hover {
    text-decoration: underline;         ◄─────── Adds an underline to each link when hovered over
}
footer {
    margin-top: 50px;
    text-align: center;
    padding: 20px 0;                             Styles the page footer
    border-top: 1px solid black;
}
```

If you like, you can use these annotations to tweak your web page code, as I describe in the next section.

7.4.3   *Customizing the home page*

If you don't like the home page that results from the code generated by ChatGPT, feel free to tweak your prompt and try again. However, if you only want to make a few small tweaks, consider editing the code manually.

First, here are some customization suggestions for the HTML code:

- In the header, you can edit the title or tagline. Just be sure not to edit or delete the associated HTML tags: <h1> and </h1> for the title, and <p> and </p> for the tagline.
- In the header, edit the link text and link filename as needed for your website files.
- Edit the section elements, adjusting the heading, description, and link as needed.
- To add a new section, copy an existing section (that is, everything between and including a single pair of <section> and </section> tags), paste the code where you want it in the main element (that is, between the <main> and </main> tags), and then adjust the heading, description, and link. (Refer to chapter 6 for more detailed instructions on adding a new section element.)
- In the footer section of the HTML code, you can add links to your social media accounts, as I described in chapter 4.

Now, here are a few customization ideas for the CSS code:

- To set the darkness of the hero image, ChatGPT uses the following code:

```
linear-gradient(rgba(0, 0, 0, 0.5), rgba(0, 0, 0, 0.5))
```

You control the darkness by adjusting the final numbers in the two rgba functions (the 0.5 values in this code). The first rgba function controls the darkness of the top half of the image, and the second rgba function controls the darkness of the bottom half. Use values closer to 0 for lighter and closer to 1 for darker. Here's a darker example:

```
linear-gradient(rgba(0, 0, 0, 0.75), rgba(0, 0, 0, 0.75))
```

- To give your text more breathing room, create some extra space between each line by adding the declaration line-height: 1.5; somewhere in the CSS code's body rule:

```
body {
    background: wheat;
    font-family: 'Lato', serif;
    font-size: 24px;
    color: #333;
    line-height: 1.5;
}
```

- If you want your page to have a different maximum width, locate the main rule in the CSS code and change the max-width value to something other than 800px. In the following example, I've changed the maximum width to 960px:

```
main {
    padding: 25px;
    max-width: 960px;
    margin: 0 auto;
}
```

- For any color value, you can change the existing color to a different color keyword.
- For any font size value, you can change the number to increase or decrease the font size. Just make sure you leave the px unit in place.
- For any padding or margin value, you can change the number to increase or decrease the padding or margins. In each case, be sure to leave the px unit in place.
- To make your page code more accessible, consider converting all px measurements to rem measurements. 1 rem is by default equivalent to 16 px, so 20 px is 1.25 rem, 24 px is 1.5 rem, 32 px is 2 rem, 48 px is 3 rem, and so on. The rem unit is more accessible because it measures font sizes relative to the default font size the browser user has defined in their browser settings.

7.5   *Building prompts for the other site pages*

Although it's possible that your interest/hobby website consists of just a single page, it's far more likely that you'll have several pages, one for each subtopic of your site's main topic. If that's the case, your next chore is to prompt ChatGPT for the code to create your other pages.

Fortunately, these other pages will have a structure very similar to your home page, with the only difference being that the `main` element will store each page's headings and text. All this means your prompt for each subtopic page will be very similar to the prompt for your home page. Note, too, that you don't need any new CSS for these subtopic pages, so you can skip the CSS part of the prompt.

Here's a generic prompt you can use:

```
I want to build a website page. I don't know how to code, so I need you to
provide the code for me.

Write the HTML code for a web page that includes the following:
 * A header element that includes the title "[page title]" and the tagline
"[page tagline]".
 * The header should also include the following links in the upper-right
corner:
[Copy your home page links here]
 * A main element that includes the text between triple quotation marks.
 """
[page content goes here]
 """
 * A footer element that includes the Copyright symbol, followed by the
current year, followed by "[your name]".
 * In the page head section, include the tag <meta charset="utf-8">.
 * In the page head section, include a reference to a stylesheet file named
"styles.css".
 * In the page head section, include a reference to the Google fonts X and Y.
 * Do not add any inline styles.
```

Note the final instruction to ChatGPT to not add inline styles, which refers to CSS code added directly to an HTML tag. In the absence of any CSS-related instructions, ChatGPT has a tendency to insert a few formatting suggestions in the form of inline styles. Because all the styling you need is already present in your styles.css file, you need to tell ChatGPT to hold off on adding any new styling that may mess up your pages.

Figure 7.12 shows an example page generated by ChatGPT for my interest site. Whatever your interest or hobby, why not enlist ChatGPT's help to share your enthusiasm with friends, family, and whoever drops by your new website? It has never been easier to show the world what you care about!

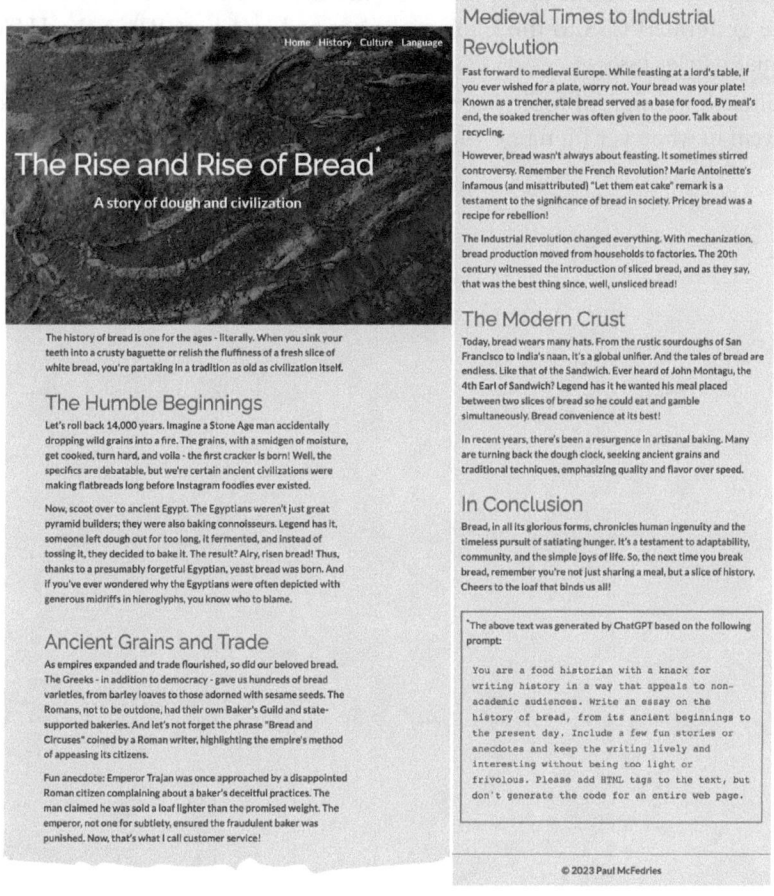

Figure 7.12   A subtopic page generated by ChatGPT

Summary

- A hero image is an eye-catching photo or illustration that takes up the entire width (and usually the entire height) of the browser window when you first land on a page.

- You can use ChatGPT to suggest writing ideas, offer tips for writing about specific topics, and help research topics.

- To get ChatGPT to write in your own voice, supply it with several examples of your writing, ask it to analyze the samples for tone and style, and then ask it to write something that emulates your writing voice.

- For best results, your page prompt should be as specific as possible, including colors, font sizes, and heading levels.

- For the website home page, save the generated HTML to the index.html file and the generated CSS to the filename suggested by ChatGPT in the HTML code, usually styles.css.
- For each website subtopic page, ask ChatGPT to create only the HTML code and save it to whatever filename you're using for the page.

Generating site forms 8

This chapter covers

- Dealing with text boxes and text areas
- Working with check boxes and radio buttons
- Adding selection lists and buttons to a form
- Using the free Getform service to have form data sent to you
- Crafting a ChatGPT prompt for building an event sign-up page
- Examining and customizing the ChatGPT-generated code

Most web pages—and all the web projects so far in this book—are read-only media, meaning their purpose is to present each visitor with information related to the page's main topic. Such pages require nothing of the visitor except their time and attention (which are big asks in these overly busy times!).

However, there are plenty of scenarios where you'll want your page to be more interactive, meaning you ask users to provide you with some information. Perhaps you want to get feedback about your website. Maybe you want to present your visitors with a survey or quiz. Or maybe you want to offer folks a way to sign up for a newsletter or register for an upcoming event. Whatever the reason, you solicit such information by offering a *form*, which is a special web page object that has fields the visitor fills in and then submits.

In this chapter, you learn how forms work, what kinds of fields you can use, and how to get form data emailed to you. You then use this information to create a detailed prompt for ChatGPT to generate the necessary code for an event signup page. This chapter also provides a high-level explanation of the code generated by ChatGPT and tips for customizing the code.

8.1   *Checking out this chapter's project*

This chapter's project is a simple web page that includes a form that enables a page visitor to sign up for an upcoming event. The final page will include the following components:

- A header element that includes the website logo, title, and tagline
- A main element that includes the event title, some info, and a form for signing up for the event
- A footer element that includes a copyright notice

Figure 8.1 shows an example of the type of page you'll build with ChatGPT's help in this chapter.

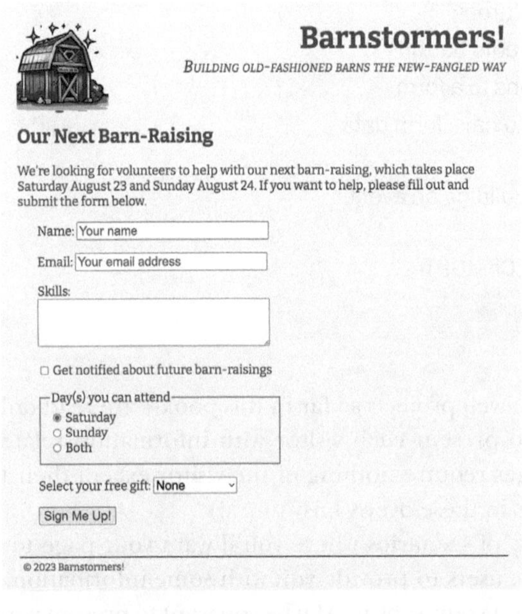

Figure 8.1   An event sign-up page generated by ChatGPT

The example form includes all the major types of form controls, which means you can easily modify the form to gather other types of information, such as site feedback or a survey or quiz. To do any of that, you need to know a bit about each type of form control. First, however, you need to learn how to get the form data sent to you.

8.2 *Getting the form data sent to you*

Unfortunately, there's no method built into HTML to have a form's data sent to you. To get the form data that a user submits, you need to set up an account with a company that provides this service. There are quite a few such companies, but for this project, I'm going to use Getform (https://getform.io). This company enables you to create a free *endpoint*, which is an address to which your form submits its data.

Although Getform has subscription plans, you may not need one because the service also offers a free tier that has the following restrictions:

- One endpoint only.
- A maximum of 50 form submissions per month.
- Getform branding is added to each form-submission email message you receive.

If one of these restrictions is a dealbreaker for you, check out Getform's paid plans at https://getform.io/pricing (plans start at US $19 per month).

8.2.1 *Setting up a Getform account*

First, follow these steps to set up a Getform account:

1 Navigate to the Getform home page (https://getform.io).
2 Click the Generate Endpoint for Free button. (If you don't see that button, click Account, Sign Up, or navigate directly to https://app.getform.io/register.)
3 Enter your name, email, and password, and then click Sign Up.
4 Go to your email inbox, open the Getform email message, and then click the link to verify your account.

8.2.2 *Creating a Getform endpoint*

With your account verified, log in to your Getform account and then follow these steps to set up your form submission endpoint:

1 Click Create in the left sidebar. Getform displays the Create dialog, shown (filled in) in figure 8.2.
2 Make sure the Form tab is selected.
3 Use the Form Endpoint Name text box to type a short but descriptive name for your form.
4 Use the Time Zone list to select your time zone.
5 Click Create.

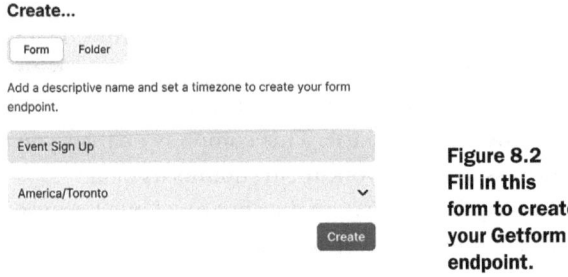

Figure 8.2
**Fill in this
form to create
your Getform
endpoint.**

Getform creates your new endpoint and then displays the endpoint's home page, an example of which is shown in figure 8.3. There are several things to notice on this page:

- You'll need the endpoint address when you prompt ChatGPT to build your form. To avoid errors, click the Copy button to the right of the address, and then paste the address into your prompt.

- To prevent spam, the example form includes the following code:

```
<input type="hidden" name="_gotcha" style="display:none !important">
```

This is an example of a *honeypot*, which is a hidden field that your users won't see (and therefore won't fill in) but a spam bot will fill in and submit. (It's called a honeypot because the spam bot can't resist it.) A filled-in honeypot field tells the Getform server that the submission must be spam. When you build your ChatGPT prompt later, you'll ask ChatGPT to include this code in your form.

- You can click Inbox at the top of this page to monitor your form submissions. But remember that Getform also sends each form submission to your email address.

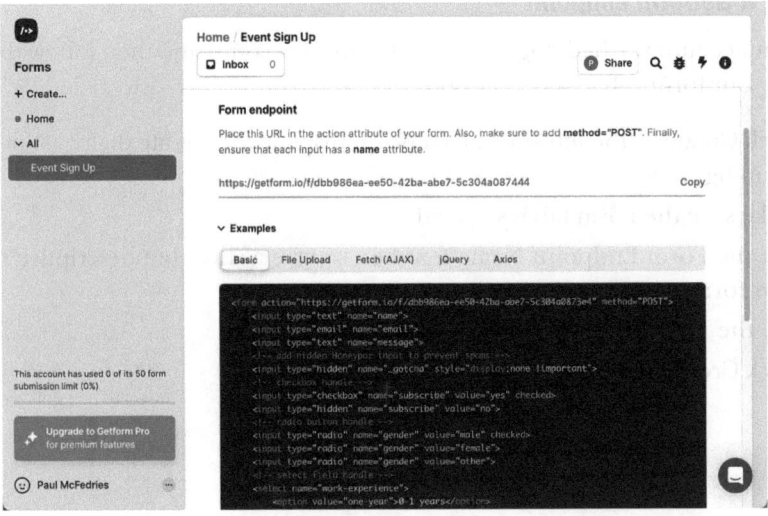

Figure 8.3   When your Getform endpoint is created, you see its home page.

8.3 Building a form

A form is a special collection of HTML elements that enables you to gather information from a user and then send that information somewhere. Each of these special HTML elements is called a *control*, and in the next few sections, you learn about the half-dozen most common and most useful form controls. Knowing what each control does and what type of information it is designed to gather will enable you to set up a prompt so ChatGPT can build the form you need.

Along the way, I'll provide you with example ChatGPT prompts for each type of control. In each example, assume that an instruction similar to the following has been included earlier in the prompt:

```
Include the code for an HTML form that has the following specifications:
```

8.3.1 Specifying the form's endpoint

In this chapter's example, you learn how to get form data sent to you by using a service called Getform. This service provides you with a unique address called an *endpoint*, which is a remote script that processes the form data. When you're instructing ChatGPT to build an HTML form, the first specification is this endpoint address. (Refer to section 8.2 to learn how to generate a unique endpoint address to use with your form.) Here's an example instruction:

```
In the form element, set the action attribute to "endpoint" and the method
attribute to "POST".
```

In this prompt, replace `endpoint` with the address provided to you by the Getform service. The `method` attribute referred to in the instruction tells the browser how to send the form data.

With that out of the way, it's time to take a closer look at the most common form controls. The first control type is the text box, discussed next.

8.3.2 Gathering text with text boxes

The most common type of form control is the *text box*, which is a rectangular area designed to hold text typed by the user. HTML offers a large collection of text box input types, each designed to hold a particular kind of information. Here are the four most common input types:

- *Text*—Holds any kind of text, which can be any combination of letters, numbers, and symbols. Here's an example instruction to include in your form prompt:

  ```
  A text box.
  ```

- *Number*—Holds numeric data only. Example instruction:

  ```
  A text box for numeric data.
  ```

- *Email*—Holds an email address only. The control also checks whether the user entered a valid email address. Here's an example instruction to ChatGPT:

```
A text box for an email address.
```

- *URL*—Holds a web address. Example instruction:

```
A text box for a web address.
```

Figure 8.4 shows an example of each input type. Notice that the Number field includes up and down arrows that the user can click to increment and decrement (respectively) the current field value.

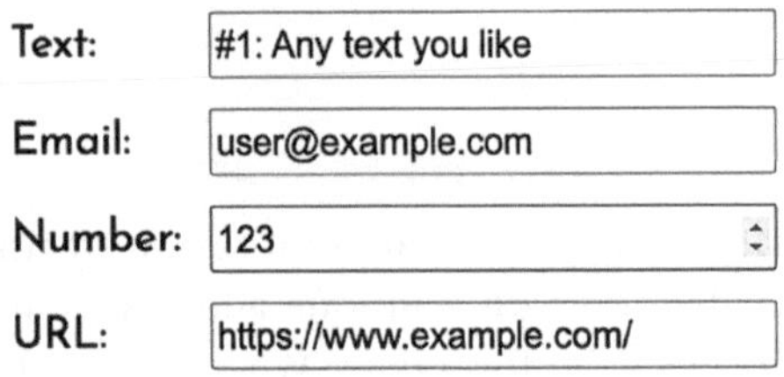

Text:	#1: Any text you like
Email:	user@example.com
Number:	123
URL:	https://www.example.com/

Figure 8.4   The four main text box input types

TIP To get ChatGPT to generate code that configures your form with the text on the left and the text boxes on the right, include the following in your prompt: "Make the form a two-column grid container with the labels in the first column and the controls in the second column."

When prompting ChatGPT to include text boxes in a form, you have control over the following for each text box:

- You can set the width of the box by specifying a size in characters. In figure 8.4, for example, each text box is 30 characters wide. Example prompt:

```
A text box that is 25 characters wide.
```

- You can specify an initial value. This value appears by default in the text box, although the user is free to edit or replace this default value. Example prompt:

```
A numeric text box with the initial value 42.
```

- You can specify a *placeholder*, which is some text that appears temporarily in the text box and that briefly tells the user what to type into the text box. As soon as the user starts typing, the placeholder text disappears. Example prompt:

```
An email text box with the placeholder text "Type your email address".
```

- You can specify a maximum and/or minimum length in characters:

```
A text box with a minimum length of 3 and a maximum length of 10.
```

- You can specify that a text box is "required" if the user must fill in a value before submitting the form:

```
An email text box that is required.
```

You may be wondering how you get ChatGPT to name each control (such as the names shown to the left of each control in figure 8.4). If you don't specify a name, ChatGPT will make one up for you. Specifying your own control names is the subject of the next section.

8.3.3 Adding labels to each control

If you examine figure 8.4 in the previous section, you can see that the items are divided into two columns: the controls are in the right column, and the left column contains short bits of text that describe each control. These short bits of text are called *labels*, and, with the exception of the button control (discussed below), you need to include a label for each field. Your labels should be short enough that they don't take up too much room on the page but descriptive enough that the user knows what they're supposed to type into each field.

When you're building your ChatGPT prompt for your form, it's best to state the label you want at the same time you state the rest of your control specifications:

```
An email address text box. Make the text box 30 characters wide and give it
the label "Email address".
```

8.3.4 Handling more text with text areas

A text box is useful for gathering relatively short informational tidbits from the user, such as their name, email address, or favorite number. However, occasionally, your form may need to solicit longer text entries, such as feedback, suggestions, questions, or even the user's bio. For these longer entries, you can add a *text area*, which is a form field that supports multiline entries. Figure 8.5 shows an example of a text area.

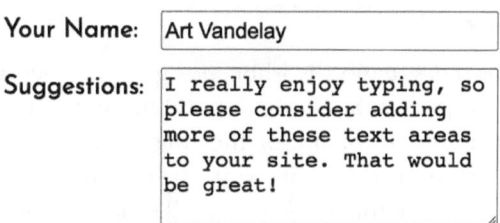

Figure 8.5   An example of a text area

When prompting ChatGPT to include a text area in a form, you can customize the text area in the following ways:

- You can set the height of the text area box by specifying the number of rows. In figure 8.5, for example, the text area's height is six rows. Example instruction to ChatGPT:

```
A text area with the label "Suggestions" and a height of six rows.
```

NOTE Whatever the height of the text area, the user is free to enter text beyond the specified number of lines. If the amount of text is greater than the height of the text area, the user can either scroll the text area vertically or resize it by dragging the lower-right corner of the box.

- You can set the width of the text area box by specifying the number of columns:

```
A text area with a width of 30 columns.
```

- A text area enables the user to type any length of entry they want. However, if you're worried about being inundated with too much text, you can specify a maximum entry size in characters:

```
A text area with a maximum length of 240 characters.
```

- If needed, you can also specify a minimum entry size in characters:

```
A text area with a minimum length of 20 characters.
```

- You can set a text area as "required" if the user must fill in a value before submitting the form:

```
A text area that is required.
```

The opposite, in a sense, of the text-heavy text area is when you need the user to choose between just two simple possibilities: yes or no, on or off, and so on. Don't use a text area or even a text box for this—HTML offers a special control to handle these one-or-the-other choices, which is the subject of the next section.

8.3.5 *Getting yes-or-no info with check boxes*

One common information-gathering situation is when you give the user an option, and the user either accepts it or rejects it. Similarly, depending on the wording and intent of the option, the user may say yes or no, or they may turn it on or off. For all these scenarios—accept/reject, yes/no, on/off—you can include in your form a control called a *check box*. This is a control that displays a small square. If the user wants to submit a positive response for the check box (accept or yes or on), they click the check box to add a checkmark inside it; if, instead, the user wants to submit a negative response for the check box (reject or no or off), they click the check box to remove its checkmark.

Figure 8.6 shows a couple of examples of check boxes. The top check box is unchecked, which means (in this case) the user doesn't want to be notified about future events. The bottom check box is checked, which means (again, in this case) the user does want to subscribe to the site's newsletter. Here's an example instruction to include in your form prompt:

```
A checkbox with the label "Get notified about future events".
```

☐ **Get notified about future events**

☑ **Subscribe to our newsletter**

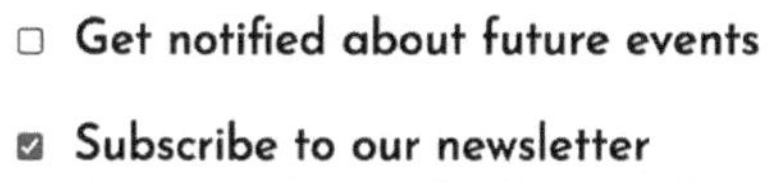

Figure 8.6   Some example check boxes

When prompting ChatGPT to include a check box in a form, you can customize the check box by specifying whether the check box is initially checked, as in this example:

```
A checkbox with the label "Subscribe to our newsletter" that is initially
checked.
```

If you want your users to choose between more than two options, HTML offers a couple of solutions, starting with radio buttons, discussed next.

8.3.6   *Choosing one of several options with radio buttons*

In the previous section, you learned about enabling your users to choose between two states by offering a check box. However, it's often the case that you want a user to choose one of three or four possibilities. For example, if an event occurs on Friday, Saturday, and Sunday, you may want the user to choose just one of those days. Similarly, for a free t-shirt giveaway, you may ask the user to choose the shirt size they want: Small, Medium, Large, or Extra Large.

When you need your visitors to choose just one of three or four options, you can add to your form a group of *radio buttons*, which is a set of HTML elements with the following characteristics:

- Each button is a small circle.
- Only one button can be selected at a time.
- The currently selected button's circle is filled in.
- All the nonselected buttons have empty circles.
- When the user clicks a nonselected button, that button's circle is filled in, and the previously selected button's circle becomes empty.

Figure 8.7 shows an example of a radio button group. The Medium radio button is currently selected.

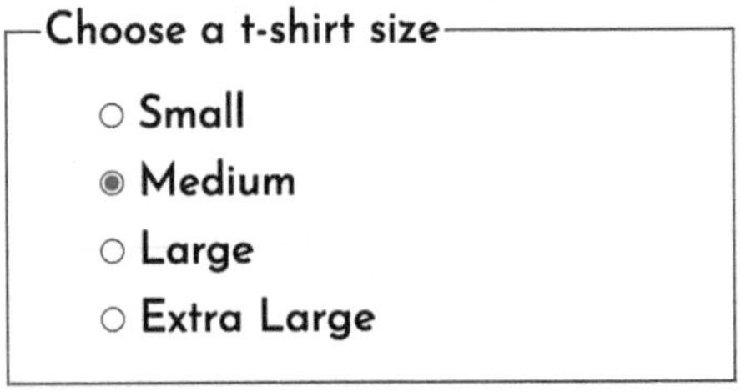

```
┌─Choose a t-shirt size──────────────────┐
│   ○ Small                              │
│   ◉ Medium                             │
│   ○ Large                              │
│   ○ Extra Large                        │
│                                        │
└────────────────────────────────────────┘
```

Figure 8.7   A group of radio buttons

When it's time to build your ChatGPT prompt for a form, you can use an instruction such as the following:

```
A group of radio buttons with the following options: "Small", "Medium",
"Large", and "Extra Large".
```

You can customize your radio buttons as follows:

- You can specify which radio button is initially selected:

```
A group of radio buttons with the following options: "Small", "Medium",
"Large", and "Extra Large". The "Medium" radio button is initially
selected.
```

- You can surround your radio button group with a "legend" element and specify a "caption" for that legend. The radio button group in figure 8.7 has such a legend with the caption `Choose a t-shirt size`. ChatGPT tends to include a legend element automatically, but you can use an instruction such as the following to specify the caption you want:

```
A group of radio buttons with the following options: "Small", "Medium",
"Large", and "Extra Large". Include a legend element with the caption
"Choose a t-shirt size".
```

If you need your users to choose from more than four options, you should put those options into a selection list, as I describe in the following section.

8.3.7   *Offering more selections with lists*

Theoretically, there's no reasonable limit on the number of radio buttons you can offer your users. Practically, however, having a large number of radio buttons can be confusing for the user and can take up too much page real estate. The general rule is to have at most four options in any group of radio buttons.

However, it's not at all unusual to have five or more options to present to your users. Perhaps you want the user to choose one day out of the seven days of the week (Monday through Sunday). Or you may ask a visitor to choose a state or country (as part of, say, gathering the user's mailing address).

For these larger collections of choices, you can put all the options you want to present to the user in a *selection list*, which by default is displayed as a dropdown list, as shown in figure 8.8. Clicking the list displays a menu of the choices you've made available to the user, as shown in figure 8.9.

What type of pet do you have?

None ⌄

Figure 8.8 A selection list initially appears as a dropdown list.

What type of pet do you have?

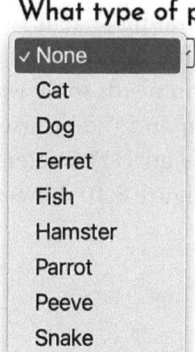

Figure 8.9 Clicking the selection list displays the available options.

Here's an example instruction you can include in your form prompt:

```
A selection list that includes the following items: "None", "Cat", "Dog",
"Ferret", "Fish", "Hamster", "Parrot", "Peeve", and "Snake".
```

When you're creating your ChatGPT form prompt, you can customize your selection lists as follows:

- You can specify which list item is initially selected:

  ```
  A selection list with the following options: "Happy", "Content",
  "Neutral", "Melancholy", and "Sad." Make "Neutral" the initially
  selected option.
  ```

- You can specify that the user is allowed to select multiple list items (by holding Ctrl (Windows) or Cmd (macOS) and clicking each item):

  ```
  A selection list with the label "Philosophers You've Read" and the
  following options: "Plato", "Aristotle", "Blaise Pascal", "Friedrich
  Nietzsche", and "Jean-Paul Sartre." Allow the user to make multiple
  selections.
  ```

- You can specify a size in rows. This converts the dropdown list to a regular list box that displays the number of rows you specified. If the number of displayed rows is smaller than the number of items in the list, the user can scroll the list box vertically. Here's an example instruction:

```
A selection list with the label "Dream Vacation" and the options "Beach
getaway", "Long-distance hike", "Mountain resort", "Urban exploration",
and "Staycation". Give the list a height of five rows.
```

Now that you're familiar with all the basic form controls, you're ready to find out how your users can submit the form.

8.3.8   *Submitting the form with a button*

When you deal with a dialog on your computer, you fill in the fields (if any) and then click a button (usually labeled OK) to tell your app or operating system that you're done with the dialog and it should process the dialog data. In a sense, an HTML form is the web page equivalent of a dialog, which means your form needs some way for the user to tell the web browser that they're done with the form and the browser should process it. The user does this by clicking a button, which is an HTML element that looks and acts just like an OK button in a computer dialog. Figure 8.10 shows an example of a form with a button.

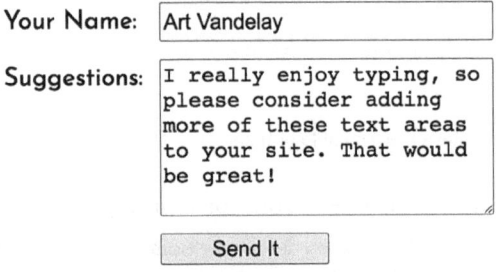

Figure 8.10   A form with a Send It button

ChatGPT will always include a button named Submit when you ask it to generate form code. To specify your preferred button name, here's an example instruction to ChatGPT that you can include in your overall form prompt:

```
A submit button element with the name "Send It".
```

Clicking a button in a form element is called *submitting* the form, and in the next section, you learn how to get the form data sent to you.

OK, you now know everything you need to know to successfully prompt ChatGPT to build a working form, as I describe in the next section.

8.4 Crafting the prompt for the event sign-up page

This chapter's project is a single page that contains a form that enables users to sign up to participate in a local barn-raising event. The form itself will use all six types of controls that I discussed earlier in this chapter: a text box, an email field, a text area, a check box, a radio button group, a selection list, and a button to submit the form.

Before continuing, you should already have a site title, tagline, and page title. You should also know which Google Fonts typefaces you want for the page text and the color scheme you want to apply. Refer to chapter 3 to learn how to get ChatGPT's help with titles, fonts, and colors.

Your prompt begins by telling ChatGPT that you want it to help you build a web page and that you don't know how to code, so it will have to generate the code for you:

```
I want to build a web page that enables page visitors to use a form to sign
up for an event. I don't know how to code, so I need you to provide the code
for me.

First, write the HTML code for a web page that includes the following:
```

You then specify the content of your page, including the following items (refer to figure 8.11):

- A header that includes your logo, site title, and tagline
- A main element that starts with the page title and is followed by some introductory text
- The form that users can submit to sign up for your event
- A footer that includes a copyright notice

Next, you instruct ChatGPT to generate the CSS for the page formatting:

```
Second, in a separate file please write the CSS code for the following:
```

You then specify the formatting, including the following:

- The page background color and text color.
- The type sizes you want to use for the site title, tagline, page title, page text, and the form controls.
- The fonts to use for the headings and regular page text.
- A maximum width for the page. This prevents the lines of text from getting too long. A maximum length of 800 px works for this page.

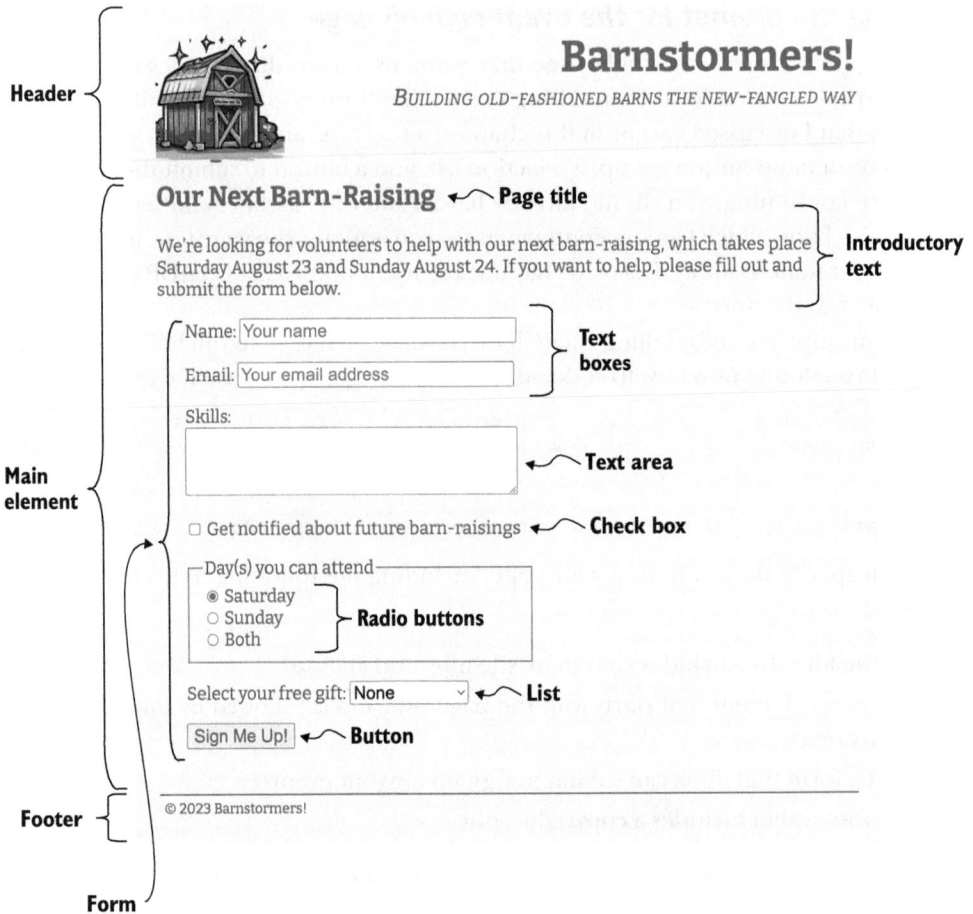

Figure 8.11   The elements of the event sign-up page

Here's an example prompt for my own event sign-up page:

```
I want to build a web page for an event sign-up page. I don't know how to
code, so I need you to provide the code for me.

First, write the HTML code for a web page that includes the following:
 * A header element that includes an image named barn.png, the title
"Barnstormers!", and the tagline "Building old-fashioned barns the new-
fangled way".
 * A main section with the heading "Our Next Barn-Raising".
 * A paragraph with the text "We're looking for volunteers to help with our
next barn-raising, which takes place Saturday August 23 and Sunday August 24.
If you want to help, please fill out and submit the form below.".
   * Include the code for an HTML form that has the following specifications:
     * In the form element, set the action attribute to "https://getform.io/f/
dbb986ea-ee50-42ba-abe7-5c304a087444" and the method attribute to "POST".
```

    * A text box with the label "Name", a width of 30 characters, and the placeholder "Your name".

    * An email field with the label "Email", a width of 30 characters, and the placeholder "Your email address".

    * A text area with the label "Skills", 3 rows, and 30 columns.

    * A checkbox with the label "Get notified about future barn-raisings".

    * A radio button group with the options "Saturday", "Sunday", and "Both". Select the "Saturday" option. Add a legend element with the caption "Day(s) you can attend".

    * A selection list with the label "Select your free gift" and the options "None", "Baseball cap", "Coffee mug", "Poster", "T-shirt", and "Tote bag".

    * The following code: `<input type="hidden" name="_gotcha" style="display:none !important">`

    * A button element with the name "Sign Me Up!".

    * Use paragraphs to separate each form control, except for the radio buttons, which should be separated by line breaks.

  * A footer element that includes the Copyright symbol, followed by the current year, followed by "Barnstormers!".

 * In the page head section, include the tag `<meta charset="utf-8">`.

 * In the page head section, include the tag `<meta name="viewport" content="width=device-width, initial-scale=1">`.

Second, in a separate file write the CSS code for the following:
 * The page has a 24px margin.
 * The page background color is cornsilk.
 * The page text color is saddlebrown.
 * Make the header image a maximum width of 150px and floated to the left.
 * The title is 48px, aligned to the right, and with no bottom margin.
 * The tagline is 26px, formatted as italic and small caps, aligned to the right, and with no top margin.
 * The main section has a top margin of 75px.
 * The main section heading font size is 30px.
 * The main section font size is 20px.
 * The form width is 400px and the left margin is 32px.
 * The form, input, textarea, select, and button font size is 20px.
 * The button text color is saddlebrown.
 * For all the page text, use the Bitter font from Google Fonts.
 * The footer has 5px padding all around, 50px top margin, and a saddlebrown top border.
 * Give the page a maximum width of 800px.

ChatGPT will first generate the HTML code, which you can copy and then paste and save to a file named index.html. In that code, you should see a line near the top similar to the following:

```
<link rel="stylesheet" type="text/css" href="styles.css">
```

This code tells the web browser to look for the CSS code in a file named styles.css, so your next task is to copy the generated CSS code and then paste it and save it to a file named styles.css (or whatever name you see in the `<link>` tag). Be sure to save styles .css file in the same folder as your index.html file. You also need to copy your header image file into the same folder. Refer to appendix A to learn more about working web page files.

I used OpenAI's ChatGPT app to submit my prompt to GPT-4. The generated code produced the page shown in figure 8.12.

Figure 8.12   My event sign-up page

If you're satisfied with the page and form generated by ChatGPT, feel free to bypass the rest of this chapter and deploy the code to the web (refer to appendix B for the details). However, if you're curious to know more about the generated web page code, proceed to the next section for a closer look.

8.5   *Examining the event sign-up page code*

You don't need to know how the web page code generated by ChatGPT works. However, if you'd like to dive a little deeper, the next couple of sections offer a brief and not-overly-technical description of the event sign-up page code that resulted from my prompt from the previous section (that page is shown in figure 8.12).

> **NOTE**   The generated HTML and CSS code for my event sign-up page are available on this book's website (www.manning.com/books/build-a-website-with -chatgpt) and in the book's GitHub repository: https://github.com/paulmcfe/ websites-with-chatgpt.

I hope my code annotations help you to understand what's happening under the hood and assist you in tweaking or customizing your own code.

8.5.1 Examining the HTML

Here's the HTML code that ChatGPT generated for my event sign-up page:

```
<!DOCTYPE html>
<html>
<head>
    <meta charset="utf-8">
    <meta name="viewport"
        content="width=device-width, initial-scale=1">
    <title>Barnstormers!</title>
    <link rel="stylesheet"
        type="text/css" href="styles.css">
</head>
<body>
    <header>
        <img src="barn.png" alt="Barnstormers logo">
        <h1>Barnstormers!</h1>
        <p>Building old-fashioned barns the new-fangled way</p>
    </header>
    <main>
        <h2>Our Next Barn-Raising</h2>
        <p>We're looking for volunteers to help with our next
            barn-raising, which takes place Saturday August 23
            and Sunday August 24. If you want to help, please
            fill out and submit the form below.</p>
        <form action="https://getform.io/f/
            dbb986ea-ee50-42ba-abe7-5c304a087444"
            method="POST">
            <p>
                <label>Name:
                <input type="text"
                    name="name"
                    size="30"
                    placeholder="Your name">
                </label>
            </p>
            <p>
                <label>Email:
                <input type="email"
                    name="email"
                    size="30"
                    placeholder="Your email address">
                </label>
            </p>
            <p>
                <label>Skills:
                <textarea name="skills"
                        rows="3"
                        cols="30">
                </textarea>
                </label>
            </p>
            <p>
```

Helps the page display properly on mobile devices

Tells the web browser where to find the CSS code

Site logo
Site title
Site tagline
Page header

Form element specifies the endpoint

Name text box

Email text box

Skills text area

```
        <label>
        <input type="checkbox"
               name="notify">
        Get notified about future barn-raisings
        </label>
    </p>
    <fieldset>
        <legend>Day(s) you can attend</legend>
        <label>
        <input type="radio"
               name="day"
               value="Saturday"
               checked>
        Saturday
        </label>
        <br>
        <label>
        <input type="radio"
               name="day"
               value="Sunday">
        Sunday
        </label>
        <br>
        <label>
        <input type="radio"
               name="day"
               value="Both">
        Both
        </label>
    </fieldset>
    <p>
        <label>Select your free gift:
        <select name="gift">
            <option value="">None</option>
            <option value="cap">Baseball cap</option>
            <option value="mug">Coffee mug</option>
            <option value="poster">Poster</option>
            <option value="shirt">T-shirt</option>
            <option value="bag">Tote bag</option>
        </select>
        </label>
    </p>
    <input type="hidden"
           name="_gotcha"
           style="display:none !important">
    <p>
        <button type="submit">Sign Me Up!</button>
    </p>
  </form>
 </main>
 <footer>© 2023 Barnstormers!</footer>
</body>
</html>
```

Check box

Radio button group
text box

Selection list

Hidden "honeypot" field

◄— Submit button

◄— Page footer

Here are a few notes to bear in mind when reading the HTML code:

- In the `form` element, notice that the `action` attribute is set to address of the Getform endpoint. (Note that I've altered the real address, so don't try to use this address in your own forms because it won't work.)
- For each form control (except the button), notice that ChatGPT also includes a `name` attribute. The web browser uses these `name` attribute values to identify each field when it submits the form. Figure 8.13 shows an example submission. Notice that the names of each field—`name`, `email`, `skills`, `day`, `gift`, and `notify`—match the `name` attribute values in the form.

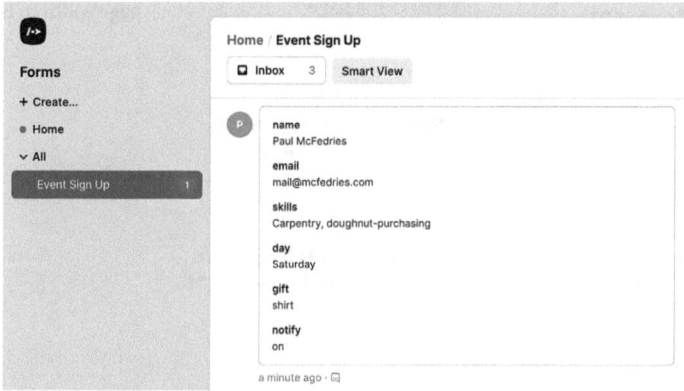

Figure 8.13   Form submissions appear on your Getform page.

- Note also that each radio button and selection list option has its own `value` attribute. When the browser submits the form, it sends the value of the currently selected radio button and list item. In figure 8.13, for example, that the submitted value for the `day` field (the radio button group) is `Saturday`, and the submitted value for the `gift` field (the selection list) is `shirt` (that is, the T-shirt item in the list).
- Just before the `button` element is an `input` element with its `type` attribute set to `hidden` and its `name` attribute set to `_gotcha`. This field is used to sniff out spam bots, which, when they submit this form, are programmed to fill in each field, including this hidden one. If the Getform service receives a form submission where this hidden field is filled in, it knows it's dealing with spam and discards the submission.

Finally, note that the HTML code includes the following line:

```
<link rel="stylesheet" href="styles.css">
```

This tag tells the web browser where to find the CSS code, which I describe in the next section.

8.5.2   *Examining the CSS*

Here's the CSS code that ChatGPT generated for my event sign-up page:

```
@import url('https://fonts.googleapis.com/css2?
    family=Bitter:ital, wght@0,400;0,700;1,400
    display=swap');
body {
    margin: 24px;
    background-color: cornsilk;
    color: saddlebrown;
    font-family: 'Bitter', serif;
    max-width: 800px;
    margin-left: auto;
    margin-right: auto;
}

header img {
    max-width: 150px;
    float: left;
}

header h1 {
    font-size: 48px;
    text-align: right;
    margin-bottom: 0;
}

header p {
    font-size: 26px;
    font-style: italic;
    font-variant-caps: small-caps;
    text-align: right;
    margin-top: 0;
}

main {
    margin-top: 75px;
}

main h2 {
    font-size: 30px;
}

main p, form {
    font-size: 20px;
}

form {
    width: 400px;
    margin-left: 32px;
}

form input, form textarea, form select, form button {
```

Loads the Bitter font from Google Fonts

Sets the page background color, text color, and font

Sets the maximum page width to 800 px

Centers the page

Sets a maximum logo width, and floats it to the left

Sets the page title font size to 48 px, and aligns it to the right

Styles the tagline with font size 26 px, italics, small caps, and right alignment

Adds a margin to the top of the main element

Sets the font size of the main heading

Styles the font size of the regular page text

Sets a width for the form

```
    font-size: 20px;
}

form button {
    color: saddlebrown;
}

footer {
    padding: 5px;
    margin-top: 50px;
    border-top: solid saddlebrown;
}
```

◄——— **Styles the font size of the form control text**

◄——— **Applies the text color to the button**

If you like, you can use these annotations to help customize your web page code, as I describe in the next section.

8.6   Customizing the event sign-up page

If the form code generated by ChatGPT isn't even close to what you want, you're better off starting a new chat session and submitting a revised prompt. However, if the form code is close to what you were looking for, it may be easier to modify it yourself.

First, here are some customization suggestions for the HTML code:

- Feel free to edit any of the page text, such as the title, the tagline, the introductory text, or any of the form labels. Be careful not to edit or delete the HTML tags that surround each bit of text (such as the <label> and </label> tags that bracket a form label).
- If you want to include a second introductory paragraph, place the edit cursor after the </p> tag that ends the existing introductory paragraph. Press Enter or Return to start a new line, type a <p> tag, type your paragraph text, and finish with a </p> tag.
- In the form code, you can edit some of the tag attribute values. For example, with a text box, you can modify the size and placeholder attribute values; with a text area, you can modify the rows and cols attribute values; and you can modify any value attribute string. In all these cases, be sure to modify only the text between the double quotation marks. Also, don't change the values of any type or name attribute in the form.
- In the footer section of the HTML code, you can add links to your social media accounts, as I describe in chapter 4.

Now, here are a few customization ideas for the CSS code:

- To give your page a different background color, use a different color keyword for the body element's background-color property.
- To use a different color for the page text, specify a different color keyword for the body element's color property.

- The CSS code uses the page text color in two other places: the `form button` element's `color` property and the `footer` element's `border-top` property. To keep your colors in harmony, you need to replace these color values with whatever color keyword you use in the previous item.

- If you want your page to have a different maximum width, change the `max-width` value to something other than `800px`.

- If you'd prefer to have the header logo on the right and the text and tagline aligned on the left, you need to make three changes:
  - In the `header img` element, change the `float` value to `right`.
  - In the `header h1` element, change the `text-align` value to `left`.
  - In the `header p` element, change the `text-align` value to `left`.

- For any font size value, you can change the number to increase or decrease the font size. Just make sure you leave the `px` unit in place.

- For any padding or margin value, you can change the number to increase or decrease the padding or margins. In each case, be sure to leave the `px` unit in place.

- To make your page code more accessible, consider converting all px measurements to rem measurements. 1 rem is by default equivalent to 16 px, so 20 px is 1.25 rem, 24 px is 1.5 rem, 32 px is 2 rem, 48 px is 3 rem, and so on. The rem unit is more accessible because it measures font sizes relative to the default font size the browser user has defined in their browser settings.

Summary

- A form is a special collection of HTML elements that enable you to gather information and then send that information somewhere (such as your email address).

- A form's endpoint is the address to which the web browser sends the form data when the user submits the form.

- A text box is a rectangular area designed to hold text typed by the user. You can set up text boxes to hold special data types, such as email addresses, numbers, and URLs.

- A label is text that describes a particular control.

- A text area is a form field that supports longer, multiline text entries.

- For yes/no or on/off types of data, use a check box.

- To enable the user to choose one of three or four options, use a radio button group.

- To enable the user to choose from among five or more options, use a selection list.

- Include a button in the form so the user can submit the form data.

- For best results, your page prompt should be as specific as possible, including colors, font sizes, and heading levels.

Adding lists to your pages

This chapter covers

- Prompting ChatGPT to build a bulleted list
- Asking ChatGPT to generate a numbered list
- Customizing your lists
- Crafting a ChatGPT prompt for building a recipe page
- Examining and customizing the ChatGPT-generated code

"Content is king" is an old (and, alas, sexist) adage from the early days of the web. It meant that what was most important on every web page was the content it contained. In other words, if you published great content, the world would beat a path to your website door.

That may have been true in the 1990s when people didn't expect much from each web page they visited. Nowadays, however, having great content doesn't amount to anything if you present that content poorly. If you've gone through any of the web projects in the previous chapters, you may have been surprised (but hopefully not dismayed) by how specific all my ChatGPT prompts have been. That level of detail is needed because otherwise, ChatGPT will generate code for pages that are decidedly unattractive: dull, cramped, and poorly laid out. Yes, you have awesome content you want to share, but to prevent visitors from leaving seconds after they arrive, you need to present that content engagingly.

In this chapter, you learn two techniques for making your content easier to read, easier to understand, and more engaging for the reader. The two techniques are bulleted lists and numbered lists, which are among the most common patterns used in modern web pages and form the basis of some of today's most popular sites. You then put your newfound list know-how to work to create a detailed prompt for ChatGPT to generate the code for a recipe page. This chapter also provides a high-level explanation of the code generated by ChatGPT and tips for customizing it.

9.1   *Checking out this chapter's project*

The project you get ChatGPT to create for you in this chapter is a basic web page that takes the reader through a recipe for making nut bars. The final page will include the following components:

- A header element that includes the website logo, title, and tagline
- A main element that begins with the recipe title and introduction
- A couple of bulleted lists containing the recipe ingredients
- A numbered list of the recipe steps
- A footer element that includes a copyright notice

Figure 9.1 shows an example of the kind of page you'll convince ChatGPT to generate for you in this chapter.

The Super Baker

The ultimate guide to super-powered baking. Learn how to make delicious treats that will boost your energy, strength, and speed.

Preparation

1. Preheat the oven to 350°F. Place one rack on the bottom shelf and another rack in the middle.
2. Cover two baking sheets with parchment paper.
3. Spread out the nuts and seeds evenly on one baking sheet.
4. Spread out the rolled oats evenly on the other baking sheet.
5. Place the nuts and seeds on the bottom rack and the oats on the middle rack.
6. Bake for 8 minutes, then remove the nuts and seeds; continue baking the oats for another 7 minutes.
7. Allow the oats, nuts, and seeds to cool. (Don't throw out the parchment paper sheets.)
8. Chop the cooled nuts.
9. Chop the dates.
10. Combine all the dry ingredients in a large bowl.
11. Prepare an 8x10 or 7x11 pan:
    i. Line the pan with one of the sheets of parchment paper from the bake.
    ii. Coat the parchment paper with oil (such as sunflower oil).
    iii. Oil one side of the other sheet of parchment paper.
12. Add the wet ingredients to a small saucepan.
13. Cook the wet ingredients on the stovetop, stirring constantly, until a quick-read thermometer inserted into the liquid reads 260°F.
14. Add to cooked liquid to the dry ingredients and mix thoroughly.
15. Add the mixture to the prepared pan.
16. Place the oiled side of the second sheet of parchment paper down on the mixture and use a spoon and/or potato masher to press the mixture into place.
17. Cool the mixture in the refrigerator for 30-60 minutes.
18. Remove from the fridge and let sit for 30-60 minutes. (You want the mixture to be warm enough that it doesn't shatter when you try to cut it.)
19. Cut into 24 pieces.

Super-Energy Nut Bars

Looking for an energy boost, either first thing in the morning or during that mid-afternoon lull? Look no further than these tasty and nutritious nut bars, which turn the energy dial up to 11. Packed full of delicious and take-you-all-the-way-to-dinner nuts and dried fruit, all combined with a give-me-energy-now hit of honey and maple syrup, these bars just might be the perfect superhero snack.

Dry Ingredients

- 200g rolled oats
- 100g peanuts
- 100g almonds
- 50g pumpkin seeds
- 50g sesame seeds
- 100g dates or other dried fruit

Wet Ingredients

- 120g honey
- 80g maple syrup
- 1 tsp vanilla extract
- ¼ tsp sea salt

Figure 9.1   A recipe page generated by ChatGPT

The example page includes two bulleted lists and a single numbered list (with a numbered sublist), but you can easily modify this project to include only a bulleted list, only a numbered list, or multiple lists of both types. This means you can create pages that include content such as top-10 lists, tutorials, documentation, travel guides, product reviews, and lists of your favorite books, movies, TV shows, games, ice cream flavors, computer book authors, and more. Before you get to all that, you need to know a bit about each type of list.

9.2   *Building a bulleted list*

A *bulleted list* is a collection of HTML elements that present multiple items as a vertical list, where each item is indented slightly from the left margin and preceded by a small black circle called a *bullet.* You use a bulleted list when you want to present several items but the order of those items isn't an essential component of the list. Figure 9.2 shows an example of a bulleted list.

The Most Common Mango Varieties

- Francis
- Haden
- Honey
- Keitt
- Kent
- Tommy Atkins

Figure 9.2   An example of a bulleted list

Here's how you'd instruct ChatGPT to generate the code for such a list:

```
Generate the HTML code for a bulleted list that includes the following items:
"Francis", "Haden", "Honey", "Keitt", "Kent", and "Tommy Atkins".
```

Here's the resulting code:

```
<ul>
    <li>Francis</li>
    <li>Haden</li>
    <li>Honey</li>
    <li>Keitt</li>
    <li>Kent</li>
    <li>Tommy Atkins</li>
</ul>
```

There are two main components to this code:

- The whole thing is surrounded by `<ul>` and `</ul>` tags (where `ul` is short for *unnumbered list*).
- Each list item is surrounded by `<li>` and `</li>` tags (where `li` is short for *list item*).

For short items (a word or a short phrase), surrounding each item with quotation marks is fine. If your list contains items with much longer text, you'll want to use the method I discuss in the next section.

9.2.1 *Handling longer list items*

Bulleted list items don't have to be single words or short phrases. You're free to include as much text as you need in each item. (That said, if you make the content of your items too long—say, more than a few sentences—your list becomes harder to read and scan.) For longer items, your prompt should separate the items clearly so ChatGPT doesn't get confused. Here's an example instruction:

```
Generate the HTML code for a bulleted list that includes the following items:
- "Sailing Alone Around the Room," by Billy Collins. The former U.S. poet
laureate at the top of his game.
- "Blue Horses," by Mary Oliver. Each poem in this collection is a gem.
- "Human Wishes," by Robert Hass. If prose poetry is more your thing, you owe
yourself these stunning examples of the form.
- "The Carrying," by Ada Limón. The current U.S. poet laureate at the top of
*her* game.
- "All of Us," by Raymond Carver. The complete poetical works of the master
of quiet desperation.
- "What the Living Do," by Marie Howe. A searingly honest search for hope
amidst overwhelming grief. Highly recommended.
```

Notice that the instruction precedes each list item with a dash (-). ChatGPT understands that a dash represents a new list item (The plus sign [+] also works.). Figure 9.3 shows how the code generated by ChatGPT from this instruction appears in a web browser.

Recommended Poetry Books

- "Sailing Alone Around the Room," by Billy Collins. The former U.S. poet laureate at the top of his game.
- "Blue Horses," by Mary Oliver. Each poem in this collection is a gem.
- "Human Wishes," by Robert Hass. If prose poetry is more your thing, you owe yourself these stunning examples of the form.
- "The Carrying," by Ada Limón. The current U.S. poet laureate at the top of *her* game.
- "All of Us," by Raymond Carver. The complete poetical works of the master of quiet desperation.
- "What the Living Do," by Marie Howe. A searingly honest search for hope amidst overwhelming grief. Highly recommended.

Figure 9.3   A bulleted list with longer list items

Does one of your bullet points itself need to have a bulleted list? That's covered in the next section.

9.2.2 *Nesting bulleted lists*

A common bulleted list pattern is to have one of the items contain its own bulleted list. This is known as a *nested* bulleted list, and it enables you to break your page info into multiple levels, which can make complex data much clearer and easier for your readership to follow.

Here's an example instruction that convinces ChatGPT to generate a bulleted list where one of the items is a nested bulleted list:

```
Generate the HTML code for a bulleted list with the following items:
- Bread
- Milk
- Fruit
 - Bananas
 - Oranges
 - Papayas
- Chocolate
```

Notice that, under the `Fruit` item, the three items are indented by one space. This indentation is enough to let ChatGPT know that you want those items rendered as a nested bulleted list. Figure 9.4 shows the code generated by ChatGPT in the web browser.

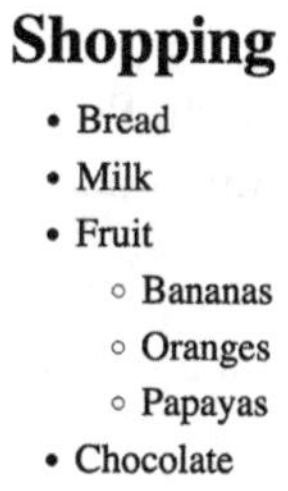

Shopping List

- Bread
- Milk
- Fruit
  - Bananas
  - Oranges
  - Papayas
- Chocolate

Figure 9.4　A bulleted list with a nested bulleted list

Here's the code behind this list:

```
<ul>
    <li>Bread</li>
    <li>Milk</li>
    <li>Fruit
        <ul>
            <li>Bananas</li>
            <li>Oranges</li>
            <li>Papayas</li>
        </ul>
    </li>
    <li>Chocolate</li>
</ul>
```

To help the reader differentiate the nested list from the main list, the web browser does two things:

- Indents the nested list items a bit more than the main list items
- Uses a hollow circle instead of a filled circle as the item bullet

That hollow circle lets you know that there are different bullet types available. The next section shows you how to specify a different bullet type for your lists.

9.2.3   *Changing the bullet type*

By default, web browsers render a bulleted list with a filled circle (also called a *disc*) as the bullet. However, that default bullet type isn't set in stone. Here's a generic prompt instructing ChatGPT to use a different bullet type:

```
Generate the HTML code for a bulleted list with the items below. Use a type
as the bullet.
- Item 1
- Item 2
- etc.
```

In your instruction, you replace `type` with one of the following:

- The word `circle` to use an unfilled circle as the bullet.
- The word `square` to use a filled square as the bullet.
- The name of any emoji character, such as Check Mark, Star, Heart, Arrow, or Smiley Face.
- The name of any other Unicode character, such as Black Right-Pointing Triangle, Rightwards Arrow, or White Diamond. (Check out www.unicode.org/charts to see the available characters—all 144,000 of them!)

Figure 9.5 shows a bulleted list that uses Check Mark emoji characters instead of the regular bullets.

Breads We Carry

- ✅ Brioche
- ✅ Ciabatta
- ✅ Marbled Rye
- ✅ Pugliese
- ✅ San Francisco Sourdough
- ✅ Ten-Grain
- ✅ Whole Wheat (100%)

Figure 9.5   A bulleted list that uses Check Mark emojis as bullets

Bulleted lists are a common sight throughout the web, but they're not the only list game in town. Numbered lists are the topic of the next section.

9.3   *Building a numbered list*

I mentioned earlier that you use a bulleted list when the order of the list items isn't an essential component of the list. However, for many collections of items, the order *is* important, and your web pages can display those items using a numbered list.

For example, if you're providing a set of step-by-step instructions, it's vital that the procedure begins with the first step and then proceeds sequentially to the final step. Similarly, for a top-10 ranking, you probably want the 10th-ranked item to appear first, followed by the 9th-ranked item, and continuing to the top-ranked item, which appears last.

Figure 9.6 shows an example of a numbered list. Here's how you'd instruct ChatGPT to generate the code for it:

```
Generate the HTML code for a numbered list with the following items:
-Inflatable Dartboard
-Water-Resistant Sponge
-Helium-Filled Paperweight
-Teflon Bath Mat
-Flame-Retardant Firewood
```

Our Bestsellers

1. Inflatable Dartboard
2. Water-Resistant Sponge
3. Helium-Filled Paperweight
4. Teflon Bath Mat
5. Flame-Retardant Firewood

Figure 9.6 An example of a numbered list

Notice that you precede each item in your list with a dash (-). You can also use a plus sign (+), an asterisk (*), or even the numeral 1 followed by a period (1.). Here's the resulting code:

```
<ol>
    <li>Inflatable Dartboard</li>
    <li>Water-Resistant Sponge</li>
    <li>Helium-Filled Paperweight</li>
    <li>Teflon Bath Mat</li>
    <li>Flame-Retardant Firewood</li>
</ol>
```

There are two main components to this code:

- The whole thing is surrounded by `<ol>` and `</ol>` tags (where ol is short for *ordered list*).
- Each list item is surrounded by `<li>` and `</li>` tags (where li is short for *list item*).

The web browser always renders numbered lists starting with the first item as number 1, but there are a couple of ways you can customize the list order. First up, in the next section you learn how to reverse the list order.

9.3.1 *Reversing the list order*

When you're using a numbered list as part of a tutorial, some product documentation, or a recipe, you want the reader to start with step 1, proceed to step 2, and continue in sequence until the final step. However, not every numbered list fits this pattern. For example, it's traditional for a top-10 list to begin at number 10, present number 9, and so on down to number 1.

To cajole ChatGPT into creating such a list, instruct it to generate a *reversed numbered list*, as in this example:

```
Generate the HTML code for a reversed numbered list with the following items:
-U.C. Santa Cruz Banana Slugs
-Delta State Fighting Okra
-Kent State Golden Flashes
-Evergreen State College Geoducks
-New Mexico Tech Pygmies
-South Carolina Fighting Gamecocks
-Southern Illinois Salukis
-Whittier Poets
-Western Illinois Leathernecks
-Delaware Fightin' Blue Hens
```

Figure 9.7 shows how the code generated by ChatGPT from this instruction is rendered in the web browser.

My Top Ten Favorite U.S. College Nicknames

10. U.C. Santa Cruz Banana Slugs
 9. Delta State Fighting Okra
 8. Kent State Golden Flashes
 7. Evergreen State College Geoducks
 6. New Mexico Tech Pygmies
 5. South Carolina Fighting Gamecocks
 4. Southern Illinois Salukis
 3. Whittier Poets
 2. Western Illinois Leathernecks
 1. Delaware Fightin' Blue Hens

Figure 9.7   A reversed numbered list

The other method you can use to change the order of a numbered list is to specify the list's starting number, which is the topic of the next section.

9.3.2   *Changing the list's starting number*

By default, a regular numbered list starts with number 1, and a reversed numbered list starts with a value equal to the number of items in the list. However, you're free to specify any starting value you like. Why would you ever want to do such a thing? One common example is when you present part of a larger list (such as a contract). If that part of the larger list starts at number 4, for example, so should the numbered list you present to the reader.

Another common example is when you start a numbered list, have a section of text, and then have a new numbered list that's meant to be a continuation of the first. Figure 9.8 shows what happens in the browser.

How to Boil Water

1. Fill a pot with water: Depending on how much water you need, fill a pot with the appropriate amount of water. Make sure not to fill it to the brim as the water can overflow when it starts to boil.
2. Place the pot on the stove: Put the pot on a burner that fits its size. A small pot on a large burner can lead to heat loss and longer boiling times.
3. Turn on the stove: Turn the knob of the stove to ignite the burner. If you're using a gas stove, you'll see a flame. If it's an electric stove, the burner will start to glow.
4. Set the heat to high: To boil water quickly, set the heat to its highest setting.

WARNING: Please be extremely careful here because multiple things are about to get dangerously hot: the water, of course, but also the pot and the stove burner.

1. Wait for the water to boil: You'll know the water is boiling when you see bubbles rising to the surface rapidly. This could take anywhere from a few minutes to over ten minutes, depending on how much water you're boiling and how powerful your stove is.
2. Turn off the stove: Once your water has reached a rolling boil (or once it's heated to your desired temperature), carefully turn off the stove.

Figure 9.8 A list, interrupted

The problem here is that the second list starts over at step 1 when it should continue with step 5. Fortunately, you can tell ChatGPT the starting value of a numbered list by including `starting at x` in your prompt, where x is the starting value you want. Here's an example:

```
Generate the HTML code for a numbered list starting at 5 with the following
items:
-Wait for the water to boil: You'll know the water is boiling when you see
bubbles rising to the surface rapidly. This could take anywhere from a few
minutes to over ten minutes, depending on how much water you're boiling and
how powerful your stove is.
-Turn off the stove: Once your water has reached a rolling boil (or once it's
heated to your desired temperature), carefully turn off the stove.
```

Figure 9.9 shows that the code generated by ChatGPT from this instruction now renders the second list correctly as a continuation of the first.

How to Boil Water

1. Fill a pot with water: Depending on how much water you need, fill a pot with the appropriate amount of water. Make sure not to fill it to the brim as the water can overflow when it starts to boil.
2. Place the pot on the stove: Put the pot on a burner that fits its size. A small pot on a large burner can lead to heat loss and longer boiling times.
3. Turn on the stove: Turn the knob of the stove to ignite the burner. If you're using a gas stove, you'll see a flame. If it's an electric stove, the burner will start to glow.
4. Set the heat to high: To boil water quickly, set the heat to its highest setting.

WARNING: Please be extremely careful here because multiple things are about to get dangerously hot: the water, of course, but also the pot and the stove burner.

5. Wait for the water to boil: You'll know the water is boiling when you see bubbles rising to the surface rapidly. This could take anywhere from a few minutes to over ten minutes, depending on how much water you're boiling and how powerful your stove is.
6. Turn off the stove: Once your water has reached a rolling boil (or once it's heated to your desired temperature), carefully turn off the stove.

Figure 9.9 The second list is now a proper continuation of the first list.

Need one of the items in a nested list to have its own numbered list? The next section tells you everything you need to know.

9.3.3 *Nesting numbered lists*

Occasionally, you need to have "substeps" in a numbered list. In a tutorial, for example, you may want to break down a particular item into multiple subitems for clarity or precision. Similarly, it's common for legal text to have numbered clauses and numbered subclauses. A collection of substeps within a larger numbered list is called a *nested* numbered list.

Here's an example prompt that asks ChatGPT to generate a numbered list where each of the two main steps has multiple substeps:

```
Generate the HTML code for a numbered list with the following items:
-Get into the starting position:
 -Place two balls in your dominant hand, one in front of the other.
 -Hold the third ball in your other hand.
 -Let your arms dangle naturally and bring your forearms parallel to the
ground (as though you were holding a tray).
-Make the first toss:
 -Of the two balls in your dominant hand, toss the front one toward your left
hand in a smooth arc.
 -Make sure the ball doesn't spin too much.
 -Make sure the ball goes no higher than about eye level.
```

Notice that in each case, the three subitems are indented by one space. This indentation tells ChatGPT that you want those items rendered as a nested numbered list. Figure 9.10 shows the code generated by ChatGPT in the web browser.

How to Juggle

1. Get into the starting position:
    1. Place two balls in your dominant hand, one in front of the other.
    2. Hold the third ball in your other hand.
    3. Let your arms dangle naturally and bring your forearms parallel to the ground (as though you were holding a tray).
2. Make the first toss:
    1. Of the two balls in your dominant hand, toss the front one toward your left hand in a smooth arc.
    2. Make sure the ball doesn't spin too much.
    3. Make sure the ball goes no higher than about eye level.

Figure 9.10 A numbered list with two nested numbered lists

Here's the code behind this list:

```
<ol>
    <li>Get into the starting position:
        <ol style="list-style-type: lower-roman;">
            <li>Place two balls in your dominant hand,
                one in front of the other.</li>
            <li>Hold the third ball in your other hand.</li>
            <li>Let your arms dangle naturally and bring
                your forearms parallel to the ground (as
                though you were holding a tray).</li>
        </ol>
```

```
        </li>
        <li>Make the first toss:
            <ol style="list-style-type: lower-roman;">
                <li>Of the two balls in your dominant hand,
                    toss the front one toward your left hand
                    in a smooth arc.</li>
                <li>Make sure the ball doesn't spin too much.</li>
                <li>Make sure the ball goes no higher than
                    about eye level.</li>
            </ol>
        </li>
    </ol>
</ol>
```

To help the reader differentiate the nested list from the main list, the web browser indents the nested items a bit more than the main list items. However, this default way of handling nested numbered lists is a bit confusing because the nested items use the same numbering scheme (1, 2, 3, etc.) as the main numbered list. Fortunately, as you learn in the next section, you can specify a different numbering style.

9.3.4 *Changing the numbering style*

By default, web browsers render a numbered list using decimal numbers (1, 2, 3, and so on). However, there are several different numbering styles you can use, such as Roman numerals. Here's a generic instruction that asks ChatGPT to use a different numbering style:

```
Generate the HTML code for a numbered list with the items below. Use style as
the numbering style.
- Item 1
- Item 2
- etc.
```

In your instruction, you replace `style` with one of the following:

- The phrase `decimal leading zero` to use decimal numbers padded by initial zeros, as needed (01, 02, 03, and so on)
- The phrase `upper roman` to use uppercase Roman numerals (I, II, III, and so on)
- The phrase `lower roman` to use lowercase Roman numerals (i, ii, iii, and so on)
- The phrase `upper alpha` to use uppercase letters (A, B, C, and so on)
- The phrase `lower alpha` to use lowercase letters (a, b, c, and so on)

Here's a revised version of the ChatGPT instruction from the previous section, asking for lowercase Roman numbers in the nested numbered lists:

```
Generate the HTML code for a numbered list with items below. Use lower roman
as the numbering style for the nested numbered lists.
-Get into the starting position:
 -Place two balls in your dominant hand, one in front of the other.
 -Hold the third ball in your other hand.
 -Let your arms dangle naturally and bring your forearms parallel to the
ground (as though you were holding a tray).
-Make the first toss:
```

```
-Of the two balls in your dominant hand, toss the front one toward your left
hand in a smooth arc.
-Make sure the ball doesn't spin too much.
-Make sure the ball goes no higher than about eye level.
```

Figure 9.11 shows the updated numbered list with the nested numbered lists using lowercase Roman numerals.

How to Juggle

1. Get into the starting position:
   i. Place two balls in your dominant hand, one in front of the other.
   ii. Hold the third ball in your other hand.
   iii. Let your arms dangle naturally and bring your forearms parallel to the ground (as though you were holding a tray).
2. Make the first toss:
   i. Of the two balls in your dominant hand, toss the front one toward your left hand in a smooth arc.
   ii. Make sure the ball doesn't spin too much.
   iii. Make sure the ball goes no higher than about eye level.

Figure 9.11 The nested numbered lists now use lowercase Roman numerals.

At this point, you know all that's required to successfully prompt ChatGPT to build a recipe page. The following section takes you through the process.

9.4   *Crafting the prompt for the recipe page*

This chapter's project is a web page that offers the reader a recipe that uses several lists:

- Two bulleted lists for two sets of ingredients
- A numbered list (with a nested numbered list) for the instructions

At this point, you should already have a site title, a tagline, and a page title, which in this case will be the name of the recipe. It will be helpful if you know which Google Fonts typefaces you want for the page text and which colors you want to use. Check out chapter 3 to learn how to prompt ChatGPT for suggested titles, fonts, and colors.

To start your prompt, tell ChatGPT that you want to construct a web page and that you want it to generate the code for you:

```
I want to build a web page for a recipe. I don't know how to code, so I need
you to provide the code for me.
```

```
First, write the HTML code for a web page that includes the following:
```

Now spell out the page content, including the following (refer to figure 9.12):

- A header that includes your logo, site title, and tagline
- A main element that starts with the page title and is followed by some introductory text
- One or more bulleted lists that detail the recipe ingredients
- One or more numbered lists that take the reader through the recipe steps
- A footer that includes a copyright notice.

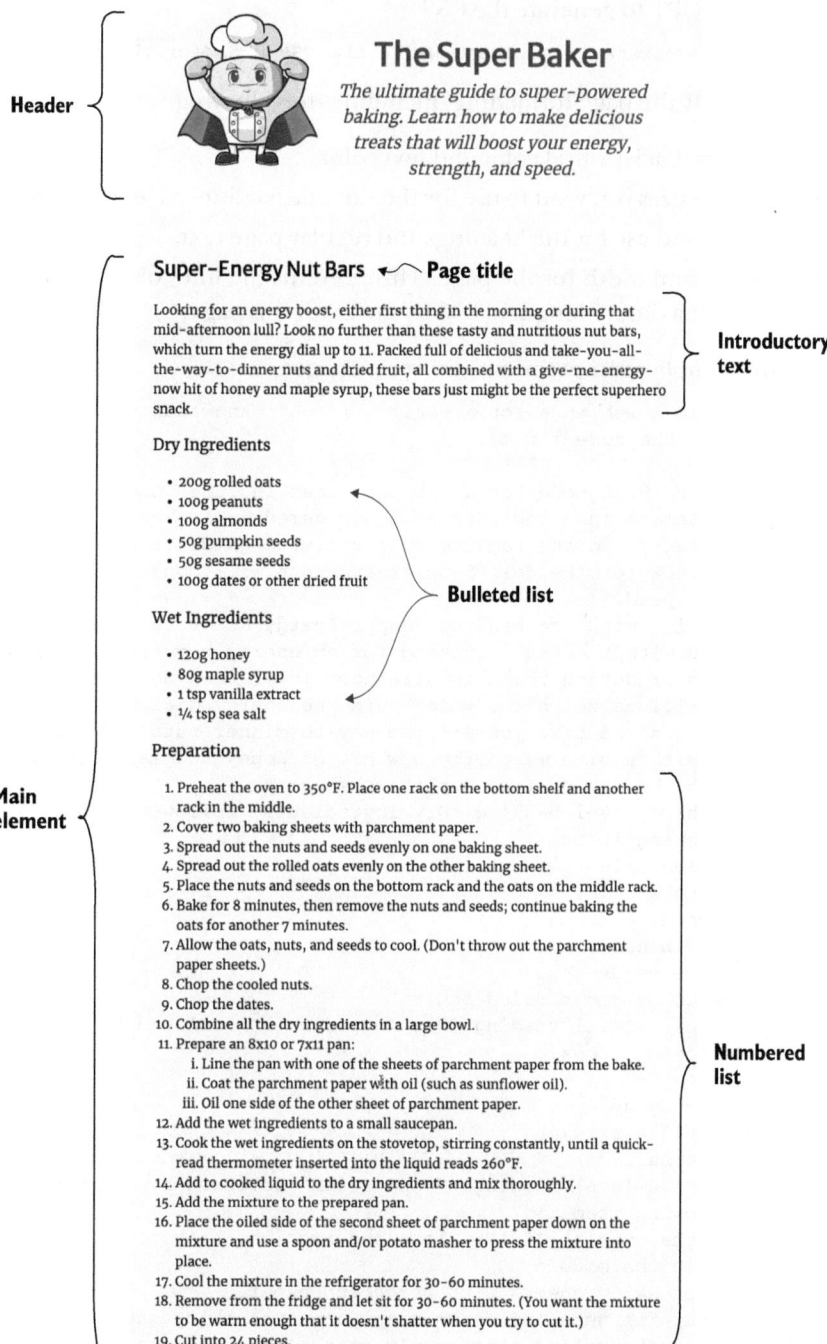

Header

The Super Baker

The ultimate guide to super-powered baking. Learn how to make delicious treats that will boost your energy, strength, and speed.

Super-Energy Nut Bars ← **Page title**

Introductory text

Looking for an energy boost, either first thing in the morning or during that mid-afternoon lull? Look no further than these tasty and nutritious nut bars, which turn the energy dial up to 11. Packed full of delicious and take-you-all-the-way-to-dinner nuts and dried fruit, all combined with a give-me-energy-now hit of honey and maple syrup, these bars just might be the perfect superhero snack.

Dry Ingredients

- 200g rolled oats
- 100g peanuts
- 100g almonds
- 50g pumpkin seeds
- 50g sesame seeds
- 100g dates or other dried fruit

Bulleted list

Wet Ingredients

- 120g honey
- 80g maple syrup
- 1 tsp vanilla extract
- ¼ tsp sea salt

Preparation

Main element

1. Preheat the oven to 350°F. Place one rack on the bottom shelf and another rack in the middle.
2. Cover two baking sheets with parchment paper.
3. Spread out the nuts and seeds evenly on one baking sheet.
4. Spread out the rolled oats evenly on the other baking sheet.
5. Place the nuts and seeds on the bottom rack and the oats on the middle rack.
6. Bake for 8 minutes, then remove the nuts and seeds; continue baking the oats for another 7 minutes.
7. Allow the oats, nuts, and seeds to cool. (Don't throw out the parchment paper sheets.)
8. Chop the cooled nuts.
9. Chop the dates.
10. Combine all the dry ingredients in a large bowl.
11. Prepare an 8x10 or 7x11 pan:
    i. Line the pan with one of the sheets of parchment paper from the bake.
    ii. Coat the parchment paper with oil (such as sunflower oil).
    iii. Oil one side of the other sheet of parchment paper.
12. Add the wet ingredients to a small saucepan.
13. Cook the wet ingredients on the stovetop, stirring constantly, until a quick-read thermometer inserted into the liquid reads 260°F.
14. Add to cooked liquid to the dry ingredients and mix thoroughly.
15. Add the mixture to the prepared pan.
16. Place the oiled side of the second sheet of parchment paper down on the mixture and use a spoon and/or potato masher to press the mixture into place.
17. Cool the mixture in the refrigerator for 30-60 minutes.
18. Remove from the fridge and let sit for 30-60 minutes. (You want the mixture to be warm enough that it doesn't shatter when you try to cut it.)
19. Cut into 24 pieces.

Numbered list

Footer

© 2023 The Super Baker

Figure 9.12 The elements of the recipe page

Next, ask ChatGPT to generate the CSS:

```
Second, in a separate file please write the CSS code for the following:
```

You then specify the page formatting, including the following:

- The page background color and text color.
- The type sizes you want to use for the site title, tagline, page title, and page text.
- The fonts to use for the headings and regular page text.
- A maximum width for the page. This prevents the lines of text from getting too long. A maximum length of 800 px works for this page.

Here's an example prompt for my own recipe page:

```
I want to build a web page for a recipe. I don't know how to code, so I need
you to provide the code for me.

First, write the HTML code for a web page that includes the following:
 * A header element that includes an image named super-baker.png, the title
"The Super Baker", and the tagline "The ultimate guide to super-powered
baking. Learn how to make delicious treats that will boost your energy,
strength, and speed.".
 * A main section with the heading "Super-Energy Nut Bars".
 * A paragraph with the text "Looking for an energy boost, either first thing
in the morning or during that mid-afternoon lull? Look no further than these
tasty and nutritious nut bars, which turn the energy dial up to 11. Packed
full of delicious and take-you-all-the-way-to-dinner nuts and dried fruit,
all combined with a give-me-energy-now hit of honey and maple syrup, these
bars just might be the perfect superhero snack."
 * Add the third-level heading "Dry Ingredients" followed by a bulleted list
with the following items:
     -200g rolled oats
     -100g peanuts
     -100g almonds
     -50g pumpkin seeds
     -50g sesame seeds
     -100g dates or other dried fruit
 * Add the third-level heading "Wet Ingredients" followed by a bulleted list
with the following items:
     -120g honey
     -80g maple syrup
     -1 tsp vanilla extract
     -¼ tsp sea salt
 * Add the third-level heading "Preparation" followed by a numbered list
with the following items:
     -Preheat the oven to 350°F. Place one rack on the bottom shelf and
another rack in the middle.
     -Cover two baking sheets with parchment paper.
     -Spread out the nuts and seeds evenly on one baking sheet.
     -Spread out the rolled oats evenly on the other baking sheet.
     -Place the nuts and seeds on the bottom rack and the oats on the middle
rack.
     -Bake for 8 minutes, then remove the nuts and seeds; continue baking the
oats for another 7 minutes.
```

　　　-Allow the oats, nuts, and seeds to cool. (Don't throw out the parchment
paper sheets.)
　　　-Chop the cooled nuts.
　　　-Chop the dates.
　　　-Combine all the dry ingredients in a large bowl.
　　　-Prepare an 8x10 or 7x11 pan:
　　　 -Line the pan with one of the sheets of parchment paper from the bake.
　　　 -Coat the parchment paper with oil (such as sunflower oil).
　　　 -Oil one side of the other sheet of parchment paper.
　　　-Add the wet ingredients to a small saucepan.
　　　-Cook the wet ingredients on the stovetop, stirring constantly, until a
quick-read thermometer inserted into the liquid reads 260°F.
　　　-Add to cooked liquid to the dry ingredients and mix thoroughly.
　　　-Add the mixture to the prepared pan.
　　　-Place the oiled side of the second sheet of parchment paper down on the
mixture and use a spoon and/or potato masher to press the mixture into place.
　　　-Cool the mixture in the refrigerator for 30-60 minutes.
　　　-Remove from the fridge and let sit for 30-60 minutes. (You want the
mixture to be warm enough that it doesn't shatter when you try to cut it.)
　　　 -Cut into 24 pieces.
　 * A footer element that includes the Copyright symbol, followed by the
current year, followed by "The Super Baker".
　 * In the page head section, include the tag <meta charset="utf-8">.
　 * In the page head section, include the tag <meta name="viewport"
content="width=device-width, initial-scale=1">.

Second, in a separate file write the CSS code for the following:
　 * The page has background color azure, a 24px margin, and a line height of
1.5.
　 * The header has text color darkred and 12px padding.
　 * Make the header image a maximum width of 250px and floated to the left.
　 * The title is 48px, centered, and with no bottom margin.
　 * The tagline is 26px, italic, centered, and with no top margin.
　 * The main section has a top margin of 75px.
　 * The main section heading font size is 30px.
　 * The main section font size is 20px.
　 * For the page headings, use the Merriweather Sans font from Google Fonts.
For the page text, use the Merriweather font from Google Fonts.
　 * For the nested numbered list, use lower roman numerals.
　 * The footer has 5px padding all around, 50px top margin, and a darkred top
border.
　 * Give the page a maximum width of 800px and center the body element within
the browser window.

ChatGPT first generates the HTML code, which you can copy and then paste and save
to a file named index.html. In that code, you should see a line near the top similar to
the following:

```
<link rel="stylesheet" type="text/css" href="styles.css">
```

This code tells the web browser to look for the CSS code in a file named styles.css, so
your next task is to copy the generated CSS code and paste it and save it to a file named
styles.css (or whatever name you see in the <link> tag). Be sure to save styles.css in the

same folder as your index.html file. You also need to copy your header image file into the same folder. Refer to appendix A to learn more about working web page files.

I used OpenAI's ChatGPT app to submit my prompt to GPT-4. The generated code produced the page shown in Figure 9.13.

The Super Baker

The ultimate guide to super-powered baking. Learn how to make delicious treats that will boost your energy, strength, and speed.

Super-Energy Nut Bars

Looking for an energy boost, either first thing in the morning or during that mid-afternoon lull? Look no further than these tasty and nutritious nut bars, which turn the energy dial up to 11. Packed full of delicious and take-you-all-the-way-to-dinner nuts and dried fruit, all combined with a give-me-energy-now hit of honey and maple syrup, these bars just might be the perfect superhero snack.

Dry Ingredients

- 200g rolled oats
- 100g peanuts
- 100g almonds
- 50g pumpkin seeds
- 50g sesame seeds
- 100g dates or other dried fruit

Wet Ingredients

- 120g honey
- 80g maple syrup
- 1 tsp vanilla extract
- ¼ tsp sea salt

Preparation

1. Preheat the oven to 350°F. Place one rack on the bottom shelf and another rack in the middle.
2. Cover two baking sheets with parchment paper.
3. Spread out the nuts and seeds evenly on one baking sheet.
4. Spread out the rolled oats evenly on the other baking sheet.
5. Place the nuts and seeds on the bottom rack and the oats on the middle rack.
6. Bake for 8 minutes, then remove the nuts and seeds; continue baking the oats for another 7 minutes.
7. Allow the oats, nuts, and seeds to cool. (Don't throw out the parchment paper sheets.)
8. Chop the cooled nuts.
9. Chop the dates.
10. Combine all the dry ingredients in a large bowl.
11. Prepare an 8x10 or 7x11 pan:
    i. Line the pan with one of the sheets of parchment paper from the bake.
    ii. Coat the parchment paper with oil (such as sunflower oil).
    iii. Oil one side of the other sheet of parchment paper.
12. Add the wet ingredients to a small saucepan.
13. Cook the wet ingredients on the stovetop, stirring constantly, until a quick-read thermometer inserted into the liquid reads 260°F.
14. Add to cooked liquid to the dry ingredients and mix thoroughly.
15. Add the mixture to the prepared pan.
16. Place the oiled side of the second sheet of parchment paper down on the mixture and use a spoon and/or potato masher to press the mixture into place.
17. Cool the mixture in the refrigerator for 30-60 minutes.
18. Remove from the fridge and let sit for 30-60 minutes. (You want the mixture to be warm enough that it doesn't shatter when you try to cut it.)
19. Cut into 24 pieces.

© 2023 The Super Baker

Figure 9.13   My recipe page

If you like the page ChatGPT came up with, you can skip the rest of this chapter and deploy the code to the web (refer to appendix B for the deployment details). However, if you want to understand the generated web page code, keep reading to get a closer look.

9.5   *Examining the recipe page code*

One of the main premises of this book is that ChatGPT is good enough at slinging web page code that even folks who don't want to know much about web development can still publish pages to the web by trusting ChatGPT to do the code part of the job. That said, there's no rule against trying to understand what the code generated by ChatGPT is doing. To that end, the next two sections take a peek behind the curtain to examine the recipe page code that resulted from my prompt from the previous section (that page is shown in figure 9.13).

NOTE The generated HTML and CSS code for my recipe page are available on this book's website (www.manning.com/books/build-a-website-with -chatgpt) and in the book's GitHub repository: https://github.com/paulmcfe/ websites-with-chatgpt.

The code annotations that follow should help you both to understand what's happening under the hood and to tweak or customize your own code.

9.5.1 Examining the HTML

Here's the ChatGPT-generated HTML code for my recipe page:

```html
<!DOCTYPE html>
<html>
<head>
    <title>The Super Baker</title>
    <meta charset="utf-8">
    <meta name="viewport"
        content="width=device-width, initial-scale=1">
    <link href="https://fonts.googleapis.com/css2?
        family=Merriweather&family=Merriweather+Sans&
        display=swap" rel="stylesheet">
    <link rel="stylesheet" type="text/css" href="styles.css">
</head>
<body>
    <header>
        <img src="super-baker.png" alt="The Super Baker Logo">
        <h1>The Super Baker</h1>
        <p>The ultimate guide to super-powered baking. Learn how to
            make delicious treats that will boost your energy,
            strength, and speed.</p>
    </header>

    <main>
        <h2>Super-Energy Nut Bars</h2>
        <p>
            Looking for an energy boost, either first thing in the
            morning or during that mid-afternoon lull? Look no further
            than these tasty and nutritious nut bars, which turn the
            energy dial up to 11. Packed full of delicious and
            take-you-all-the-way-to-dinner nuts and dried fruit, all
            combined with a give-me-energy-now hit of honey and maple
            syrup, these bars just might be the perfect superhero snack.
        </p>
        <h3>Dry Ingredients</h3>
        <ul>
            <li>200g rolled oats</li>
            <li>100g peanuts</li>
            <li>100g almonds</li>
            <li>50g pumpkin seeds</li>
            <li>50g sesame seeds</li>
            <li>100g dates or other dried fruit</li>
        </ul>
```

Annotations:
- Helps the page display properly on mobile devices
- Loads the Merriweather and Merriweather Sans fonts from Google Fonts
- Tells the web browser where to find the CSS code
- Site logo
- Site title
- Site tagline
- Page header
- Recipe title
- Recipe introduction
- Bulleted list for the dry ingredients

```
<h3>Wet Ingredients</h3>
<ul>
    <li>120g honey</li>
    <li>80g maple syrup</li>
    <li>1 tsp vanilla extract</li>
    <li>¼ tsp sea salt</li>
</ul>
```

Bulleted list for the wet ingredients

```
<h3>Preparation</h3>
<ol>
    <li>Preheat the oven to 350°F. Place one rack on the bottom
        shelf and another rack in the middle.</li>
    <li>Cover two baking sheets with parchment paper.</li>
    <li>Spread out the nuts and seeds evenly on one baking sheet.</li>
    <li>Spread out the rolled oats evenly on the other baking
        sheet.</li>
    <li>Place the nuts and seeds on the bottom rack and the oats on
        the middle rack.</li>
    <li>Bake for 8 minutes, then remove the nuts and seeds; continue
        baking the oats for another 7 minutes.</li>
    <li>Allow the oats, nuts, and seeds to cool. (Don't throw out the
        parchment paper sheets.)</li>
    <li>Chop the cooled nuts.</li>
    <li>Chop the dates.</li>
    <li>Combine all the dry ingredients in a large bowl.</li>
    <li>Prepare an 8x10 or 7x11 pan:</li>
    <ol>
        <li>Line the pan with one of the sheets of parchment paper
            from the bake.</li>
        <li>Coat the parchment paper with oil (such as sunflower
            oil).</li>
        <li>Oil one side of the other sheet of parchment paper.</li>
    </ol>
    <li>Add the wet ingredients to a small saucepan.</li>
    <li>Cook the wet ingredients on the stovetop, stirring constantly,
        until a quick-read thermometer inserted into the liquid reads
        260°F.</li>
    <li>Add to cooked liquid to the dry ingredients and mix
        thoroughly.</li>
    <li>Add the mixture to the prepared pan.</li>
    <li>Place the oiled side of the second sheet of parchment paper
        down on the mixture and use a spoon and/or potato masher to
        press the mixture into place.</li>
    <li>Cool the mixture in the refrigerator for 30-60 minutes.</li>
    <li>Remove from the fridge and let sit for 30-60 minutes. (You
        want the mixture to be warm enough that it doesn't shatter
        when you try to cut it.)</li>
    <li>Cut into 24 pieces.</li>
</ol>
</main>

<footer>
    &copy; 2023 The Super Baker
</footer>
</body>
</html>
```

Numbered list for the recipe preparation

Nested numbered list

Page footer

Note that the HTML code includes the following line:

```
<link rel="stylesheet" href="styles.css">
```

This tag tells the web browser where to find the CSS code, which I describe in the next section.

9.5.2 *Examining the CSS*

Here's the ChatGPT-generated CSS code for my recipe page:

```
body {
    background-color: azure;
    margin: 24px;
    line-height: 1.5;
    font-family: 'Merriweather', serif;
    max-width: 800px;
    margin-left: auto;
    margin-right: auto;
}
```

> Sets the page background color, margin, line height, and font

> Centers the page

> Sets the maximum page width to 800 px

```
header {
    color: darkred;
    padding: 10px;
    text-align: center;
}
```

> Sets the header text color, padding, and alignment

```
header img {
    max-width: 250px;
    float: left;
}
```

> Sets a maximum logo width, and floats it to the left

```
header h1 {
    font-size: 48px;
    margin-bottom: 0;
    font-family: 'Merriweather Sans', sans-serif;
}
```

> Sets the page title font size, bottom margin, and font

```
header p {
    font-size: 26px;
    margin-top: 0;
    font-style: italic;
}
```

> Styles the tagline font size, top margin, and italics

```
main {
    margin-top: 75px;
    font-size: 20px;
}
```

> Adds a margin to the top of the main element, and sets the font size

```
main h2 {
    font-size: 30px;
    font-family: 'Merriweather Sans', sans-serif;
}
```

> Sets the font size and the font of the recipe title

```
ol ol {
    list-style-type: lower-roman;
```

> Styles the nested numbered list to use lowercase Roman numerals

```
}

footer {
    padding: 5px;
    margin-top: 50px;
    border-top: 1px solid darkred;
}
```

Styles the footer padding, top margin, and top border

If you like, you can use these annotations to help customize your web page code, as I describe in the next section.

9.6   *Customizing the recipe page*

If you really don't like the page ChatGPT created for you, try revising your prompt and submitting it in a new chat session. If the page is close to what you were looking for, consider tweaking the code yourself.

I'll begin with a few suggestions for modifying the HTML:

- It's safe to edit any of the page text, including the title, tagline, headings, or introductory text or any of the bulleted or numbered list items. Just make sure you don't accidentally edit or delete the HTML tags on each side of the text (such as the <li> and </li> tags that surround a bulleted or numbered list item).
- Feel free to add one or more introductory paragraphs. For each new paragraph, follow this procedure:
  a In your text editor, position the cursor immediately after the </p> tag that ends the existing introductory paragraph.
  b Press Enter or Return to start a new line.
  c Type a <p> tag, and then press Enter or Return. Most text editors insert a </p> tag automatically.
  d Type your paragraph text.
  e If your text editor didn't do so already, type a </p> tag to finish your paragraph element.
- If you're building a site around recipes (or something similar), you'll want a navigation element so visitors can easily find your other pages. Check out chapter 6 to learn how to prompt ChatGPT for links and a navigation bar.
- In the footer section of the HTML code, you can add links to your social media accounts, as I describe in chapter 4.

Here are a few customization ideas for the CSS code:

- If you'd prefer another numbering scheme for the nested numbered list, change the ol element's list-style-type property value to a different keyword, such as lower-alpha.
- For a different background color, replace the value of the body element's background-color property with another color keyword.

- For a different header text color, replace the value of the `header` element's `color` property with another color keyword.

- If you want your page to have a different maximum width, change the `max-width` value to something other than `800px`.

- If you'd prefer to have the header logo on the right, in the `header img` element, change the `float` value to `right`.

- For any font size value, you can change the number to increase or decrease the font size. Just make sure you leave the `px` unit in place.

- For any padding or margin value, you can change the number to increase or decrease the padding or margins. In each case, be sure to leave the `px` unit in place.

- To make your page code more accessible, consider converting all px measurements to rem measurements. 1 rem is by default equivalent to 16 px, so 20 px is 1.25 rem, 24 px is 1.5 rem, 32 px is 2 rem, 48 px is 3 rem, and so on. The rem unit is more accessible because it measures font sizes relative to the default font size the browser user has defined in their browser settings.

Summary

- A bulleted list is a collection of HTML elements that present multiple items as a vertical list, where each item is indented slightly from the left margin and preceded by a small black circle called a bullet.

- You use a bulleted list when you want to present several items but the order of those items isn't an essential component of the list.

- A numbered list is a collection of HTML elements that present multiple items as a vertical list, where each item is indented slightly from the left margin and preceded (usually) by a number.

- You use a numbered list when you want to present several items and the order of those items is an essential component of the list.

- A bulleted or numbered list that resides inside another bulleted or numbered list is said to be nested within that list.

- For best results, your page prompt should be as specific as possible, including colors, font sizes, and heading levels.

- Save the generated HTML to the index.html file and the generated CSS to the filename suggested by ChatGPT in the HTML code, usually styles.css.

10

Setting up
a photo gallery

This chapter covers

- Using images on a web page
- Working with thumbnail versions of images
- Displaying images in a lightbox
- Laying out a page using Flexbox
- Crafting a ChatGPT prompt for building a photo gallery page
- Examining and customizing the ChatGPT-generated code

After you learned a few image basics in chapter 4, the projects in this book have mostly included a single image: a site logo in the page header. That's a great start, but you no doubt know from your own online gadabouts that images are everywhere on the web. A well-placed and well-chosen photo or artwork can really perk up a page and offer some welcome eye candy for text-weary visitors.

In this chapter, you learn a bit more about images and how they work on the web, which will enable you to incorporate additional images on your pages. Go big or go home, as the saying goes—so this chapter goes big with images by showing you not only how to build a working photo gallery that you can use to show off your photographic skills but also how to use a modern layout technique to make your page look awesome. You then put all this image and layout list know-how to work to create a detailed prompt for ChatGPT to generate the code for the photo gallery.

This chapter also provides annotated versions of the ChatGPT-generated HTML and CSS to help you understand how the photo gallery works. You also get a few useful tips for customizing the code.

10.1 Checking out this chapter's project

As I mentioned in the introduction, this chapter's project is a single-page photo gallery. The final page will include the following components:

- A header element that includes the website logo and title
- A main element that begins with the gallery title and instructions for using the gallery
- Nine reduced-size versions of the photos, where clicking one of these images displays a larger-size version of the image
- A footer element that includes a copyright notice

Figure 10.1 shows an example photo gallery created with code supplied by ChatGPT. You can use this kind of layout for other types of content, including a product catalog, artist portfolio, or design sampler or a gallery of current or completed projects, team members, upcoming events, testimonials, or clients. The common denominator in each of these projects is that they consist of a collection of images (perhaps with some text as well), so you need to know a bit more about how images work on the web.

Figure 10.1   A photo gallery generated by ChatGPT

10.2　*A closer look at images*

If you've used a word processor or presentation program, you've probably created lots of documents that include images. In each case, the app offers something like an Insert Picture command that enables you to choose the image you want, which is added directly into the document at the spot you choose.

Surprisingly, web page code doesn't work the same way. There's no HTML equivalent of the Insert Picture command that embeds an image directly into the page. Instead, you upload the image to your website as a separate file and then insert into your page text a special HTML tag that tells the browser where to locate the image. When the browser comes across this tag, it retrieves the image file from the server and displays the image on the page in the location you specified.

10.2.1　*Checking out the <img> tag*

The special tag that gets the browser to add an image to a web page is the `<img>` tag, which uses the partial syntax shown in figure 10.2.

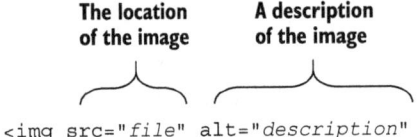

The location of the image　　**A description of the image**

```
<img src="file" alt="description"
```

Figure 10.2　You insert an image into a web page using the `<img>` tag.

This version of the `img` element has two attributes:

- `src="file"`—For the `src` (short for *source*) attribute, you replace `file` with the location of the image file. To keep things simple, I'm only going to show the two most common possibilities:
  - If the image file is in the same directory as the HTML file, replace `file` with the name of the image file. For example, if your image file is logo.png, your `<img>` tag will look like this:

    ```
    <img src="logo.png" alt="">
    ```
  - If the image is in a subdirectory, replace `file` with the image's directory name and filename, separated by a backslash (/). For example, if you've created a subdirectory named images, and your image file is logo.png, your `<img>` tag will look like this:

    ```
    <img src="images/logo.png" alt="">
    ```
- `alt="description"`—For the `alt` (short for *alternative*) attribute, you replace `description` with a word or short phrase that describes the image; this can be used in place of the image if the image file can't be displayed. Alt text (as it is often called) is also used by screen readers and Braille apps to give their users some idea of what the image is. Here's an example:

    ```
    <img src="images/logo.png" alt="Ampersand Photography logo">
    ```

Technically, your web page is invalid unless each <img> tag has an alt attribute present. Having an invalid page means your page may not render properly in the web browser, but mostly it means your page will be less accessible to people using assistive technologies such as screen readers. Fortunately, ChatGPT-generated <img> tags usually include the alt attribute, but the description is almost always trivial and unhelpful. Therefore, you should always include the alt text you want in your prompt. Here's an example instruction to ChatGPT:

```
Add an image named "old-road-marker.jpg", which is stored in the
"images" subdirectory. For the alt attribute, use the following: "A
photo with a very old road marker in the foreground that reads 'Appleby
12 Miles'".
```

Here's an example <img> tag generated by ChatGPT from such a prompt:

```
<img src="images/old-road-marker.jpg"
     alt="A photo with a very old road marker in the
     foreground that reads 'Appleby 12 Miles'">
```

TIP If your page uses decorative or other nonessential images, set the alt attribute equal to the empty string (""). That way, your page is still valid, but you're not annoying people using assistive technology (such as screen readers) who don't want to hear descriptions of purely decorative images.

If you don't yet have the image you want to use but know the image's final dimensions, you can insert a placeholder image to occupy the same space on the page until the image is ready to use. The net section provides the details.

10.2.2 Adding placeholder images

You probably know that in the world of text, a *placeholder* is some text that temporarily marks a place where some permanent word or phrase will eventually appear. In the previous section, for example, the syntax for the <img> tag used the placeholders *file* and *description* for the values of the src and alt attributes, respectively.

You can also use placeholders with images. In this case, the placeholder image takes up the same amount of space as the permanent image that will eventually be added to the page, which is very useful if you want to build your page but don't have the image (or images) you need.

You have several ways to add placeholder images, but the easiest is to use a placeholder server, such as https://placehold.co. Here's an example instruction to ChatGPT to add a placeholder image:

```
Insert a placeholder image from placehold.co. The image dimensions are width
300px and height 200px.
```

Here's an example <img> tag generated by ChatGPT from this prompt:

```
<img src="https://placehold.co/300x200" alt="Placeholder image" width="300"
height="200">
```

Figure 10.3 shows how this placeholder appears on a web page.

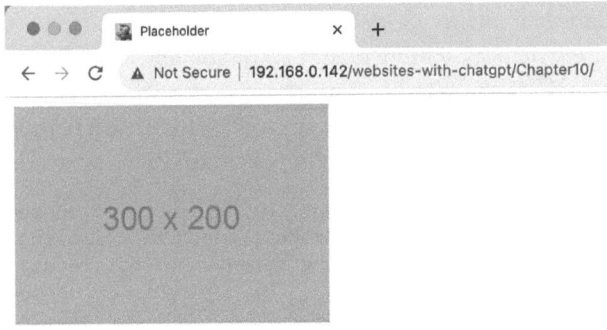

Figure 10.3   An example placeholder image from placehold.co

10.2.3 *Working with image thumbnails*

To really show off your photographs, you need to display them at a relatively large size. However, depending on the file format (refer to chapter 4) and other factors, such as the camera you used, the full-size file can be quite large—at least several megabytes. That's bad enough for a single image, but your photo gallery will have multiple images (nine in this project); it's asking too much for gallery visitors to download such a massive amount of data. (This is especially true for folks coming to your page via a slow internet connection or a limited mobile data plan.)

For a project such as a photo gallery, a better strategy for all your users is to initially display a reduced-size version—known in the trade as a *thumbnail*—of each photo. The idea is to set up your page so that clicking a thumbnail will temporarily display a large-size version of the photo. (The size the user sees depends on the dimensions of the browser window.)

> **NOTE**   There are no hard-and-fast rules about the size of your thumbnails. A page designed to hold dozens of images may use thumbnails that are only 50 or 75 pixels wide, whereas for a photo gallery like the one you get ChatGPT to help you build in this chapter, thumbnails that are around 300 pixels wide work well.

Before proceeding, you should create your thumbnail versions of your photos. First up, the Windows instructions.

CREATING A THUMBNAIL USING THE WINDOWS PHOTOS APP

If you're using Windows 11, you can make a copy of the original photo file and then use the Photos app to resize the copy to your preferred thumbnail dimensions. In this project, I assume your thumbnail versions include the text *-thumbnail* as part of the filename. For example, if the full-size version is named image01.jpg, its thumbnail version is named image01-thumbnail.jpg.

Follow these steps to create a thumbnail version of a photo using the Photos app:

1 Use File Explorer to locate the photo you want to work with.

2 Click the file, click Copy in the toolbar, and then click Paste to create a copy of the photo.

3 Click the copied file, click Rename (or press F2), and then edit the filename to remove the *-Copy* text added by Windows and replace it with `-thumbnail`. (So, you should end up with a filename along the lines of image01-thumbnail.jpg.)

4 Double-click the copied and renamed image file to load the image into the Photos app.

5 Click See More (the three dots in the toolbar), and then click Resize Image to open the Resize dialog, shown in figure 10.4.

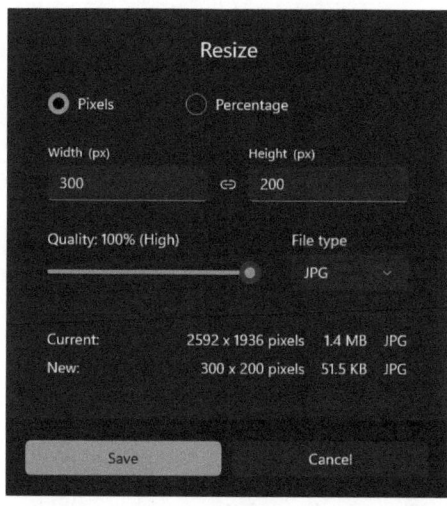

Figure 10.4   Use the Resize dialog to create a thumbnail version of your photo.

6 Make sure the Pixels option is selected.

7 Use the Width text box to set the thumbnail's width in pixels. (Note that the Height value changes automatically to maintain the aspect ratio—that is, the ratio of the image's width to its height—which is what you want. Alternatively, you can set the Height value, and the Width will change automatically.)

8 Click Save.

If you use a Mac instead of a Windows PC, your version of the steps is next.

CREATING A THUMBNAIL USING THE MACOS PREVIEW APP

If you're running macOS, you can use Finder to copy the original photo file and then use Preview to resize the copy to your preferred thumbnail width and height. This project assumes the thumbnail copies include the text *-thumbnail* in the filename. For example, if the full-size photo file is named image01.jpg, the thumbnail version should be named image01-thumbnail.jpg.

Follow these steps to create a thumbnail version of a photo in macOS:

1   Use Finder to locate and click the photo you want to work with.

2   Choose Edit > Copy, and then choose Edit > Paste to create a copy of the photo.

3   Click the copied file, press Enter, and then edit the filename to remove the *copy* text added by Finder and replace it with `-thumbnail`. (So, you should end up with a filename like image01-thumbnail.jpg.)

4   Double-click the copied and renamed image file to load the image into Preview.

5   Choose Tools > Adjust Size to open the dialog shown in figure 10.5.

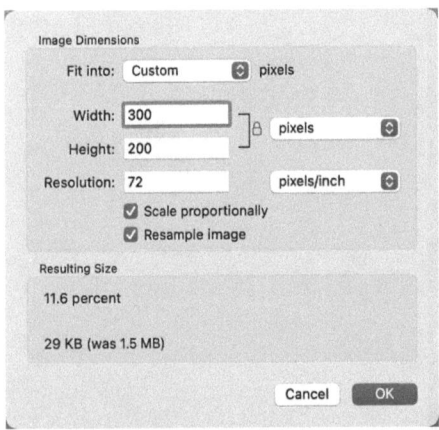

Figure 10.5   Use this dialog to create a thumbnail version of your photo.

6   Make sure the Pixels item is selected in the list to the right of the Width and Height text boxes.

7   Use the Width text box to set the thumbnail's width in pixels. (Note that the Height value changes automatically to maintain the aspect ratio—that is, the ratio of the image's width to its height—which is what you want. Alternatively, you can set the Height value, and the Width will change automatically.)

8   Click OK.

Next you learn how to enhance your thumbnail versions with some explanatory text.

10.2.4 *Adding image captions*

You may prefer that your photo gallery show only the thumbnail versions of each image. However, you can make the experience a bit more friendly for your visitors if you provide a short caption for each image. The caption doesn't have to be anything elaborate: just a brief title or description of the photo.

You can add captions in multiple ways, but the most straightforward is to ask ChatGPT to turn your image into a *figure* and then provide a *figure caption*. Here's the generic HTML that ChatGPT generates:

```
<figure>
    <img src="file" alt="description">
    <figcaption>Caption text</figcaption>
</figure>
```

Here, `Caption text` is the caption, which appears just below the image. Here's an example instruction to ChatGPT:

```
Add an image named "old-road-marker.jpg", which is stored in the "images"
subdirectory. Make it a figure with a caption. For the alt attribute, use
the following: "A photo with a very old road marker in the foreground that
reads 'Appleby 12 Miles'". For the caption, use the following: "An old road
marker".
```

Here's an example figure and caption generated by ChatGPT from such a prompt:

```
<figure>
    <img src="images/old-road-marker.jpg"
        alt="A photo with a very old road marker in the
             foreground that reads 'Appleby 12 Miles'">
    <figcaption>An old road marker</figcaption>
</figure>
```

Figure 10.6 shows how it looks in the browser.

An old road marker

Figure 10.6   A figure with a caption

With your thumbnail versions created and your captions composed, you're ready to check out how your visitors can see the large-size version of each photo.

10.3   *Implementing a lightbox overlay*

As you learn shortly (refer to section 10.5), when someone visits the photo gallery, the page at first shows a grid of nine thumbnail images. How does the user see a large-size version of a photo?

There are a bunch of ways to solve that problem. For example, you can set up each thumbnail image as a link that, when clicked, loads the large-size version of the photo. That approach works, but clicking a link takes the user out of your photo gallery, so they need to navigate back to see more photos. Believe me, no one wants to see your photos that badly!

A better solution is to ask ChatGPT to create a *lightbox*, which is a special element that has the following characteristics:

- It's created on the fly.
- It takes up the entire width and height of the browser window.
- It's slightly transparent.
- It's displayed on top of the existing web page, which is why it's called an "overlay."

For example, figure 10.7 shows a simple version of a photo gallery with three thumbnails. When the user clicks a thumbnail, the following things happen:

1 The lightbox element is created.
2 The new lightbox element is given an img element.
3 That img element is filled with the large-size version of the photo.
4 The lightbox is displayed by overlaying it on the page.

Figure 10.7   A simple photo gallery with three thumbnails

The result is that the user now sees the large-size version of the photo, which fills all or most of the browser window. For example, if I click the rightmost thumbnail in figure 10.7, the browser displays a larger version of the photo, as shown in figure 10.8. Notice that the gallery appears faintly in the spaces to the left and right of the lightbox. This

Figure 10.8   Clicking a thumbnail displays the lightbox, which contains the larger version of the photo.

lets the user know they haven't left the gallery. To return to the gallery, the user only has to click anywhere in the page, which removes the lightbox and redisplays the photo gallery.

If all this seems like it would be hideously complex to code, remember that you don't have to lift a finger beyond preparing your thumbnail images. You can ask ChatGPT to implement all the lightbox functionality with an instruction similar to the following:

```
Please provide the HTML, CSS, and JavaScript code to implement a lightbox-
style overlay for the images on this page. The thumbnails have names such
as image01-thumbnail.png, image02-thumbnail.png, image03-thumbnail.png, and
so on. Each full-size image uses the same name as its thumbnail but without
"-thumbnail", as in image01.png, image02.png, image03.png, and so on. All the
image files are stored in the "images" subdirectory.
```

The sharp-eyed reader will have noticed the instruction to provide "JavaScript code" in this prompt. What's that all about? The next section solves the mystery.

10.4   *The lightbox: Powered by JavaScript*

Up to this point in the book, you've seen that you can get pretty far with just HTML and CSS. These are powerful technologies that, when generated successfully by ChatGPT with detailed prompts, can produce attractive and useful web pages.

However, there are many things that HTML and CSS, potent as they are, just can't do. A lightbox is a good example. Yes, you can use HTML and CSS to create and style the lightbox, but once you click a thumbnail, HTML and CSS fall down on the job:

- They can't create new elements.
- They can't load the full-size version of the clicked thumbnail into the lightbox img element.
- They can't display the hidden lightbox.
- They can't remove the lightbox when the user clicks it.

Fortunately, there's a third major web page technology that can handle these types of tasks and many more: JavaScript. This is a programming language that's built into the web browser and is designed to add interactivity and dynamism to otherwise-inert web page elements. In this project, JavaScript essentially does two things:

- It adds a "click" event handler to each image. An *event handler* is JavaScript code that runs automatically when a specified event occurs. In this case, the event is the user clicking on an image in the photo gallery.
- In the event handler, JavaScript builds and then displays the lightbox.

And, happily for you, that's all you need to know about it. ChatGPT will handle the rest.

10.5 *Laying out the gallery with Flexbox*

When you add items to a web page, the default layout behavior for most elements is to flow vertically down the page, one element after the next. That has worked out well for the projects you've seen so far in this book, but it won't work for the photo gallery. Why not? Because with your images rendered as figures, they too will flow vertically down the page, one after the other.

That's not the end of the world, for sure, but it's not a great look, and it's not convenient for folks who visit your page. Figure 10.9 shows a version of the photo gallery where the photos are displayed this way.

You can prevent this default behavior by asking ChatGPT to lay out the photo gallery using a web page technique called *Flexbox*. This is a complex technology, but all you need to know for now is that when you turn a web page element into a Flexbox container, the items lose their rigid default layout behavior and adapt themselves to the browser's current dimensions. For this project, you can prompt ChatGPT to use Flexbox with a simple instruction:

```
Make the gallery a Flexbox container. Center the content and enable it to
wrap.
```

To see the result of this instruction, check out the final photo gallery layout, which appears later, in figure 10.10.

At this point, you know all that's required to successfully prompt ChatGPT to build a photo gallery. The following section takes you through the process.

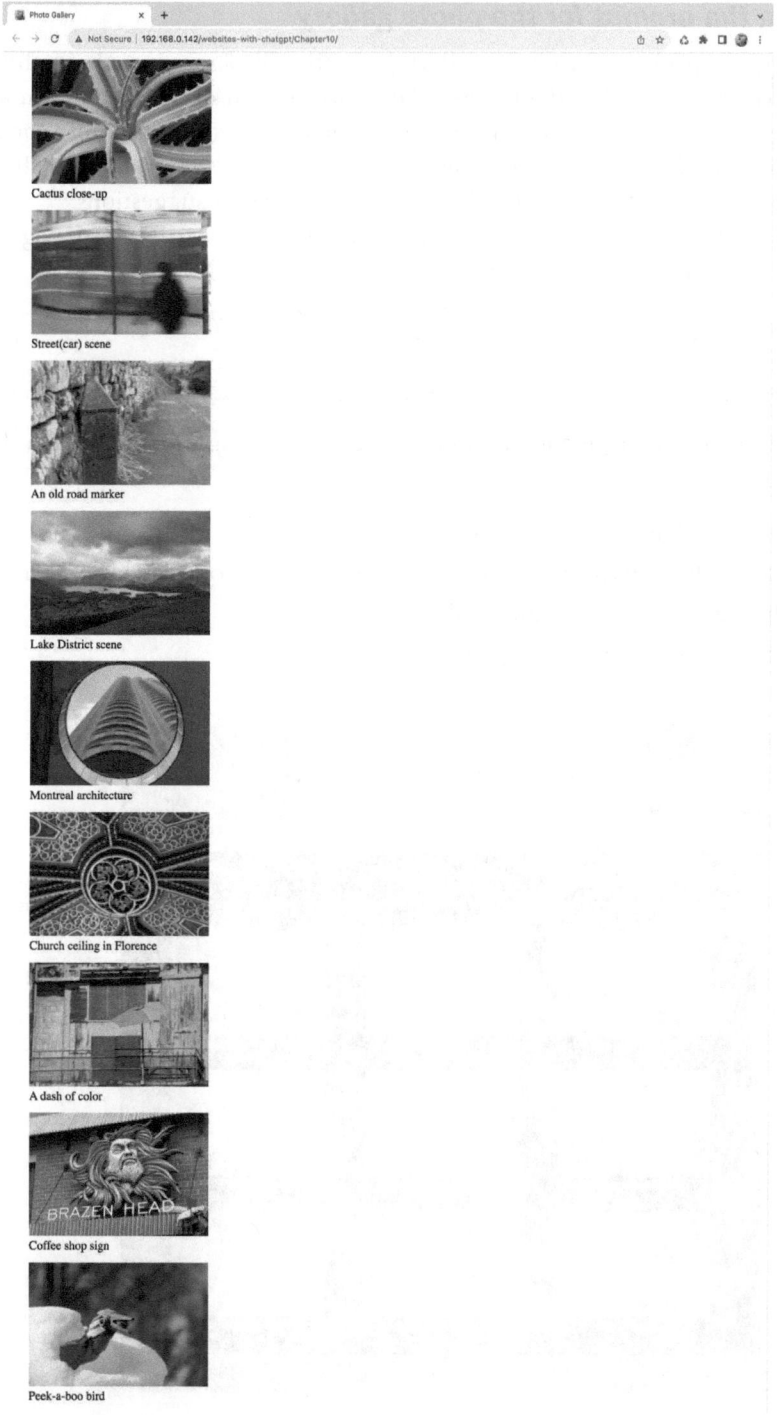

Figure 10.9 By default, your photo figures will run vertically down the page, one after the other.

10.6 *Crafting the prompt for the photo gallery*

This chapter's project is a photo gallery page that displays nine photo thumbnails, each of which, when clicked, displays a large-size version of the photo. I'm assuming you already have a site logo and title, know which fonts you want to use for the page headings and text, and have a color scheme ready to apply. Head back to chapter 3 to learn how to prompt ChatGPT for title, typeface, and color suggestions.

To start your prompt, tell ChatGPT that you want to construct a web page and that you want it to generate the code for you:

```
I want to build a web page for a photo gallery. I don't know how to code, so
I need you to provide the code for me.

First, write the HTML code for a web page that includes the following:
```

Now outline out the page content, item by item, including the following (refer to figure 10.10):

- A header that includes your logo and site title
- A main element that starts with the page title and is followed by some instructions
- The gallery of photo thumbnails
- A footer that includes a copyright notice

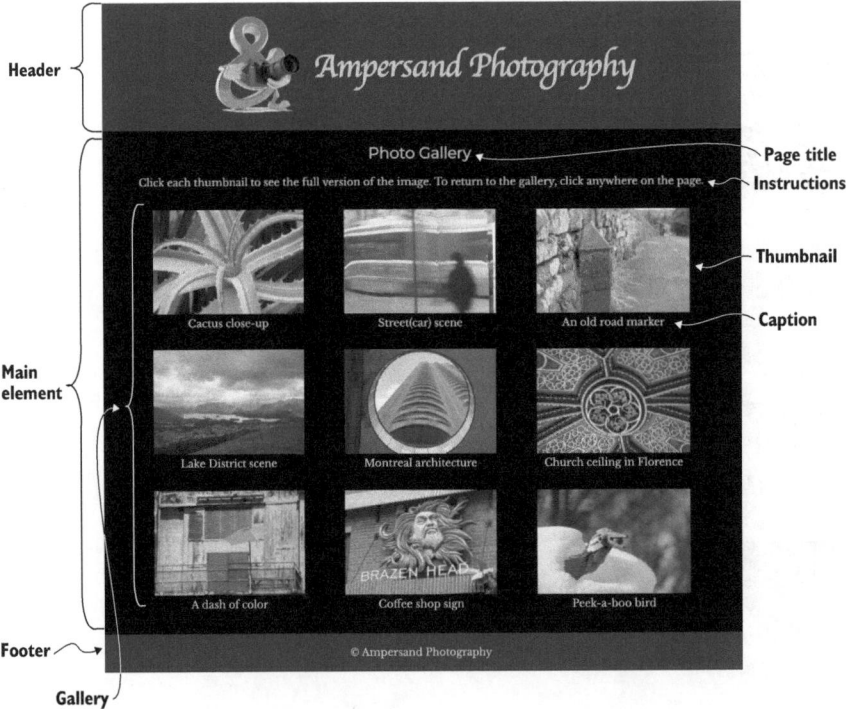

Figure 10.10 The elements of the photo gallery page

Next, ask ChatGPT to generate the CSS:

Second, in a separate file please write the CSS code for the following:

You then specify the page formatting, including the following:

- The page background color and text color
- The type sizes you want to use for the headings and page text
- The fonts to use for the headings and regular page text
- Which elements should be Flexbox containers (in this project, these will be the header, the gallery, and the lightbox overlay)

Finally, you instruct ChatGPT to provide the HTML, CSS, and JavaScript code for a lightbox-style overlay to display the large-size photos.

Here's an example prompt for my own photo gallery:

I want to build a web page for a photo gallery. I don't know how to code, so I need you to provide the code for me.

First, write the HTML code for a web page that includes the following:
 * A header element that includes an image named logo.png, which is stored in the "images" subdirectory, and the title "Ampersand Photography".
 * A main section with the heading "Photo Gallery".
 * A paragraph with the text "Click each thumbnail to see the full version of the image. To return to the gallery, click anywhere on the page."
 * A gallery element that contains the following images, each of which is stored in the "images" subdirectory, and with each image rendered as a figure with the specified alt text and caption:
 * An image named "image01-thumbnail.jpg" with the alt text "Macro photograph of a cactus" and the caption "Cactus close-up".
 * An image named "image02-thumbnail.jpg" with the alt text "A blurry reflection of a passing streetcar and a person walking" and the caption "Street(car) scene".
 * An image named "image03-thumbnail.jpg" with the alt text "A photo with a very old road marker in the foreground that reads 'Appleby 12 Miles'" and the caption "An old road marker".
 * An image named "image04-thumbnail.jpg" with the alt text "A photo taken from the top of a Lake District fell looking down on a town and a lake" and the caption "Lake District scene".
 * An image named "image05-thumbnail.jpg" with the alt text "A Montreal tower shot from below through a hole" and the caption "Montreal architecture".
 * An image named "image06-thumbnail.jpg" with the alt text "The ornate ceiling of a church in Florence, Italy" and the caption "Church ceiling in Florence".
 * An image named "image07-thumbnail.jpg" with the alt text "A cheerful, bright, sky-blue umbrella sitting improbably on a dingy, dirty balcony." and the caption "A dash of color".
 * An image named "image08-thumbnail.jpg" with the alt text "A large, ornate, Zeus-like head over the words 'Brazen Head'" and the caption "Coffee shop sign".

```
 * An image named "image09-thumbnail.jpg" with the alt text "A metal bird
sculpture with its head peeking out of a snow bank" and the caption "Peek-a-
boo bird".
 * A footer element that includes the Copyright symbol, followed by
"Ampersand Photography".
 * In the page head section, include the tag <meta charset="utf-8">.
 * In the page head section, include the tag <meta name="viewport"
content="width=device-width, initial-scale=1">.

Second, in a separate file write the CSS code for the following:
 * The page has background color black and no margin.
 * The page text uses font size 20px, the color gold, and the Libre
Baskerville font from Google Fonts.
 * The header has background color maroon and 24px padding.
 * Make the header a Flexbox container with centered content.
 * The title is 64px, centered, uses the generic "cursive" font, and has 16px
padding on the left.
 * The main section has centered text and a 24px margin.
 * The main section heading has font size 30px and uses the Montserrat font
from Google Fonts.
 * Make the gallery a Flexbox container. Center the content and enable it to
wrap.
 * The footer has background color maroon, 24px padding, and centered text.

Third, provide the HTML, CSS, and JavaScript code to implement a lightbox-
style overlay for the images in the gallery. Each full-size image uses the
same name as its thumbnail, but without "-thumbnail". For example, for
the image01-thumbnail.jpg thumbnail file, the full-size image filename is
image01.jpg.
```

In each of my tests with this prompt, ChatGPT generated this code in four stages:

1 ChatGPT generated some—but crucially, not all—of the HTML code. When it
came to generating the figure elements, ChatGPT generated the code for just
the first figure, followed by a comment similar to this:

```
<!-- repeat for each image -->
```

I don't think so! Later, I used the following prompt to ask ChatGPT to provide the
complete HTML code:

```
Please provide the complete HTML code, including all the images
specified in the original prompt.
```

When that was done, I saved the full HTML code as index.html. In that file, you
should see two references to external files:

  – The first reference is in the head section and is for the CSS file; the reference is
    a <link> tag that should look something like this:

```
<link rel="stylesheet" type="text/css" href="styles.css">
```

- The second reference is near the bottom of the HTML code and is for the JavaScript file; the reference is a `<script>` tag that should look something like this:

```
<script src="script.js"></script>
```

2 ChatGPT generated the code for the CSS, which you need to save to the same filename that appears in the `<link>` tag (usually styles.css).

3 ChatGPT generated the code for the JavaScript, which you need to save to the same filename that appears in the `<script>` tag (usually script.js)

4 ChatGPT generated more CSS code for the lightbox overlay. You need to copy that code and then paste it at the bottom of your CSS file.

I used OpenAI's ChatGPT app to submit my prompt to GPT-4. The generated code produced the page shown in figure 10.11. Clicking a thumbnail produces a larger version of the image, as shown in figure 10.12.

Figure 10.11 My photo gallery

Figure 10.12 Clicking a thumbnail displays a larger-size version of the photo.

If you're happy with your page, feel free to bypass the rest of this chapter and deploy the code to the web (refer to appendix B to learn how to deploy your page). However, if you want to understand the generated web page code, keep reading to get a closer look.

10.7 *Examining the photo gallery code*

If you'd like to have at least some idea of what ChatGPT generated on your behalf, the next three sections provide you with a brief look at the HTML and CSS code that underlies the photo gallery page shown earlier in figure 10.11, as well as the JavaScript code that enables the lightbox overlay demonstrated in figure 10.12.

> **NOTE** The generated HTML and CSS code for my photo gallery are available on this book's website (www.manning.com/books/build-a-website-with-chatgpt) and in the book's GitHub repository: https://github.com/paulmcfe/websites-with-chatgpt.

The code annotations that follow should help you understand how the photo gallery works and can make it easier to modify or customize your own code.

10.7.1 *Examining the HTML*

Here's an annotated version of the HTML code that ChatGPT produced for my photo gallery:

```
<!DOCTYPE html>
<html lang="en">
<head>
    <meta charset="utf-8">
    <meta name="viewport"
        content="width=device-width, initial-scale=1">
    <link href="https://fonts.googleapis.com/css?
        family=Montserrat|
        Libre+Baskerville&display=swap"
        rel="stylesheet">
```

Helps the page display properly on mobile devices

Loads the Montserrat and Libre Baskerville fonts from Google Fonts

```
    <link rel="stylesheet" href="styles.css">
    <title>Ampersand Photography</title>
</head>
<body>
    <header>
        <img src="images/logo.png"
            alt="Ampersand Photography Logo">
        <h1>Ampersand Photography</h1>
    </header>
    <main>
        <h2>Photo Gallery</h2>
        <p>
            Click each thumbnail to see the full version of the image.
            To return to the gallery, click anywhere on the page.
        </p>
        <div class="gallery">
            <figure>
                <img src="images/image01-thumbnail.jpg"
                    alt="Macro photograph of a cactus"
                    class="thumbnail">
                <figcaption>Cactus close-up</figcaption>
            </figure>
            <figure>
                <img src="images/image02-thumbnail.jpg"
                    alt="A blurry reflection of a passing streetcar
                        and a person walking"
                    class="thumbnail">
                <figcaption>Street(car) scene</figcaption>
            </figure>
            <figure>
                <img src="images/image03-thumbnail.jpg"
                    alt="A photo with a very old road marker in the
                        foreground that reads 'Appleby 12 Miles'"
                    class="thumbnail">
                <figcaption>An old road marker</figcaption>
            </figure>
            <figure>
                <img src="images/image04-thumbnail.jpg"
                    alt="A photo taken from the top of a Lake District
                        fell looking down on a town and a lake"
                    class="thumbnail">
                <figcaption>Lake District scene</figcaption>
            </figure>
            <figure>
                <img src="images/image05-thumbnail.jpg"
                    alt="A Montreal tower shot from below through a hole"
                    class="thumbnail">
                <figcaption>Montreal architecture</figcaption>
            </figure>
            <figure>
                <img src="images/image06-thumbnail.jpg"
                    alt="The ornate ceiling of a church in Florence,
                        Italy"
                    class="thumbnail">
                <figcaption>Church ceiling in Florence</figcaption>
            </figure>
```

Tells the web browser where to find the CSS code

Site logo · Page header
Site title

Page title

Instruction paragraph

Figure image · Photo gallery figure
Figure caption

Photo gallery

```
        <figure>
            <img src="images/image07-thumbnail.jpg"
                alt="A cheerful, bright, sky-blue umbrella sitting
                    improbably on a dingy, dirty balcony."
                class="thumbnail">
            <figcaption>A dash of color</figcaption>
        </figure>
        <figure>
            <img src="images/image08-thumbnail.jpg"
                alt="A large, ornate, Zeus-like head over the words
                    'Brazen Head'"
                class="thumbnail">
            <figcaption>Coffee shop sign</figcaption>
        </figure>
        <figure>
            <img src="images/image09-thumbnail.jpg"
                alt="A metal bird sculpture with its head peeking
                    out of a snow bank"
                class="thumbnail">
            <figcaption>Peek-a-boo bird</figcaption>
        </figure>
    </div>
</main>
<footer>
    &copy; Ampersand Photography
</footer>

<script src="script.js"></script>
</body>
</html>
```

Note that the HTML code includes the following line:

```
<link rel="stylesheet" href="styles.css">
```

This tag tells the web browser where to find the CSS code, which I describe in the next section.

10.7.2 Examining the CSS

Here's an annotated version of the CSS code that ChatGPT produced for my photo gallery:

```
body {
    background-color: black;
    margin: 0;
    font-size: 20px;
    color: gold;
    font-family: 'Libre Baskerville', serif;
}

header {
    background-color: maroon;
    padding: 24px;
    display: flex;
    justify-content: center;
    align-items: center;
```

Annotations (right margin):
- Photo gallery
- Page footer
- Tells the web browser where to find the JavaScript code
- Styles the page background color, margin, text size, text color, and font
- Styles the header background color and padding
- Sets the header as a Flexbox container with centered content

```
}

h1 {
    font-size: 64px;
    font-family: cursive;
    padding-left: 16px;
}
```

Styles the page title font size, font, and left padding

```
h2 {
    font-size: 30px;
    font-family: 'Montserrat', sans-serif;
}
```

Styles the font size and font of the page title

```
main {
    margin: 24px;
    text-align: center;
}
```

Styles the main element with a margin, and centers the text

```
.gallery {
    display: flex;
    flex-wrap: wrap;
    justify-content: center;
    align-items: center;
}
```

Sets the gallery as a Flexbox container with centered content and wrapping

```
footer {
    background-color: maroon;
    padding: 24px;
    text-align: center;
}
```

Styles the footer background color and padding, and centers the text

```
.overlay {
    position: fixed;
    top: 0;
    left: 0;
    width: 100%;
    height: 100%;
    background-color: rgba(0, 0, 0, 0.8);
    display: flex;
    justify-content: center;
    align-items: center;
}
```

Positioned in the top-left corner of the window

Takes up the full width and height

Slightly transparent

Flexbox container with centered content

Styles the lightbox overlay

```
.overlay img {
    max-width: 90%;
    max-height: 90%;
}
```

Styles the larger image to use 90% of the lightbox width and height

In the HTML code listing from earlier in this chapter, note the following line near the bottom:

```
<script src="script.js"></script>
```

This tag tells the web browser where to find the JavaScript code, which I annotate in the next section.

10.7.3 *Examining the JavaScript*

If you're careful, it's fine to make small tweaks to the HTML and CSS code. However, I strongly suggest you leave ChatGPT's JavaScript code alone. The code is complex, and an injudicious edit could render the lightbox unusable.

If you happen to know a bit of JavaScript, however, you may be interested in how ChatGPT solved the lightbox problem, so here's an annotated version of the JavaScript code that ChatGPT generated for my photo gallery:

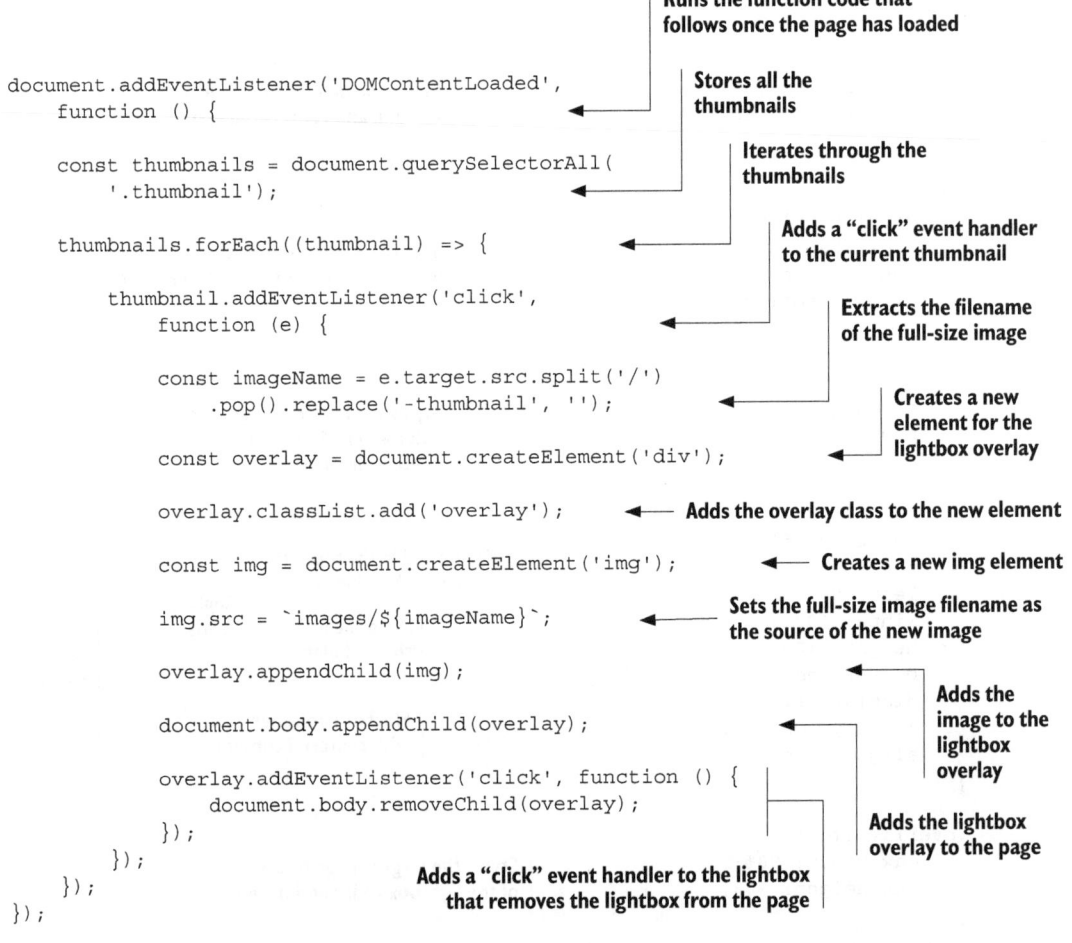

If you like, you can use the HTML and CSS annotations from the previous two sections to help customize your web page code, as I describe in the next section.

10.8 Customizing the photo gallery

Using the previous sections' annotations as a guide, I'm going to take you through a few relatively simple code customizations you can make by opening the HTML and CSS files in your text editor. If your page isn't close to what you want, however, you're better off rewriting your prompt and submitting it to ChatGPT in a new session.

For the HTML code, here are a few suggested customizations:

- You can edit what little text there is on the page, including the title, the heading, and the instruction text. Just make sure you only edit the text and not the HTML tags that surround the text (such as the `<figcaption>` and `</figcaption>` tags around each figure caption).
- Feel free to change the alternative text for any image by editing that `img` tag's `alt` attribute value. Make sure you don't accidentally delete the double quotation marks that surround the `alt` value.
- If you want to include a second introductory paragraph, place the edit cursor after the `</p>` tag that ends the existing introductory paragraph. Press Enter or Return to start a new line, type a `<p>` tag, type your paragraph text, and finish with a `</p>` tag.
- You may want to build out your site by creating multiple photo galleries (or whatever), with each page dedicated to a particular theme or category. Ask ChatGPT to create one page at a time, modifying your prompt as needed. If you go this route, you'll want a navigation element that enables users to visit each page. Refer to chapter 6 to learn how to prompt ChatGPT for links and a navigation bar.
- In the footer section of the HTML code, you can add links to your social media accounts, as I describe in chapter 4.

Now, here are a few customization ideas for the CSS code:

- To use another page background color, specify a different color keyword for the `body` element's `background-color` property.
- To use another background color for the header and footer, specify a new color keyword for the `header` and `footer` elements' `background-color` property.
- To use a different color for the page text, specify a different color keyword for the `body` element's `color` property.
- To adjust the transparency of the lightbox overlay, edit the `.overlay` class's `background-color` property. Specifically, modify the final value in the `rgba()` function, where `1.0` is completely opaque and `0.0` is completely transparent.
- For any font size value, you can change the number to increase or decrease the font size. Just make sure you leave the `px` unit in place.
- For any padding or margin value, you can change the number to increase or decrease the padding or margins. In each case, be sure to leave the `px` unit in place.

- To make your page code more accessible, consider converting all px measurements to rem measurements. 1 rem is by default equivalent to 16 px, so 20 px is 1.25 rem, 24 px is 1.5 rem, 32 px is 2 rem, 48 px is 3 rem, and so on. The rem unit is more accessible because it measures font sizes relative to the default font size the browser user has defined in their browser settings.

Summary

- In HTML, you use the `img` element to tell the web browser to insert an external image file into the page.
- In the `<img>` tag, use the `src` attribute to tell the browser where to find the image file; use the `alt` attribute to add a short phrase that describes the image, particularly for people using screen readers and Braille apps.
- When working with image thumbnails, it's best to create a separate thumbnail file that has the smaller dimensions you want to use.
- To include a caption, surround the `img` element with a `figure` element, and add the caption to the `figcaption` element.
- A lightbox overlay is a web page element created on the fly to display a large-size version of a clicked thumbnail.
- When you don't want page items laid out vertically on the page, turn the element into a Flexbox container.
- For best results, your page prompt should be as specific as possible, including colors, font sizes, and heading levels.
- Save the generated HTML to the index.html file and the generated CSS to the filename suggested by ChatGPT in the HTML code, usually styles.css.

11

Creating a portfolio page

This chapter covers

- Building user interface cards
- Adding a drop-shadow effect
- Rounding card corners
- Making the page responsive
- Crafting a ChatGPT prompt for building a portfolio page
- Examining and customizing the ChatGPT-generated code

One of the best reasons for setting up a home on the web is to showcase your personal work or the work of a team, department, or company. Quite a few of this book's projects have served that goal: the personal home page (chapter 3), the online journal (chapter 5), the interest or hobby website (chapter 7), and the photo gallery (chapter 10).

In this chapter, you learn yet another page structure for promoting the activities of a person, group, or organization: the portfolio page. This page uses images, headings, and text to create an efficient and popular page component designed to showcase whatever you want other people to see. You also learn various ways to customize this component and some techniques that can make your portfolio look its best, not only on a large monitor but also on smaller screens—even smartphones. You then put all this new HTML and CSS know-how to work to create a detailed prompt that enables ChatGPT to generate the web page code for your portfolio page.

This chapter provides annotated versions of the ChatGPT-generated HTML and CSS to help you understand how the portfolio page works. You also get a few useful tips for customizing the code.

11.1   Getting to know this chapter's project

This chapter's project is a portfolio page. The final page will include the following components:

- A header element that includes a logo and title
- A main element that begins with the portfolio title
- Six cards, each of which shows an item from the portfolio
- A footer element that includes a copyright notice

Figure 11.1 shows an example portfolio page created with code supplied by ChatGPT.

Figure 11.1   A portfolio page generated by ChatGPT

The example page is a portfolio for a book designer, but you can use this kind of layout for many other types of content:

- *Art*—Paintings, photographs, illustrations, fashion, architecture, interior design, writing
- *Work*—Projects, products, events, news, key metrics, educational courses
- *People*—Team members, clients, user profiles, testimonials

In short, this is a very versatile layout, and you will start learning how to build it in the next section.

11.2 Building the portfolio page

If you do creative work—illustration, writing, music, fine art—you owe it to yourself and your career to put yourself out there and tell the world how talented you are. How do you do that? Social media is the standard way of blowing your own horn these days. That's fine, but when you use someone else's platform to talk yourself up, you're giving up lots of control over how you present yourself. It's always better to control your own message, and the best way to do that is to build your own online presence. For creative types, that online stake in the ground should include a portfolio page that showcases your best or most recent work.

A *portfolio page* is a web page designed to show off some of (or even all) your creative work. It's the online equivalent of the hard-copy portfolio that starving artists have been lugging around from patron to patron and employer to employer for decades. The main idea of a portfolio page is to show off your creative work to people who may want to buy it or hire you to do your creative thing.

However, even if you're not an artist, a portfolio page is still a great layout for showcasing many different types of items, such as products, courses, and employees. The main component of a portfolio page is the card, which you learn about next.

11.2.1 Building a card

A *card*—sometimes called a *user interface card* or a *UI card*—is a special collection of HTML tags and CSS properties meant to succinctly and efficiently convey information about something, which could be a work of art, an event, a project, a person, or whatever items are in your portfolio. A typical card includes some or all of the following:

- *Image*—A photo, illustration, or other image that provides a preview or representation of the item
- *Heading*—The title or name of the item
- *Text*—A brief description of the item
- *Button or link*—An element that enables the reader to learn more about the item or perform an action, such as subscribing to or purchasing the item

There are many ways to organize a card's information, but two layouts are common. The first common layout has the image on top, followed by the heading, the text, and then the button or link. Figure 11.2 shows an example.

I Fell In Love With ChatGPT

I designed this book for Moughton-Hifflin's new line of AI-themed romance books.

Learn more

Figure 11.2
A typical card layout with the information running from the top of the card to the bottom

To prompt ChatGPT to create a card that uses this layout, you'd use an instruction similar to the following:

```
Generate the code for a card with a maximum width of 350px. At the top of
the card add the image portfolio01.jpg from the images subfolder. Below the
image add the second-level heading "I Fell In Love With ChatGPT", followed by
the text "I designed this book for Moughton-Hifflin's new line of AI-themed
romance books", followed by a "Learn more" link to the file portfolio01.html.
Center the text in the card.
```

The second common layout has the image on one side (it could be the left or right), with the heading, text, and button or link on the other side. Figure 11.3 shows an example.

Figure 11.3
A typical card layout with the image on the left and the text on the right

To prompt ChatGPT to create a card that uses this layout, you'd use an instruction like the following:

```
Generate the code for a card with a maximum width of 500px. On the left side
of the card, add the image portfolio01.jpg from the images subfolder. On the
right side of the card,  add the second-level heading "I Fell In Love With
ChatGPT", followed by the text "I designed this book for Moughton-Hifflin's
new line of AI-themed romance books", followed by a "Learn more" link to the
file portfolio01.html.
```

If the designer in you isn't happy with the whitespace around the image, you learn how to fix that in the next section.

11.2.2 *Making the image extend to the card edges*

One common and attractive card tweak is to have the image extend all the way out to the edges of the card:

- *If the image is at the top of the card*—The image extends all the way to the top, left, and right edges.
- *If the image is on the left side of the card*—The image extends all the way to the top, left, and bottom edges.
- *If the image is on the right side of the card*—The image extends all the way to the top, right, and bottom edges.

You can ask ChatGPT to configure the card this way by adding something like the following to the card prompt from the previous section:

```
Make sure there is no margin or padding around the image so that it extends
all the way to the top, left, and right edges of the card.
```

This instruction is suitable for a card with the image on top and results in a card that looks like the one shown in figure 11.4.

I Fell In Love With ChatGPT

I designed this book for Moughton-Hifflin's
new line of AI-themed romance books.

Learn more

**Figure 11.4
A card layout
where the image
extends to the
edges of the
card**

Another useful card customize is a drop-shadow, discussed in the next section.

11.2.3 *Adding a shadow*

Notice in figures 11.2, 11.3, and 11.4 that each card has a subtle shadow effect. This is called a *drop-shadow* because it makes the card appear as though it is raised slightly off the page and therefore has a shadow that "drops" onto the background. There are two things to note about these drop-shadow examples:

- ChatGPT automatically adds the drop-shadow even when your prompt doesn't specify one. If you don't want a drop-shadow, you need to include an instruction such as the following in your prompt:

  ```
  Don't add a drop-shadow to the card.
  ```

- The shadow that ChatGPT creates is attractive, but it may not be to your taste. For example, you may prefer to have the shadow extend to the right of the card by the same amount it extends below the card.

The CSS property that creates the drop-shadow effect is called `box-shadow`, and its syntax is shown in figure 11.5. There are four values you can play around with here:

- `x-offset`—The amount (in pixels) that the shadow is shifted either to the right (any positive value) or to the left (any negative value) relative to the card
- `y-offset`—The amount (in pixels) that the shadow is shifted either down (any positive value) or up (any negative value) relative to the card
- `blur`—The amount (in pixels) that the shadow is blurred, where 0 means no blur and higher values make the shadow progressively blurrier
- `alpha`—A value between 0 and 1 that defines the transparency of the shadow, where 0 means completely transparent and 1 means completely opaque

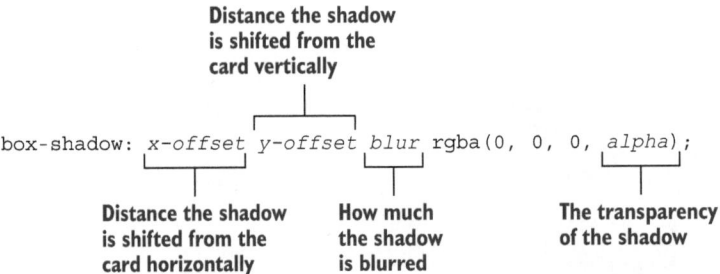

Figure 11.5   The syntax of the `box-shadow` property

Here's an example instruction to ChatGPT to add a custom shadow to a card:

```
Add a drop-shadow effect to the card where both the x and y offset are 8px,
the blur is 4px, and the transparency is 0.5.
```

NOTE Although in this chapter you apply a drop-shadow only to the portfolio cards, in practice you can add a drop-shadow to any page element that creates a block, including a paragraph, heading, `div` element, or bulleted or numbered list.

This instruction will produce a box-shadow declaration similar to the following:

```
box-shadow: 8px 8px 4px rgba(0, 0, 0, 0.5);
```

NOTE Sometimes ChatGPT generates a `box-shadow` value that includes an extra number (usually 0) between the `blur` number and the `rgba()` function. This extra parameter determines the *spread* of the shadow, which is a measure of the size of the shadow relative to the card (where 0 means the shadow is the same size as the card and higher pixel values expand the size of the shadow).

Another effect you can apply to your cards is to round the corners, which is the topic of the next section.

11.2.4 Rounding the corners

Examining figures 11.2, 11.3, and 11.4, notice that the corners of each card are rounded, which gives the card a softer, more approachable feel. There are two things to note about these rounded corners:

- ChatGPT automatically rounds the card corners even when your prompt doesn't ask it to. If you don't want rounded corners, you need to include an instruction such as the following in your prompt:

  ```
  Don't round the corners of the card.
  ```

- The amount of curvature is variable, and you can also apply the curvature only to specific corners.

The CSS property that rounds the corners is called `border-radius`, and its syntax is shown in figure 11.6.

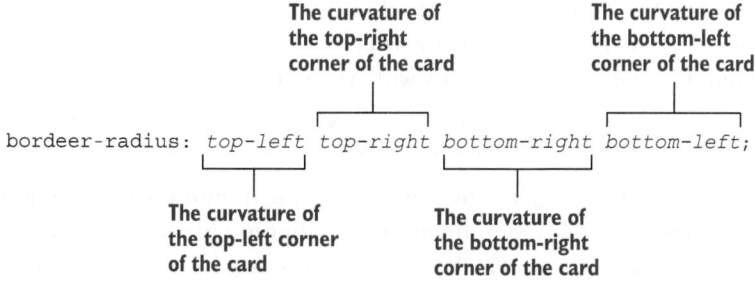

Figure 11.6 The syntax of the `border-radius` property

You can adjust four values:

- `top-left`—The amount (as pixels or a percentage) of curvature to apply to the top-left corner of the card
- `top-right`—The amount (as pixels or a percentage) of curvature to apply to the top-right corner of the card
- `bottom-right`—The amount (as pixels or a percentage) of curvature to apply to the bottom-right corner of the card
- `bottom-left`—The amount (as pixels or a percentage) of curvature to apply to the bottom-left corner of the card

> **TIP**   A short form that ChatGPT often generates is `border-radius: value`, where `value` is the amount (as pixels or a percentage) of curvature to apply to all four corners of the card.

Here's an example instruction to ChatGPT to add custom rounded corners to a card:

```
Round only the top-left and top-right corners of the card by 10px.
```

This instruction will produce a `box-shadow` declaration similar to the following:

```
border-radius: 10px 10px 0 0;
```

The final design idea you need to investigate for a portfolio page is ensuring that the page displays well on any size screen, which is the subject of the next section.

11.2.5 *Making your page responsive*

As described in chapter 10, the default layout behavior for box-like web page elements such as headers, footers, navigation areas, headings, and paragraphs is to flow vertically down the page: the second element below the first, the third element below the second, and so on. Each item of the portfolio example will also be one of these box-like elements: the `div` element. This means if you settle for the default layout, your portfolio items will display as a vertical pile, which isn't the most attractive or efficient look.

The solution I proposed in chapter 10 was to use Flexbox, which turns a web page element into a Flexbox container: items in that container lose their rigid default layout behavior and adapt themselves to the browser's current dimensions. For this project, you can prompt ChatGPT to use Flexbox with a simple instruction:

```
Make the portfolio container a Flexbox container. Enable the content to wrap
and give each card a minimum width of 250px and a maximum width of 300px.
```

Note that this prompt includes instructions that set the minimum and maximum width of the cards because you don't want them to get either too big or too small.

Enabling the content in the Flexbox container—that is, your portfolio cards—to wrap means your layout will adapt itself to the current dimensions of the browser window. A layout that does that is called *responsive* and means your portfolio will look good on everything from large monitors to tiny smartphone screens.

However, to make your page look its best on the smallest screens, your HTML code needs to include the following tag between the <head> and </head> tags:

```
<meta name="viewport" content="width=device-width, initial-scale=1">
```

This tag does two things:

- By setting width=device-width, you're telling the browser to set the width of the page to be the same as the width of whatever device the page is being displayed on.
- By setting initial-scale=1, you're telling the browser to display the page initially without zooming in or out.

To ensure this tag is included in the code, your ChatGPT prompt should include an instruction similar to the following:

```
In the page head section, include the tag <meta name="viewport"
content="width=device-width, initial-scale=1">
```

Later, after I show you the final portfolio page layout (refer to figure 11.7), I'll also show you how the page displays on both a tablet (figure 11.8) and a smartphone (figure 11.9) to verify that the page is, indeed, responsive.

> **NOTE** You can also work with a special CSS property called a *media query* to make your pages even more responsive to different screen sizes. You learn how to work with media queries in chapter 12.

Now you know everything you need to prompt ChatGPT to build a portfolio page, as described in the following section.

11.3 Crafting the prompt for the portfolio page

This chapter's project is a portfolio page that displays six cards that feature the works of a fictional book designer. Before proceeding, I assume you have the following at hand:

- One or more of the following: a page logo, title, and tagline
- The names of the typefaces you want to use for the page headings and the page text
- The names of the colors you want to apply to the page backgrounds and text

Refer to chapter 3 to learn more about each of these design elements and how to prompt ChatGPT for title, typeface, and color suggestions.

To start your prompt, tell ChatGPT that you want to construct a web page and that you want it to generate the code for you:

```
I want to build a portfolio web page. I don't know how to code, so I need you
to provide the code for me.

First, write the HTML code for a web page that includes the following:
```

Now go through the page content, item by item, including the following (refer to figure 11.7):

- A header that includes your logo and title
- A main element that starts with the page title
- The portfolio container
- The portfolio cards
- A footer that includes a copyright notice

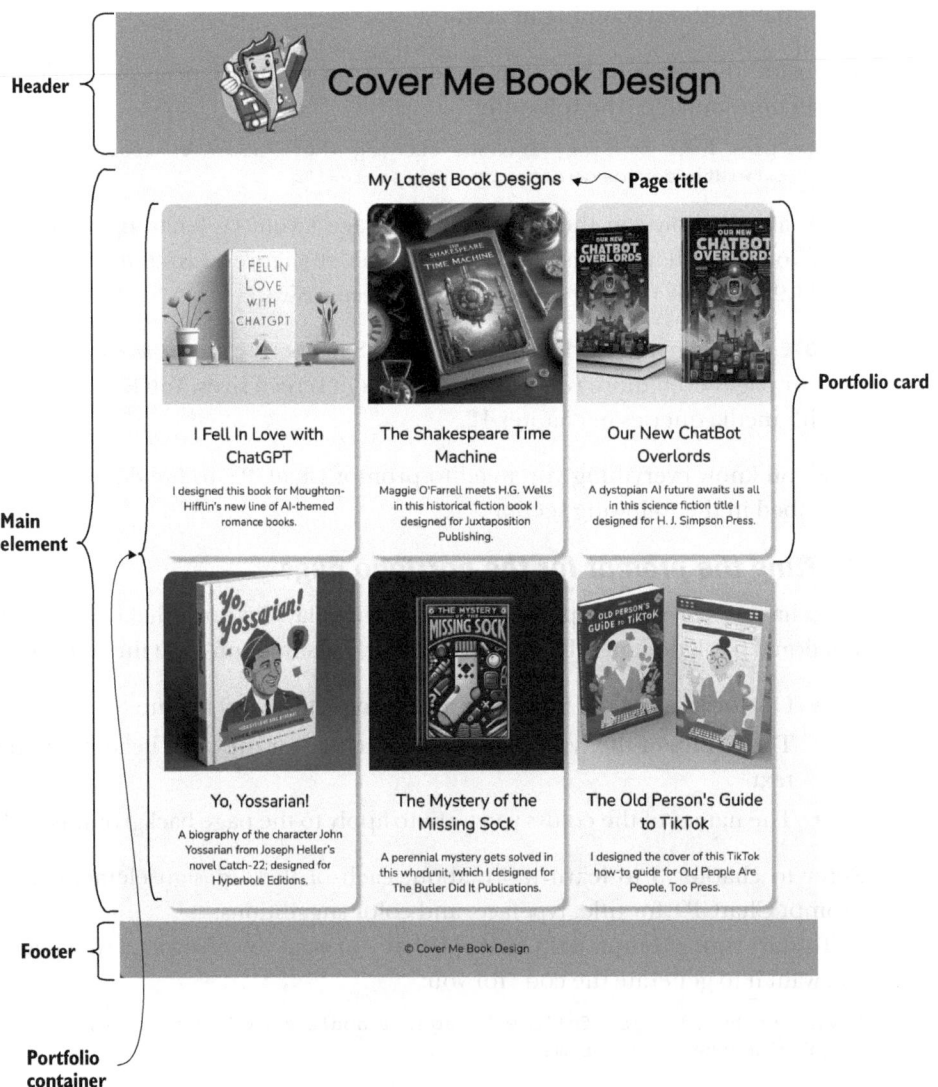

Figure 11.7   The sections of the portfolio page

Next, ask ChatGPT to generate the CSS:

```
Second, in a separate file please write the CSS code for the following:
```

You then specify the page formatting, including the following:

- The page background color and text color
- The type sizes you want to use for the headings and page text
- The fonts to use for the headings and regular page text
- Which elements should be Flexbox containers (in this project, these will be the header and the portfolio container)

Here's an example prompt for my own portfolio page:

```
I want to build a web page for a photo gallery. I don't know how to code, so
I need you to provide the code for me.

First, write the HTML code for a web page that includes the following:
 * A header element that includes an image named logo.png, which is stored in
the "images" subdirectory, and the title "Cover Me Book Design".
 * A main section with the heading "My Latest Book Designs".
 * A container with six UI cards, each of which has an image at the top,
followed by a second-level heading, followed by some text. Here are the
specifics for each of the six cards:
 * Card 1: The image portfolio01.jpg in the images subfolder; the heading
"I Fell In Love with ChatGPT"; the text "I designed this book for Moughton-
Hifflin's new line of AI-themed romance books."
 * Card 2: The image portfolio02.jpg in the images subfolder; the heading
"The Shakespeare Time Machine"; the text "Maggie O'Farrell meets H.G. Wells
in this historical fiction book I designed for Juxtaposition Publishing."
 * Card 3: The image portfolio03.jpg in the images subfolder; the heading
"Our New ChatBot Overlords"; the text "A dystopian AI future awaits us all in
this science fiction title I designed for H. J. Simpson Press."
 * Card 4: The image portfolio04.jpg in the images subfolder; the heading
"Yo, Yossarian!"; the text "A biography of the character John Yossarian from
Joseph Heller's novel Catch-22; designed for Hyperbole Editions."
 * Card 5: The image portfolio05.jpg in the images subfolder; the heading
"The Mystery of the Missing Sock"; the text "A perennial mystery gets solved
in this whodunit, which I designed for The Butler Did It Publications."
 * Card 6: The image portfolio06.jpg in the images subfolder; the heading
"The Old Person's Guide to TikTok"; the text "I designed the cover of this
TikTok how-to guide for Old People Are People, Too Press."
 * A footer element that includes the Copyright symbol, followed by "Cover Me
Book Design".
 * In the page head section, include the tag <meta charset="utf-8">.
 * In the page head section, include the tag <meta name="viewport"
content="width=device-width, initial-scale=1">.

Second, in a separate file write the CSS code for the following:
 * The page has background color mintcream and no margin.
 * The page text uses font size 20px and the Nunito font from Google Fonts.
 * The header has background color coral and 24px padding.
 * Make the header a Flexbox row container with centered content and allow
the content to wrap.
```

* The title is 64px, uses the Poppins font from Google Fonts, and has 16px padding on the left.
* The main section has centered text and a 24px margin.
* The main section heading has font size 30px and uses the Poppins font from Google Fonts.
* Make the portfolio a Flexbox container. Enable the content to wrap and add a gap between items of 16px.
* Give each card a minimum width of 200px and a maximum width of 350px.
* For each card image, make sure there is no margin or padding around the image so that it extends all the way to the top, left, and right edges of the card.
* Add 16px padding to the left and right of the card text.
* Style the cards with a drop-shadow where both the x and y offsets are 8px, the blur is 4px, and the transparency is 0.3.
* Style the cards with a border radius of 20px.
* The footer has background color coral, 16px padding, and centered text.

I used OpenAI's ChatGPT app to submit my prompt to GPT-4. The generated code produced the page shown in figure 11.8.

Figure 11.8   My portfolio page

Figure 11.8 shows how the page looks on a desktop monitor. To ensure that your page is behaving responsively, you need to test it with some smaller screens. For example, figure 11.9 shows the portfolio part of the page on a tablet-sized screen: the portfolio has adapted to the smaller screen size by going down to a two-column layout.

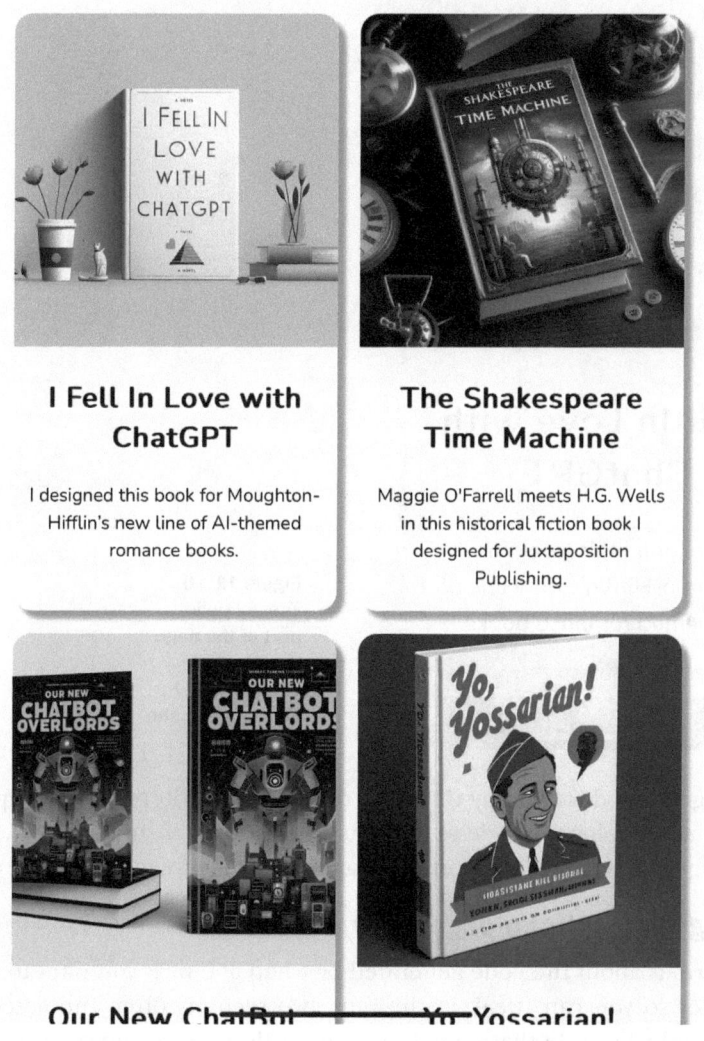

Figure 11.9 **The portfolio part of the page uses a two-column layout on a tablet screen.**

Of course, you should also test your page on a smartphone screen, as shown in figure 11.10. In this case, the portfolio has adapted to the even smaller screen size by reducing itself to a single-column layout.

My Latest Book Designs

I Fell In Love with ChatGPT

I designed this book for Moughton-Hifflin's new line of AI-themed romance books.

Figure 11.10
The portfolio part of the page uses a single-column layout on a smartphone screen.

If the code generated for you by ChatGPT does the job, you're free to skip the rest of this chapter and deploy the code to the web (as I describe in appendix B). However, if you want to get a handle on the portfolio page code, keep reading to get a closer look.

11.4 *Examining the portfolio page code*

If you're curious about the code generated by ChatGPT, or if you want to understand it a bit better so you can tweak it, the next two sections offer annotated guides to the HTML and CSS code that lie behind the portfolio page shown earlier in figures 11.8–11.10.

NOTE The generated HTML and CSS code for my portfolio page are available on this book's website (www.manning.com/books/build-a-website-with -chatgpt) and in the book's GitHub repository: https://github.com/paulmcfe/ websites-with-chatgpt.

I'll begin in the next section with the HTML code.

11.4.1 *Examining the HTML*

Here's an annotated version of the HTML code that ChatGPT generated for my portfolio page:

```
<!DOCTYPE html>
<html lang="en">
<head>
    <meta charset="utf-8">
    <meta name="viewport"
        content="width=device-width, initial-scale=1">
    <link rel="stylesheet" href="styles.css">
    <title>Cover Me Book Design</title>
</head>
<body>
    <header>
        <img src="images/logo.png"
            alt="Cover Me Book Design Logo">
        <h1>Cover Me Book Design</h1>
    </header>

    <main>
        <h1>My Latest Book Designs</h1>
        <div class="portfolio">

            <div class="card">
                <img src="images/portfolio01.jpg"
                    alt="I Fell In Love with ChatGPT"
                    class="card-image">
                <h2>I Fell In Love with ChatGPT</h2>
                <p>I designed this book for Moughton-Hifflin's new
                    line of AI-themed romance books.
                </p>
            </div>

            <div class="card">
                <img src=»images/portfolio02.jpg»
                    alt="The Shakespeare Time Machine"
                    class="card-image">
                <h2>The Shakespeare Time Machine</h2>
                <p>Maggie O'Farrell meets H.G. Wells in this historical
                    fiction book I designed for Juxtaposition Publishing.
                </p>
            </div>

            <div class="card">
                <img src=»images/portfolio03.jpg»
                    alt="Our New ChatBot Overlords"
                    class="card-image">
                <h2>Our New ChatBot Overlords</h2>
                <p>A dystopian AI future awaits us all in this science
                    fiction title I designed for H. J. Simpson Press.
                </p>
```

Annotations:
- **Helps the page display properly on mobile devices**
- **Tells the web browser where to find the CSS code**
- **Site logo** / **Site title** — **Page header**
- **Page title**
- **Card image**
- **Card title**
- **Card text** — **Portfolio card**
- **Portfolio**

```
        </div>

        <div class="card">
            <img src=»images/portfolio04.jpg»
                alt="Yo, Yossarian!"
                class="card-image">
            <h2>Yo, Yossarian!</h2>
            <p>A biography of the character John Yossarian from
                Joseph Heller's novel Catch-22, designed for
                Hyperbole Editions.
            </p>
        </div>

        <div class="card">
            <img src=»images/portfolio05.jpg»
                alt="The Mystery of the Missing Sock"
                class="card-image">
            <h2>The Mystery of the Missing Sock</h2>
            <p>A perennial mystery gets solved in this whodunit,
                which I designed for The Butler Did It Publications.
            </p>
        </div>

        <div class="card">
            <img src=»images/portfolio06.jpg»
                alt="The Old Person's Guide to TikTok"
                class="card-image">
            <h2>The Old Person's Guide to TikTok</h2>
            <p>I designed the cover of this TikTok how-to guide for
                Old People Are People, Too Press.
            </p>
        </div>
    </div>
</main>

<footer>
    <p>&copy; Cover Me Book Design</p>
</footer>
</body>
</html>
```

(Annotation: "Portfolio" marks the portfolio section. "Page footer" marks the footer section.)

Note that the HTML code includes the following line:

```
<link rel="stylesheet" href="styles.css">
```

This tag tells the web browser where to find the CSS code, which I describe in the next section.

11.4.2 *Examining the CSS*

Here's an annotated version of the CSS code that ChatGPT generated for my portfolio page:

```
@import url('https://fonts.googleapis.com/css2?]
family=Nunito&family=Poppins&display=swap');
```

Imports the Nunito and Poppins typefaces from Google Fonts

```css
body {
    background-color: mintcream;
    margin: 0;
    font-size: 20px;
    font-family: 'Nunito', sans-serif;
}
```

Styles the page background color, margin, and text size and font

```css
header {
    background-color: coral;
    padding: 24px;
    display: flex;
    justify-content: center;
    align-items: center;
    flex-wrap: wrap;
}
```

Styles the header background color and padding

Sets the header as a Flexbox container with centered, wrapped content

```css
header h1 {
    font-size: 64px;
    font-family: 'Poppins', sans-serif;
    padding-left: 16px;
}
```

Styles the page title font size, font, and left padding

```css
main {
    text-align: center;
    margin: 24px;
}
```

Styles the main element with a margin and centers the text

```css
main h1 {
    font-size: 30px;
    font-family: 'Poppins', sans-serif;
}
```

Styles the font size and font of the page title

```css
.portfolio {
    display: flex;
    flex-wrap: wrap;
    justify-content: center;
    gap: 24px;
}
```

Sets the portfolio as a Flexbox container with wrapping, centered content, and a gap between items

Styles each card with a minimum and maximum width

```css
.card {
    min-width: 200px;
    max-width: 350px;
    box-shadow: 8px 8px 4px rgba(0, 0, 0, 0.3);
    border-radius: 20px;
    overflow: hidden;
}
```

Styles the card with a drop-shadow

Styles the card with rounded corners

Ensures the image's corners are also rounded

```css
.card img {
    width: 100%;
    margin: 0;
    padding: 0;
}
```

Styles each card image to extend to the card edges

```css
.card h2, .card p {
    padding: 0 16px;
```

Adds 16 px left and right padding to the card text

```
}

footer {
    background-color: coral;
    padding: 16px;
    text-align: center;
}
```

Styles the footer background color and padding and centers the text

You can refer to the HTML and CSS annotations from the previous two sections to help customize your web page code, as I describe in the next section.

11.5   *Customizing the portfolio page*

Here are some customization suggestions for the HTML code:

- In the header, you can edit the title. Just be sure not to edit or delete the associated HTML tags, <h1> and </h1>.
- If you're building a site that includes multiple portfolios, you'll want a navigation area so visitors can easily find your other pages. Refer to chapter 6 to learn how to prompt ChatGPT for links and a navigation bar.
- In the main section, you can edit the page title, but don't mess with the associated HTML tags, <h1> and </h1>.
- If you want to include one or more extra introductory paragraphs, add them just below the <h1> tag in the main element. Ensure that each paragraph renders properly by surrounding it with a <p> tag at the beginning and a </p> tag at the end:

```
<main>
    <h1>My Latest Book Designs</h1>
    <p>
        Type your introductory paragraph text here.
    <p>
    <div class="portfolio">
    etc.
```

- In the footer section of the HTML code, you can add links to your social media accounts, as I describe in chapter 4.

Now, here are a few customization ideas for the CSS code:

- If you're not a fan of the drop-shadow effect, you can remove it by looking for the following code and deleting the box-shadow declaration:

```
.card {
    min-width: 200px;
    max-width: 350px;
    box-shadow: 8px 8px 4px rgba(0, 0, 0, 0.3);
    border-radius: 20px;
    overflow: hidden;
}
```

- If you go without the drop-shadow, you still need some way to make your card stand out from the page background. The easiest way to do that is to add a border (refer to chapter 5) around the card. At the same spot in the CSS code where the `box-shadow` declaration appeared, add the `border` declaration, as shown below (with the values adjusted to suit your own portfolio):

```
.card {
    min-width: 200px;
    max-width: 350px;
    border: 5px solid coral;
    border-radius: 20px;
    overflow: hidden;
}
```

- If you prefer your card text to be left-aligned, you can change that by finding the following code in the CSS and changing the `text-align` value from `center` to `left`:

```
main {
    text-align: center;
    margin: 24px;
}
```

- For any color value, you can change the existing color to a different color keyword.
- For any font size value, you can change the number to increase or decrease the font size. Just make sure you leave the `px` unit in place.
- For any padding or margin value, you can change the number to increase or decrease the padding or margins. In each case, be sure to leave the `px` unit in place.
- To make your page code more accessible, consider converting all px measurements to rem measurements. 1 rem is by default equivalent to 16 px, so 20 px is 1.25 rem, 24 px is 1.5 rem, 32 px is 2 rem, 48 px is 3 rem, and so on. The rem unit is more accessible because it measures font sizes relative to the default font size the browser user has defined in their browser settings.

Summary

- A card is a special collection of HTML tags and CSS properties that's meant to efficiently convey information about an item: a work of art, an event, a project, a person, and so on.
- Most cards include an image of the item, the title or name of the item, a brief description of the item, and a button or link that enables the reader to learn more about the item or perform an action related to the item.
- The two most common card layouts are vertical, where the card elements are laid out top to bottom (image, title, text, link), and horizontal, where the card

elements are laid out left to right (usually with the image on the left and the text on the right).

- You can use the `box-shadow` property to add a drop-shadow to a card.
- You can use the `border-radius` property to round the corners of a card.
- For best results, your page prompt should be as specific as possible, including colors, font sizes, and heading levels.
- Save the generated HTML to the index.html file and the generated CSS to the filename suggested by ChatGPT in the HTML code, usually styles.css.

Building an
article page

There are as many reasons to set up a web page as there are people who want to establish some kind of web presence. However, most of these reasons can be gathered under two broad umbrellas: self-expression and information sharing. So far in this book, you've worked on several projects related to self-expression: the personal home page (chapter 3), the online journal (chapter 5), the photo gallery (chapter 10), and the portfolio page (chapter 11). You've also worked on projects related to information sharing: the book club page (chapter 4), the information website (chapter 6), the interest or hobby website (chapter 7), the event sign-up page (chapter 8), and the recipe page (chapter 9).

This chapter introduces you to another information-sharing page structure: the article page. This page uses common HTML structures such as a header, navigation bar, sidebar, and footer, all arranged around the star of the page: a long article containing several sections. This chapter is going to be a bit more "hands-on" than previous projects because it's easier to add sections, headings, and paragraphs and mark up that text (that is, add the appropriate HTML tags) for the reader by hand than it is to rely on ChatGPT to do everything. Not to worry, though: you'll still take advantage of ChatGPT's coding know-how to create the basic structure for your article page and add some extra bells and whistles that will make your article stand out from the crowd.

12.1   *Getting to know this chapter's project*

This chapter's project is an article page. The final page will include the following components:

- A header element that includes a logo, title, and tagline
- A navigation bar with links to other sections of the site
- A main element that contains an article element with a title
- Multiple section elements within the article, each with its own heading and paragraphs
- A sidebar element with related information
- A footer element that includes a copyright notice

Figure 12.1 shows a (partial) example article page created with code and text supplied by ChatGPT.

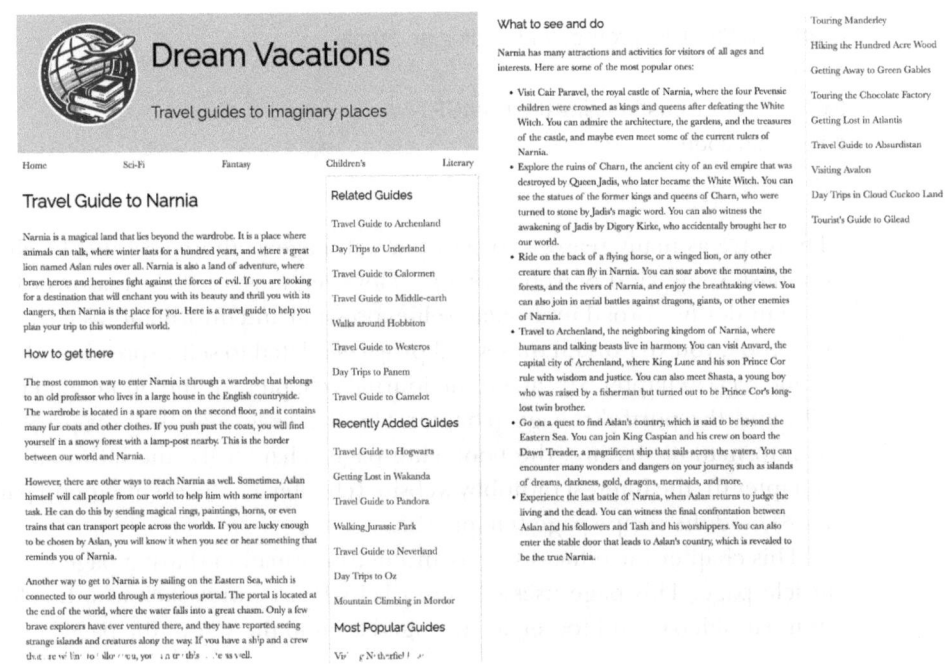

Figure 12.1   An article page generated by ChatGPT

The example page is a fictional travel article for an imaginary place from a work of literature (Narnia, the primary setting of C.S. Lewis's fantasy series *The Chronicles of Narnia*), but you can use the article layout for many other types of content: news items, essays, blog posts, reviews, biographies, historical accounts, and so on. You start learning how to build the article layout in the next section.

12.2 Building the article page

How do you know when an article is the page layout you need? Examine the main content you want to display on the page, and ask yourself the following questions:

- Is the writing focused on a single topic?
- Is the writing divided into multiple subtopics?

If the answer is "Yes" to both questions, the article layout you learn about in this chapter will be a fine showcase for your writing.

Before you learn how to lay out a page as an article, you should step back a bit and review the HTML page layout elements you've encountered in this book's earlier chapters. This will help you understand the overall layout of the article page.

12.2.1 Reviewing the HTML page layout elements

In most of this book's projects, the HTML that ChatGPT has generated has laid out the page using some or all of the following elements:

- `header`—Defines a page area that contains introductory content. This content is most often the site title (which should be marked up with a heading element, such as `h1`), but it can also include things such as a site logo and a tagline. Here's an example (from chapter 9):

```
<header>
    <img src="super-baker.png" alt="The Super Baker Logo">
    <h1>The Super Baker</h1>
    <p>The ultimate guide to super-powered baking. Learn how to
        make delicious treats that will boost your energy,
        strength, and speed.</p>
</header>
```

- `nav`—Defines a page area that contains navigation content, such as links to other sections of the site. This element can be anywhere on the page but typically appears right after the page's `header` element. Here's an example (from chapter 6):

```
<nav>
    <a href="index.html">Home</a>
    <a href="blog.html">Blog</a>
    <a href="faq.html">FAQ</a>
    <a href="about.html">About</a>
    <a href="contact.html">Contact</a>
</nav>
```

- main—Creates a container for the content that's unique to the current page. Whereas the header, nav, and footer elements are often common to all or most of the pages on the site, the main element is meant to mark up the content that's unique. You can have only one main element per page. It typically appears after the header and nav elements, as shown here (from chapter 6):

```
<header>
    <h1>Antediluvian Word Preservation Society</h1>
    <p>Preserving words from the past for the future</p>
</header>
<nav>
    <a href="index.html">Home</a>
    <a href="blog.html">Blog</a>
    <a href="faq.html">FAQ</a>
    <a href="about.html">About</a>
    <a href="contact.html">Contact</a>
</nav>
<main>
    Unique page content goes here
</main>
```

- section—Contains any part of a page that you'd want to see in an outline of the page. That is, if part of the page consists of a heading element (such as h2 or h3) followed by some text, you'll surround the heading and its text with <section> and </section> tags, like so (from chapter 6):

```
<section>
    <h2>This week's challenge</h2>
    <p>
        Your challenge this week is to use the word tomfoolery
        — foolish or silly behavior — at least once in each
        of the following: in conversation, in an email message,
        in a text message, and in a business meeting (virtual or
        real-world). Good luck and let us know how you make out!
    </p>
</section>
```

- p—Marks up a chunk of text as a paragraph. A section element typically consists of one or more paragraphs, although you can also add paragraphs to any other element, particularly the header, main, and footer elements.

- footer—Defines a page area that contains closing content, such as a copyright notice, address, and contact information. Here's an example (from chapter 4):

```
<footer>
    <p>Copyright 2023 Code & Prose</p>
    <p>
        <a href="https://www.facebook.com/CodeAndProse">
        <i class="fab fa-facebook-square"></i></a>
        <a href="https://www.instagram.com/codeandprose">
        <i class="fab fa-instagram"></i></a>
        <a href="https://twitter.com/codenprose">
        <i class="fab fa-twitter-square"></i></a>
    </p>
</footer>
```

Figure 12.2 shows an abstract page layout that demonstrates how these elements appear on a page. Notice that it includes two HTML page layout elements I didn't cover in this section: `article` and `aside`. Not surprisingly, the `article` element plays a vital role in this chapter's article page layout, so I cover it in detail next.

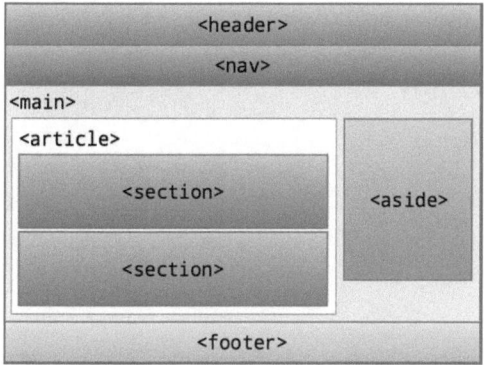

Figure 12.2   A conceptual layout that includes the basic HTML layout elements

12.2.2 *Working with the article element*

You use the `article` element to mark up a complete, self-contained composition. The model here is a newspaper or magazine article, but this element can also apply to a review, a blog entry, a forum post, or an essay. Most pages have a single `article` element nested within the `main` element. That `article` element usually contains the following:

- A title, usually marked up as a second-level heading (that is, an `h2` element)
- One or more introductory `p` elements (paragraphs)
- One or more `section` elements
- Within each of those `section` elements, a third level-heading (that is, an `h3` element) followed by one or more `p` elements

None of this is set in stone. For example, it's perfectly fine for an `article` element to contain only a title and one or more paragraphs. However, for the purposes of this chapter, the article page layout uses these elements. Here's the generic structure you'll be using:

```
<main>
    <article>
        <h2>Article Title</h2>
        <p>Introductory paragraph</p>
        <section>
            <h3>Section 1 heading</h3>
            <p>
                Section 1 paragraph 1
```

```
        </p>
        <p>
            Section 1 paragraph 2
        </p>
        <p>
            etc.
        </p>
    </section>
    <section>
        <h3>Section 2 heading</h3>
        <p>
            Section 2 paragraph 1
        </p>
        <p>
            Section 2 paragraph 2
        </p>
        <p>
            etc.
        </p>
    </section>
    <section>
        <h3>Section 3 heading</h3>
        <p>
            Section 3 paragraph 1
        </p>
        <p>
            Section 3 paragraph 2
        </p>
        <p>
            etc.
        </p>
    </section>
    </article>
</main>
```

In general, you can get ChatGPT to generate the code for an `article` element by including an instruction similar to the following in your prompt:

```
In the main section, add an article element where the article title is
"[title]" as a second-level heading.
```

The second new HTML page layout element shown earlier in figure 12.2 is `aside`, which you learn about next.

12.2.3 *Including a sidebar on your page*

You use the `aside` element to mark up a page sidebar area that contains content indirectly related to the page's unique content (in this chapter's layout, that unique content refers to what appears in the `article` element). Here are a few use cases for such a sidebar:

- A list of links to site pages related to the page's main content
- The latest site news

- A social media feed
- One or more advertisements

An `aside` element can appear anywhere within the `main` element (and can appear multiple times on the page). In this chapter's article page layout, the `aside` element appears right after the page's `article` element, as shown in the following example:

```
<main>
    <article>
        <h2>Article Title</h2>
        <p>Introductory paragraph</p>
        <section>
            <h3>Section 1 heading</h3>
            <p>
                Section 1 paragraph 1
            </p>
            <p>
                Section 1 paragraph 2
            </p>
            <p>
                etc.
            </p>
        </section>
        <section>
            <h3>Section 2 heading</h3>
            <p>
                Section 2 paragraph 1
            </p>
            <p>
                Section 2 paragraph 2
            </p>
            <p>
                etc.
            </p>
        </section>
        <section>
            <h3>Section 3 heading</h3>
            <p>
                Section 3 paragraph 1
            </p>
            <p>
                Section 3 paragraph 2
            </p>
            <p>
                etc.
            </p>
        </section>
    </article>
    <aside>
        <h3>Aside heading</h3>
        <p>
            Aside paragraph 1
```

```
        </p>
        <p>
            Aside paragraph 2
        </p>
        <p>
            etc.
        </p>
    </aside>
</main>
```

In general, to have ChatGPT generate the code for an `aside` element, include an instruction similar to the following in your prompt:

```
At the bottom of the main section, add an aside element where the aside title
is "[title]" as a third-level heading.
```

As part of this chapter's more hands-on approach, in the next couple of sections, you learn how to add new items to your page rather than asking ChatGPT to generate those items.

12.2.4 *Adding new sections to the article*

Articles can be either short or long. For a short article, it's no problem to include the text and headings in your ChatGPT prompt and let the model do the heavy lifting for you. However, that approach doesn't work all that well for lengthy articles because your prompts end up being extremely long. That length can cause two problems:

- You may exceed the maximum number of characters allowed in a prompt.
- The longer the prompt, the more likely it is that ChatGPT will lose its way when generating a response.

For these reasons, in this chapter's project, you're only going to ask ChatGPT to create a skeleton of the page layout. You'll then put some flesh on those bones by adding the rest of the article content by hand.

The HTML code returned by ChatGPT will look, in part, like this:

```
<main>
    <article>
        <h2>Travel Guide to Narnia</h2>
        <!-- Article content goes here -->
    </article>
</main>
```

Here are the steps to follow to add a new `section` element to the article:

1 Open the HTML file in a text editor.
2 Position the cursor immediately after the `<!-- Article content goes here -->` text placeholder, as shown in figure 12.3.

```
24        <main>
25            <article>
26                <h2>Travel Guide to Narnia</h2>
27                <!-- Article content goes here -->
28            </article>
```

Position the cursor here.

Figure 12.3   Position the cursor as shown here.

3 Press Enter or Return to start a new line.

4 Type `<section>`. If you're using a code editor, it should automatically add the `</section>` tag (although you may need to press Tab to make this happen). If not, type `</section>`, and then position the cursor between the `<section>` and `</section>` tags.

5 Press Enter or Return. You now have a new `section` element ready to go, as shown in figure 12.4.

```
24        <main>
25            <article>
26                <h2>Travel Guide to Narnia</h2>
27                <!-- Article content goes here -->
28                <section>
29                    |
30                </section>
```

Figure 12.4   The new `section` element, ready to be filled in

6 Type `<h3>`. If you're using a code editor, it should automatically add the `</h3>` tag (although you may need to press Tab to make this happen). If not, type `</h3>` and then position the cursor between the `<h3>` and `</h3>` tags.

7 Type the section heading or title, as shown in figure 12.5. (You're not adding the paragraphs just yet. I cover that in the next section.)

```
24        <main>
25            <article>
26                <h2>Travel Guide to Narnia</h2>
27                <!-- Article content goes here -->
28                <section>
29                    <h3>How to get there</h3>
30                </section>
31            </article>
```

Figure 12.5   Type a title or heading for the new section.

8 To add more sections, position the cursor immediately after the `</section>` tag of the `section` element you just added and then follow steps 3 through 7.

Your new `section` elements have headings but no text. You'll remedy that situation next.

12.2.5 *Adding new paragraphs to the article, section, or aside*

Whether you're working on your page's `article` element, any `section` element, or the `aside` element, you'll often need to add another paragraph. Here are the steps to do this:

1 Open the HTML file in a text editor.

2 Position the cursor immediately after the end tag of the element after which you want to add the paragraph. For example, if you're working in a `section` element that currently only has an `h3` element heading, you'll position the cursor immediately after the `</h3>` tag, as shown in figure 12.6.

```
24    <main>
25        <article>
26            <h2>Travel Guide to Narnia</h2>
27            <!-- Article content goes here -->
28            <section>
29                <h3>How to get there</h3>
30            </section>
31        </article>
```
Position the cursor here.

Figure 12.6   Position the cursor after the end tag of the element after which you want to add the paragraph.

3 Press Enter or Return to start a new line.

4 Type `<p>`. If you're using a code editor, it should automatically add the `</p>` tag (although you may need to press Tab to make this happen). If not, type `</p>` and then position the cursor between the `<p>` and `</p>` tags.

5 Press Enter or Return. You now have a new `p` element ready for text, as shown in figure 12.7.

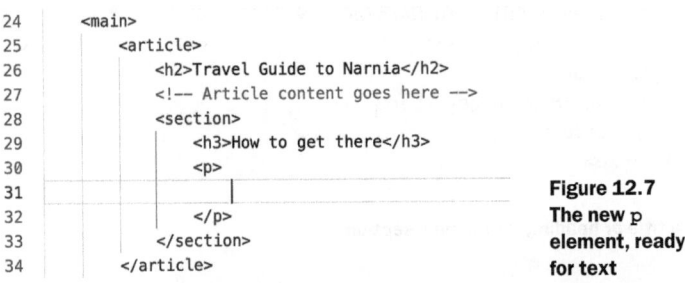

```
24    <main>
25        <article>
26            <h2>Travel Guide to Narnia</h2>
27            <!-- Article content goes here -->
28            <section>
29                <h3>How to get there</h3>
30                <p>
31
32                </p>
33            </section>
34        </article>
```

Figure 12.7
The new p
element, ready
for text

6 Type the paragraph text, as shown in figure 12.8.

```
24    <main>
25        <article>
26            <h2>Travel Guide to Narnia</h2>
27            <!-- Article content goes here -->
28            <section>
29                <h3>How to get there</h3>
30                <p>
31                    The most common way to enter Narnia is through a
                     wardrobe that belongs to an old professor who
                     lives in a large house in the English countryside.
                     The wardrobe is located in a spare room on the
                     second floor, and it contains many fur coats and
                     other clothes. If you push past the coats, you
                     will find yourself in a snowy forest with a
                     lamp-post nearby. This is the border between our
                     world and Narnia.|
32                </p>
33            </section>
34        </article>
```

Figure 12.8   Type a title or heading for the new section.

7 For each new paragraph you want to add, position the cursor immediately after the current paragraph's `</p>` tag and then follow steps 3 through 6.

As you're typing your paragraph text, you may come across special words or phrases that you want the web browser to display in either bold or italics. You learn how to do that in the next section.

12.2.6 *Marking up special words and phrases*

Certain words or phrases in your text are "special" in the sense that they stand apart in some way from the rest of the text. For example, you may want to emphasize a particular word, which you'd normally do by formatting the word with italic type. Similarly, a particular phrase may be important, so to ensure that the reader doesn't miss it, you'd normally format the phrase using bold type.

Although it's certainly possible to instruct ChatGPT to add italics and bold where needed, that can be problematic in many circumstances:

- Your text may use a word or phrase multiple times.
- You may want only the first instance of a word or phrase marked up.
- Your text may include many different words or phrases you want marked up.

In each case, you'd somehow have to find a way to ensure that ChatGPT marked up what you wanted, a task that's not easy to do in practice. Instead, it's actually straightforward to do the marking up yourself manually as you enter your text. The next few sections provide the details.

MARKING UP IMPORTANT TEXT

On your web page, you may want to be sure the reader sees a particular word, phrase, or sentence because it's important. This text may be a vital instruction, a crucial condition, or a similarly significant passage that needs to stand out from the regular text because you don't want the reader to miss it. In HTML, you mark text as important by using the strong element:

```
<strong>important text goes here</strong>
```

All browsers render the text between the `<strong>` and `</strong>` tags in a bold font. The following example shows some web page code with an important passage marked up with the strong element, and figure 12.9 shows that text displayed in bold in the web browser:

```
<p>
    As you enter the room, notice the big, red button to your right.
    <strong>Never press that button!</strong>
</p>
```

As you enter the room, notice the big, red
button to your right. **Never press that button!**

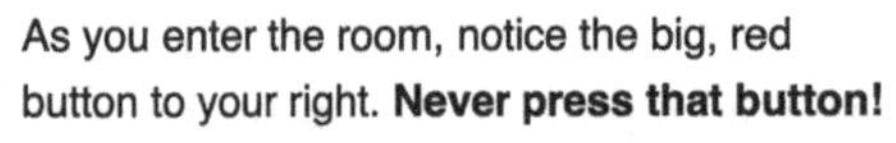

Figure 12.9   Text marked up with the strong element appears as bold in the browser.

A similar markup scenario is the keyword, discussed next.

MARKING UP KEYWORDS

In some cases, you want to draw attention to a word or phrase not because it's important per se but because the text in question plays a role that makes it different from regular text. That text could be a product name, a company name, or an interface element, such as the text associated with a check box or command button. Again, the text you're working with isn't crucial, but it's different in some way, so you want it to look different from the regular page text.

> **TIP** Other candidates for web page keywords include the name of a person (such as the infamous "boldface names" that appear in celebrity gossip columns) and the first few words or the opening sentence of an article.

Each of these items indicates a *keyword* (or *key phrase*) that has meaning beyond the regular page text. In HTML, this type of item is marked up with the b element:

```
<b>keyword</b>
```

Web browsers render the text between the `<b>` and `</b>` tags in a bold font, as shown in the following example and figure 12.10:

```
<p>
    To save your work, pull down the <b>File</b> menu
    and then click <b>Save</b>.
</p>
```

To save your work, pull down the **File** menu and
then click **Save**.

Figure 12.10 Keywords marked up with the b element appear as bold in the browser.

At this point, I imagine you're scratching your head and wondering what the difference is between the `strong` element and the `b` element, because both render as bold
text. That's a fair point, and I'll admit the difference is subtle. I should say it's *semantic* because HTML uses these two separate elements to differentiate between important text and keywords. Why bother? Because it's expected that in the future, screen
readers and other assistive devices will use this semantic distinction to help the visually
impaired make sense of web pages.

MARKING UP EMPHASIZED TEXT

It's often important to emphasize certain words or phrases on a page. This emphasis
tells the reader to read or say the text with added stress. In HTML, you add emphasis to
a word or phrase by marking it up with the `em` (for emphasis) element:

```
<em>text</em>
```

Web browsers render the text between the `<em>` and `</em>` tags in italics, as shown in
the following example and figure 12.11:

```
<p>
    When mixing pie pastry, it's <em>vital</em> that
    your butter is as cold as possible.
</p>
```

When making pie pastry, it's *vital* that your butter is
as cold as possible.

Figure 12.11 Text marked up with the em element is rendered as italic in the browser.

> **NOTE** What's the difference between the `strong` element and the `em` element?
> You use `strong` when the text in question is inherently crucial for the reader;
> you use `em` when the text in question requires enhanced stress to get a point
> across.

MARKING UP ALTERNATIVE TEXT

It's common in prose to need markup for a word or phrase to indicate that it has a
voice, mood, or role that's different from that of the regular text. Common examples
of alternative text are book and movie titles. In HTML, this type of semantic text is
marked up with the `i` (for italics) element:

```
<i>text</i>
```

NOTE   Other examples of alternative text include publication names, technical terms, foreign words and phrases, and a person's thoughts.

Web browsers render such text in italics, as shown in the following example and figure 12.12:

```
<p>
    Let's visit the land of Narnia, first introduced to us by
    C.S. Lewis in <i>The Lion, the Witch, and the Wardrobe</i> (1950).
</p>
```

Let's visit the land of Narnia, first introduced to us by
C.S. Lewis in *The Lion, the Witch, and the Wardrobe*
(1950).

Figure 12.12   **Alternative text marked up with the i element is rendered as italic in the browser.**

You can nest these text-level elements within other text-level elements for extra effect. For example, you can mark up a sentence as important by using the strong element, and within that sentence, you can mark up a word with emphasis by using the em element. The browser will render that word as both bold and italic.

12.2.7 *Starting the article with a drop cap*

You can make your articles stand out from the crowd by starting them with a *drop cap*: the first letter of the first paragraph, formatted to appear much larger than the rest of the paragraph text and positioned so that sits below the text baseline and "drops" a few lines into the paragraph. To get ChatGPT to create a drop cap for you, include an instruction similar to the following in your prompt:

```
Create the HTML and CSS code that renders the following text as a paragraph
with a dark red drop cap: "Starting an article doesn't have to be boring!
Get your text off to a great beginning by rocking the opening paragraph with
a giant first letter. You can use either a <i>raised cap</i> (also called a
<i>stick-up cap</i> or simply an <i>initial</i>) that sits on the baseline,
or you can use a <i>drop cap</i> that sits below the baseline and nestles
into the text."
```

Here's the HTML generated by ChatGPT:

```
<p>
    <span class="drop-cap">S</span>tarting an article doesn't have to be
    boring! Get your text off to a great beginning by rocking the opening
    paragraph with a giant first letter. In particular, you can use a
    <i>drop cap</i> that sits below the baseline and nestles into the text.
</p>
```

The keys are the <span> and </span> tags that surround the first letter of the paragraph. The span element uses the drop-cap class, which looks like this in the CSS code:

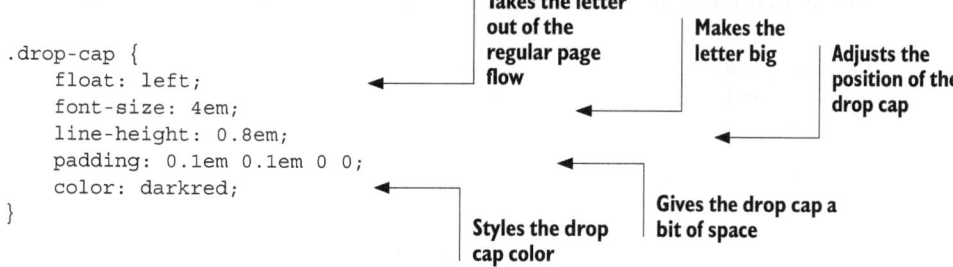

```
.drop-cap {
    float: left;
    font-size: 4em;
    line-height: 0.8em;
    padding: 0.1em 0.1em 0 0;
    color: darkred;
}
```

Takes the letter out of the regular page flow

Makes the letter big

Adjusts the position of the drop cap

Gives the drop cap a bit of space

Styles the drop cap color

Figure 12.13 shows how the drop cap looks in the browser.

S tarting an article doesn't have to be boring! Get your text off to a great beginning by rocking the opening paragraph with a giant first letter. In particular, you can use a *drop cap* that sits below the baseline and nestles into the text.

Figure 12.13   An opening paragraph of an article with a drop cap

Drop caps are a great way to add a professional flair to your web pages. Just remember that you only use a drop cap for the first letter of the first paragraph of an article.

12.2.8 *Laying out the article with CSS Grid*

When I introduced Flexbox in chapter 10, I mentioned that the default way the web browser lays out HTML block-level elements—including the header, nav, main, section, aside, footer, and p elements—is by stacking them on top of each other. The first block is on top, the second block sits below it, the third block goes below that, and so on. It's not a very inspiring look!

Flexbox enables you to break out of that default layout in one dimension (horizontally *or* vertically), but if you want to lay out your page in two dimensions (horizontally *and* vertically), you need to turn to a different layout technique called CSS Grid.

The good news about CSS Grid is that you can ask ChatGPT to generate all the required code for you by including a simple instruction in the CSS part of your prompt:

```
The header is a two-column CSS Grid container with the logo in the left
column and the site title and tagline in the right column.
```

That's it! However, for the purposes of this chapter's project, I'll mention one important aspect of the CSS Grid code that ChatGPT generates. If you refer to figure 12.2, notice these two things:

- Within the main element, the aside element is laid out to the right of the article element.
- The article element takes up more horizontal space than the aside element.

This is all done with CSS Grid. To understand how it works, first examine the HTML:

```
<main>
    <article>
        Article content goes here
    </article>

    <aside>
        Aside content goes here
    </aside>
</main>
```

Normally the web browser would stack the article element on top of the aside element, and both would be the full width of the main element. You can break out of that default layout with an instruction to ChatGPT similar to the following:

```
The main element is a two-column CSS Grid container where the article element
column is twice the width of the aside element column.
```

In this case, the resulting CSS Grid code puts the aside element to the right of the article element and adjusts the widths of the elements by defining a two-column grid for the main element:

```
main {
    display: grid;                         ◄──  Sets up the main
    grid-template-columns: 2fr 1fr;             element as a grid
}                                               container

                                          ◄──  Divides the grid container
                                               into two columns
```

The article element comes first in the HTML, so it is assigned to the left column, and the article element is assigned to the right column. The key here is the 2fr 1fr value for the grid-template-columns property. This strange-looking value defines the relative widths of the two columns as follows:

1   Take all the horizontal space available to the main element.
2   Divide that horizontal space evenly into three portions.
3   Give two of those portions to the first column.
4   Give the remaining portion to the second column.

This gives you a bit of freedom to adjust these relative widths to suit your own page. For example, if you'd prefer that the article element have three units of the available space and the aside element just one unit, you can modify the rule like so:

```
main {
    display: grid;
    grid-template-columns: 3fr 1fr;
}
```

As you learn in the next section, although CSS Grid makes your page responsive to browser window size changes, it's not quite enough to make the article page display well on all screens.

12.2.9 Adjusting the article page layout for small screens

The `fr` units I introduced in the previous section are known as *relative* measurements because the value of, say, `1fr` depends on the available width (assuming you're working with grid columns) in the grid container. This makes your page responsive because when the width of the grid container changes (perhaps because the width of the browser window changes), the widths of the columns change automatically relative to the new width.

That works well for relatively large screens (say, tablets, laptops, and desktops), but it can be a problem on small screens, such as a smartphone in portrait mode. To understand what I mean, examine figure 12.14, which is this chapter's article page displayed on a smartphone. Notice in particular that the two columns are narrow, making the text difficult to read.

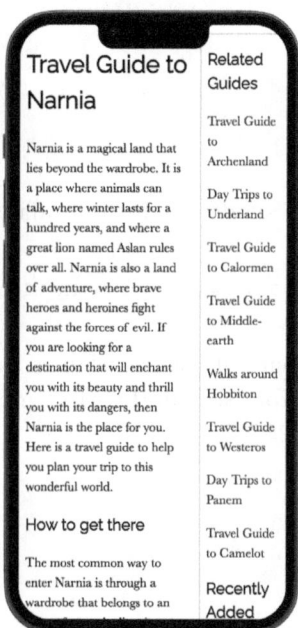

Figure 12.14 On a smartphone screen, the text columns can become too narrow for comfortable reading.

This may seem like an unsolvable problem, but with CSS you can create what's known as an *adaptive layout*, which is a layout that changes its properties based on some feature of the device screen, such as its width. With an adaptive layout, you can solve the problem shown in figure 12.14 by asking questions about the width of the browser viewport (the part of the browser window that displays the web page).

For example, you may ask, "Is the viewport width less than 500 pixels?" If the answer is no, you leave the layout as it is; if the answer is yes, you can tell the browser to display the article as a single column, where the `aside` element comes after the `article` element but both take up the full width of the screen.

You can ask these and many other types of questions by defining media queries in your CSS. A *media query* is an expression accompanied by a code block consisting of one or more style rules. The expression interrogates some feature of the screen, such as its width. If that expression is true for the current device, the browser applies the media query's style rules; if the expression is false, the browser ignores the media query's rules.

Here's the general syntax for a media query:

```
@media (expression) {
    Rules to apply if expression is true go here
}
```

The `expression` is most often `min-width` or `max-width` followed by a colon and a value. For example, if you want to apply styles on a screen no wider than a specified value, use `max-width`. The following code tells the browser to display the `main` element as a one-column grid whenever the screen width is less than or equal to 500 px:

```
@media (max-width: 500px) {
    main {
        display: grid;
        grid-template-columns: 1fr;
    }
}
```

To ask ChatGPT to include a media query in your CSS code, you include an instruction such as the following in your prompt:

```
For screens with width less than or equal to 500px, make the main element a
one-column grid.
```

Similarly, if you want to apply styles on a screen that's at least as wide as a specified value, use `min-width`. The following code sets the font size on the `h1` element whenever the screen width is greater than or equal to 1,024 px:

```
@media (min-width: 1024px) {
    h1 {
        font-size: 72px;
    }
}
```

To ask ChatGPT to include this media query in your CSS code, you include an instruction such as the following in your prompt:

```
For screens with width greater than or equal to 1024px, make the h1 element
font size 72px.
```

Later, after I show you the final article page layout (refer to figure 12.16), I'll also show you how the page displays on a smartphone (figure 12.17) to verify that the page has, indeed, adapted to the smaller screen by switching to a one-column layout.

Now you know everything you need to prompt ChatGPT to build an article page, as described in the following section.

12.2.10 *Crafting the prompt for the article page*

This chapter's project is an article page that displays a travel guide for a place from a work of literature. Before proceeding, I assume you have the following at hand:

- The header content, such as the website logo, title, and tagline
- The Google Fonts typefaces you want to use for the headings and text
- The keywords of the colors you want to use for the page backgrounds and text

Refer to chapter 3 to learn more about each of these design elements and how to prompt ChatGPT for title, typeface, and color suggestions.

To start your prompt, tell ChatGPT that you want to construct a web page and that you want it to generate the code for you:

```
I want to build a web page for an article. I don't know how to code, so I
need you to provide the code for me.

First, write the HTML code for a web page that includes the following:
```

Now go through the page content, item by item, including the following (refer to figure 12.15):

- A header that includes your website logo, title, and tagline
- A navigation element with links to other site areas
- A main element that includes an `article` element and an `aside` element arranged in two columns
- A footer that includes a copyright notice

Figure 12.15   The sections of the article page

Notice that in this project, you're not going to include the page content—that is, the sections and paragraphs that form the article and the paragraphs that form the sidebar—in your prompt. Instead, once you have the page skeleton shown in figure 12.15, you'll add the content manually, as I explain in section 12.3.

Next, ask ChatGPT to generate the CSS:

Second, in a separate file please write the CSS code for the following:

You then specify the page formatting, including the following:

- The page background color and text color
- The type sizes you want to use for the headings and page text
- The fonts to use for the headings and regular page text
- That the layout should use CSS Grid
- That the layout should adapt to smaller screens

Here's an example prompt for my own article page:

I want to build a web page for an article. I don't know how to code, so I need you to provide the code for me.

First, write the HTML code for a web page that includes the following:
* A header element that includes an image named logo.png, which is stored in the "images" subdirectory, the site title "Dream Vacations" and the site tagline "Travel guides to imaginary places".
* A navigation element that includes the following links:
* Home (links to index.html)
* Sci-Fi (links to sci-fi.html)
* Fantasy (links to fantasy.html)
* Children's (links to childrens.html)
* Literary (links to literary.html)
* A main section that contains an article element and an aside element.
* The article element title is the second-level heading "Travel Guide to Narnia".
* The aside element title is the third-level heading "Related Guides".
* A footer element that includes the Copyright symbol, followed by "Dream Vacations, LLC".
* In the page head section, include the tag <meta charset="utf-8">.
* In the page head section, include the tag <meta name="viewport" content="width=device-width, initial-scale=1">.

Second, in a separate file write the CSS code for the following:
* The page text uses font size 20px and the Baskerville font from Google Fonts.
* The header has background color lightblue and 24px padding.
* The site title is 64px and uses the Raleway font from Google Fonts.
* The site tagline is 32px and uses the Raleway font from Google Fonts.
* The second-level heading is 36px and uses the Raleway font from Google Fonts.
* The third-level headings are 24px and use the Raleway font from Google Fonts.
* The article title and the aside title have a 10px top margin.

```
* The aside has a 1px, solid, lightblue border.
* The nav, article, aside, and footer elements have 10px padding.
* The footer has a 1px, lightblue top border and a 10px top margin.
* The page has a maximum width of 800px and is centered within the browser
window.
* Style all links with color midnightblue and no underline.
* Lay out the page as follows:
 * The header is a two-column CSS Grid container with the logo in the left
column and the site title and tagline in the right column.
 * The navigation bar is a row Flexbox container.
 * The main element is a two-column CSS Grid container; the article element
column is twice the width of the aside element column; there is a gap of 10px
between the columns.
* For screens with width less than or equal to 500px, do the following:
 * Convert each two-column grid into a one-column grid.
 * Make the site title 40px and the site tagline 24px.
 * Give the site logo a maximum width of 150px.
 * Center the header content.
```

I used Copilot in Precise mode to submit my prompt. The generated code produced the page shown in figure 12.16.

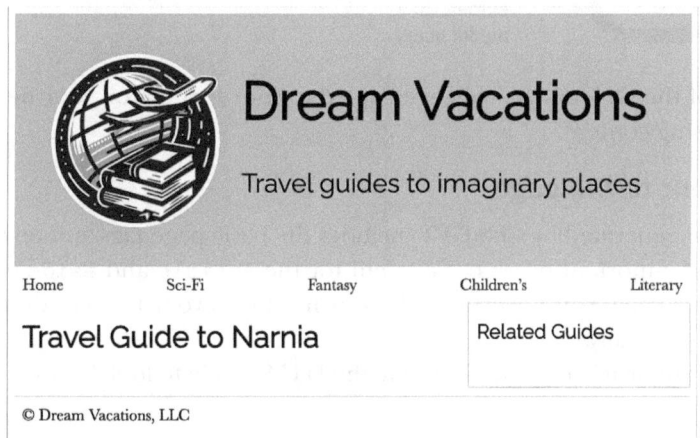

Figure 12.16 My article page before adding the content

Figure 12.16 shows how the page looks on a desktop monitor. To check that the media query in the prompt is working properly, you need to load the page using a smartphone browser, as shown in figure 12.17. In this case, the media query has adapted the page as follows:

- The header is now a one-column grid container.
- The maximum size of the site logo has been reduced.
- The font size of the site title and tagline have been reduced.
- The main element is now a one-column grid container.

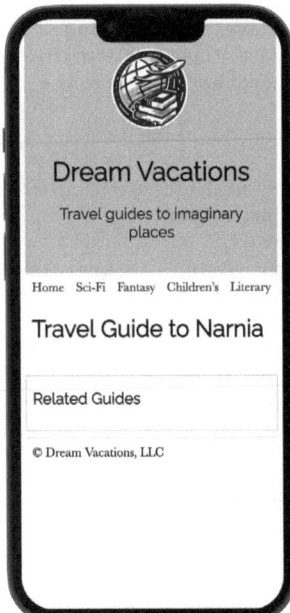

**Figure 12.17
The article
skeleton adapted
to a smartphone
screen via a
media query**

With the code of the skeleton article page copied to your text editor, your next task is
to fill in the missing content.

12.3   *Adding content to the page*

The HTML code generated by ChatGPT includes the basic page tags and text, but it's
missing the most important parts: the content for the `article` and `aside` elements.
To complete your page, you need to load index.html into your text editor and then
add the content manually.

First, to add your article content, examine the HTML code to look for the following
tags:

```
<article>
    <h2>Travel Guide to Narnia</h2>
    <!-- Article content goes here -->
</article>
```

The key line here is `<!-- Article content goes here -->`, which is a placeholder for the article content. (The tags `<!--` and `-->` create a *comment*, which is text
that describes the HTML code but doesn't appear when the page is displayed in the
browser.) You type your content below that line. In most cases, you'll add the following:

- A set of `<p>` and `</p>` tags below the article title (the `h2` element) and the text for
  your article introduction between those tags. Feel free to add two or more such
  paragraphs as needed.

- After the introductory paragraph (or paragraphs), add one or more `section` elements, each of which has a third-level (`h3`) heading, followed by one or more paragraphs (with each one between a set of `<p>` and `</p>` tags).

Once your article is complete, add your sidebar content. To begin, examine the HTML code to look for the following tags:

```
<aside>
    <h3>Related Guides</h3>
    <!-- Related guides go here -->
</aside>
```

Again, the important line here is `<!—Related guides go here -->` (your text will be different depending on the heading you used in your prompt). This line is a place-holder for the `aside` content. You type your content below that line, and your content may be a set of paragraphs, a list of links, or something else related to the article. Feel free to add new `h3` elements as needed by your content. Figure 12.18 shows the top part of my article page fleshed out with content.

Figure 12.18   My article page, now with added content

If you're happy with your article page, you may prefer to skip the rest of this chapter and deploy your page to the web (as I describe in appendix B). If you want to know more about the article page code, keep reading.

12.4   Examining the article page code

The next two sections offer annotated guides to the HTML and CSS code behind the article skeleton page shown earlier in figures 12.16 and 12.17. I'll begin in the next section with the HTML code.

> **NOTE**   The generated HTML and CSS code for my article page are available on this book's website (www.manning.com/books/build-a-website-with-chatgpt) and in the book's GitHub repository: https://github.com/paulmcfe/websites-with-chatgpt.

12.4.1   Examining the HTML

Here's an annotated version of the HTML code that ChatGPT generated for my article page:

```
<!DOCTYPE html>
<html>
<head>
    <meta charset="utf-8">
    <meta name="viewport"                              Helps the page display
        content="width=device-width, initial-scale=1">  properly on mobile devices
    <title>Dream Vacations</title>
    <link rel="stylesheet" type="text/css" href="styles.css">   Tells the web
</head>                                                          browser where to
<body>                                                          find the CSS code
    <header>
        <img src="images/logo.png" alt="Logo">        Site logo
        <div>
            <h1>Dream Vacations</h1>                   Site title         Page header
            <p>Travel guides to imaginary places</p>
        </div>                                         Site tagline
    </header>
    <nav>
        <a href="index.html">Home</a>
        <a href="sci-fi.html">Sci-Fi</a>
        <a href="fantasy.html">Fantasy</a>            Navigation bar
        <a href="childrens.html">Children's</a>
        <a href="literary.html">Literary</a>
    </nav>
    <main>                                             Article
        <article>                                      title
            <h2>Travel Guide to Narnia</h2>                         Article
            <!-- Article content goes here -->                     element      Main
        </article>                      Placeholder for                          element
        <aside>                         the article content
            <h3>Related Guides</h3>                    Aside        Aside
            <!-- Related guides go here -->            title        element
        </aside>                        Placeholder for
    </main>                             the aside content
    <footer>
        © Dream Vacations, LLC                                     Page footer
    </footer>
```

```
</body>
</html>
```

Note that the HTML code includes the following line:

```
<link rel="stylesheet" href="styles.css">
```

This tag tells the web browser where to find the CSS code, which I describe in the next section.

12.4.2 Examining the CSS

Here's an annotated version of the CSS code that ChatGPT generated for my article page:

```
@import url('https://fonts.googleapis.com/css2?family=
➡Baskerville:wght@400&family=Raleway:wght@400&display=swap');
```
Imports the Baskerville and Raleway typefaces from Google Fonts

```
body {
    font-size: 20px;
    font-family: 'Baskerville', serif;
    max-width: 960px;
    margin: 0 auto;
}
```
Styles the text size and font, sets the maximum width, and centers the page

```
header {
    display: grid;
    grid-template-columns: auto 1fr;
    background-color: lightblue;
    padding: 24px;
}
```
Sets up the header as a two-column grid

Styles the header background color and padding

```
header h1 {
    font-size: 64px;
    font-family: 'Raleway', sans-serif;
}
```
Styles the site title font size and font

```
header p {
    font-size: 32px;
    font-family: 'Raleway', sans-serif;
}
```
Styles the site tagline font size and font

```
nav {
    display: flex;
    justify-content: space-between;
}
```
Sets the nav as a Flexbox container with the items evenly spaced

```
a {
    color: midnightblue;
    text-decoration: none;
}
```
Sets the color of the links and removes the underline

```
main {
    display: grid;
    grid-template-columns: 2fr 1fr;
    gap: 10px;
```
Sets up the main element as a two-column grid

```
}

article h2, aside h3 {
    margin-top: 10px;
}

aside {
    border: 1px solid lightblue;
}

nav, article, aside, footer {
    padding: 10px;
}

h2 {
    font-size: 36px;
    font-family: 'Raleway', sans-serif;
}

h3 {
    font-size: 24px;
    font-family: 'Raleway', sans-serif;
}

footer {
    border-top: 1px solid lightblue;
    margin-top: 10px;
}

@media (max-width: 500px) {
    header {
        grid-template-columns: 1fr;
        text-align: center;
    }

    header img {
        max-width: 150px;
        margin-left: auto;
        margin-right: auto;
        display: block;
    }

    header h1 {
        font-size: 32px;
    }

    header p {
        font-size: 24px;
    }

    main {
        grid-template-columns: 1fr;
    }
}
```

◄── **Adds a margin above the article and aside titles**

◄── **Styles the aside with a border**

◄── **Adds padding to the nav, article, aside, and footer elements**

| **Styles the h2 font size and font**

| **Styles the h3 font size and font**

| **Styles the footer with a top border and margin**

The media query for screens 500 px wide and less

You can refer to the HTML and CSS annotations from the previous two sections to help customize your web page code, as I describe in the next section.

12.5 *Customizing the article page*

Here are some customization suggestions for the HTML code:

- If you'd prefer to have the sidebar on the left, you need to change both the HTML and the CSS. First, in the HTML code, move the `aside` element so it comes just before the `article` element:

```
<main>
    <aside>
        <h3>Related Guides</h3>
        <!-- Related guides go here -->
    </aside>
    <article>
        <h2>Travel Guide to Narnia</h2>
        <!-- Article content goes here -->
    </article>
</main>
```

  Second, in the CSS, switch the `main` element's `grid-template-columns` value from `2fr 1fr` to `1fr 2fr`, as shown here:

```
main {
    display: grid;
    grid-template-columns: 1fr 2fr;
    gap: 10px;
}
```

- In the header, you can edit the title and tagline. Just be sure not to edit or delete the associated HTML tags, `<h1>` and `</h1>` and `<p>` and `</p>`.
- In the main section, you can edit the article title, but don't mess with the associated HTML tags, `<h2>` and `</h2>`.
- In the footer section of the HTML code, you can add links to your social media accounts, as I describe in chapter 4.

Now, here are a few customization ideas for the CSS code:

- For any color value, you can change the existing color to a different color keyword.
- For any font size value, you can change the number to increase or decrease the font size. Just make sure you leave the `px` unit in place.
- For any padding or margin value, you can change the number to increase or decrease the padding or margins. In each case, be sure to leave the `px` unit in place.
- To make your page code more accessible, consider converting all px measurements to rem measurements. 1 rem is by default equivalent to 16 px, so 20 px is 1.25 rem, 24 px is 1.5 rem, 32 px is 2 rem, 48 px is 3 rem, and so on. The rem unit is more accessible because it measures font sizes relative to the default font size the browser user has defined in their browser settings.

Summary

- Use an article layout if the writing is focused on a single topic and can be divided into multiple subtopics.
- The main HTML page layout elements are `header`, `nav`, `main`, `article`, `aside`, `footer`, and `p`.
- Use the `article` element to mark up a complete, self-contained composition, similar to a newspaper or magazine article. This element can also apply to a review, a blog entry, a forum post, or an essay.
- Use the `aside` element to mark up a page sidebar area that contains content that's indirectly related to the page's unique content, such as a list of links to related site pages, the latest site news, a social media feed, or advertisements.
- Use the `strong` element to mark up important text, use the `b` element to mark up keywords, use the `em` element to add emphasis to text, and use the `i` element to mark up alternative text.
- Use CSS Grid to lay out a page in two dimensions.
- For best results, your page prompt should be as specific as possible, including colors, font sizes, and heading levels.
- Save the generated HTML to the index.html file and the generated CSS to the filename suggested by ChatGPT in the HTML code, usually styles.css.

Coding an interactive course catalog

13

This chapter covers

- Getting Excel data ready to use on the web
- Learning about the JSON data format
- Using ChatGPT to convert Excel data to JSON
- Using JSON data to make a web page interactive
- Crafting a ChatGPT prompt to a course catalog page
- Examining and customizing the ChatGPT-generated code

The projects you've seen so far in this book have produced useful and reasonably attractive web pages. However, you may have noticed one thing that's common to the pages you've built with the help of ChatGPT: that's right, they just kind of sit there. Granted, there's nothing wrong with a page that doesn't do much, if that page offers information that's useful, informative, or fun. However, it can really add to a page's appeal if the page is interactive in some way. And by "interactive," I mean readers can manipulate the page to change what data is displayed. For example, on a page with lots of data, you might include controls that enable users to display just a subset of the data or to search the data.

In this chapter, you first learn how to get data onto a web page without having to configure a web server, a hideously complex task that you'll be grateful you can skip. In particular, this chapter shows you how to take data from an Excel file and turn it into a format that can be loaded into a page. The example data is a set of college courses, and the goal is a page that enables visitors to search, sort, and filter this data. You then put all this to work to create a detailed prompt for ChatGPT to generate the code for a course catalog web page.

This chapter provides annotated versions of the ChatGPT-generated HTML, CSS, and JavaScript to help you understand how the course catalog works. You also get a few useful tips for customizing the code.

13.1   Checking out this chapter's project

As I mentioned in the introduction, this chapter's project is a single-page course catalog for a fictional university. The final page will include the following components:

- A header element that includes the website logo and title
- A main element that begins with the controls for filtering, sorting, and searching the catalog
- For each course, a vertical element—sometimes called a *tile*—that displays the course image, title, ID, instructor, department, semester, and description
- A footer element that includes a copyright notice

Figure 13.1 shows an example course catalog created with code supplied by ChatGPT. The example page is a collection of tiles, each of which holds the information for a college course, this kind of layout can be used for other types of content, such as a product catalog, a list of available services, customer orders, or just about any type of structured data. The common denominator in each of these projects is that the underlying web page data resides originally in an Excel spreadsheet file, so you need to know how to get data from Excel into a format the web browser can understand.

Figure 13.1 A course catalog generated by ChatGPT

13.2 Getting data from Excel

When you want to display data on a web page, one of the most common problems is data in a format that's not compatible with the web. The data could be in a table in a word processing document, a presentation, text in a text file, or scattered notes in a note-taking app. In this project, I assume the data is in an Excel file, and getting that data ready is the subject of the next section.

13.2.1 Getting your Excel data ready

Excel is a very common application for light database needs because it's familiar to most people, data entry is relatively straightforward, and the row-and-column format of a worksheet mirrors the row-and-column format required by most data. To use Excel data on the web, you need to convert it to a suitable format. I'll get to that conversion soon, but for now, you need to make sure your Excel data is ready. Here, "ready" means the Excel data must have the following characteristics:

- The data is either a range or a range that has been converted to a table.
- If the data is a range (that is, not a table), one of the following must be true:
  - There is no other data on the worksheet.
  - The data resides in a named range.
- Each column of data has a unique heading.

Figure 13.2 shows the Excel data I'll be using as an example for this project. The data is a collection of college courses and store the following for each course:

- The course ID
- The course title
- A description of the course
- The name of the course instructor
- The name of the department offering the course
- The semester in which the course is offered

The data resides in a regular Excel range; there is no other data in the worksheet, and each column has a unique heading.

Before you learn how to convert such Excel data to a usable format, you need to understand that format, which is the topic of the next section.

	A	B	C	D	E	F
1	Course ID	Title	Description	Instructor	Department	Semester
2	AI101	The Art of Chatting: Building Conversational AIs	Dive into the quirky world of chatbots and virtual companions. Le	Prof. Kaitlyn Wong	Artificial Intelligence	1
3	AI102	Robot Overlords 101: An Introduction to AI Ethics	Explore the moral dilemmas of our future robot overlords. From c	Prof. Thiago Silva	Artificial Intelligence	2
4	AI103	Dreaming in Code: AI for Creative Minds	Unleash the power of AI to create art, music, and literature. Learn	Prof. Anika Singh	Artificial Intelligence	3
5	AI201	Time-Traveling AIs: The Future of Historical Research	Venture into the past with AI as your guide. Discover how artificia	Prof. Lerato Mbeki	Artificial Intelligence	1
6	AI202	Cooking with AIs: Culinary Arts of the Future	Spice up your cooking skills with AI assistants. Learn how to collal	Prof. Kaitlyn Wong	Artificial Intelligence	2
7	AI203	AI in Wonderland: Programming the Imagination	Dive down the rabbit hole to explore AI systems that can imagine,	Prof. Thiago Silva	Artificial Intelligence	3
8	AI301	The Emotional Circuit: Building Empathetic AIs	Can machines feel? This course examines the development of AI t	Prof. Anika Singh	Artificial Intelligence	1
9	AI302	Mind Melding: The Intersection of AI and Telepathy	Explore the futuristic realm where AI meets telepathy. Learn abou	Prof. Lerato Mbeki	Artificial Intelligence	2
10	AI401	The AI Zoo: Designing Digital Ecosystems	Create virtual habitats where digital creatures evolve and interact.	Prof. Kaitlyn Wong	Artificial Intelligence	3
11	AI402	Ghost in the Machine: AI and Paranormal Research	Investigate the uncanny valley with AI. Learn how artificial intellig	Prof. Sven Eriksson	Artificial Intelligence	1
12	AR101	Magic Lenses: An Introduction to Augmented Reality	Peek into the looking glass of AR. Learn how to blend digital fanta	Prof. Amina Patel	Augmented Reality	1
13	AR102	Virtual Graffiti: Painting the Town with AR	Unleash your inner artist on a city-scale canvas. This course teach	Prof. Yuto Nakamura	Augmented Reality	2
14	AR103	AR for Wizards and Warriors: Creating Fantasy Worlds	Craft enchanting realms where dragons fly overhead and treasure	Prof. Elena Kuznetsova	Augmented Reality	3
15	AR201	Fashion Forward: The Future of Wearables and AR	Project your inner style into the world with AR wearables. Design	Prof. Elena Kuznetsova	Augmented Reality	1
16	AR202	Ghost Hunters: AR for Exploring the Paranormal	Equip yourself with AR to seek spirits and specters. This course gu	Prof. Amina Patel	Augmented Reality	2
17	AR203	Educational Illusions: Learning Enhanced with AR	Transform classrooms into interactive learning environments. Dis	Prof. Carlos Rivera	Augmented Reality	3
18	AR301	Augmented Athletics: Sports Training with AR	Elevate your game with virtual coaches and performance overlays	Prof. Carlos Rivera	Augmented Reality	1
19	AR302	The ARt of Storytelling: Immersive Narratives	Dive into stories that surround you. Learn to craft narratives whe	Prof. Elena Kuznetsova	Augmented Reality	2
20	AR401	Spatial Computing: Designing Interfaces for AR	Rethink how we interact with digital information. This course cov	Prof. Amina Patel	Augmented Reality	3
21	AR402	The Architect's Guide to AR: Building the Invisible	Construct digital structures that coexist with reality. From virtual	Prof. Fatima Al-Farsi	Augmented Reality	1
22	AD101	Autopilots and Artifacts: The Basics of Autonomous Devices	Embark on a journey with self-piloting gadgets. Learn the A to Z of aut	Prof. Thiago Silva	Autonomous Devices	1
23	AD102	Robots with Personality: AI and Machine Learning for Autonomo	Dive into the digital psyche of robots. Explore how AI and machine lea	Prof. Kaitlyn Wong	Autonomous Devices	2
24	AD103	Drones and the Art of Aerial Acrobatics	Soar through the skies with advanced drone piloting. Master the art o	Prof. Anika Singh	Autonomous Devices	3
25	AD201	Underwater Explorers: Autonomous Submarines and Oceanograp	Plunge into the deep blue with autonomous submarines. Discover the	Prof. Sven Eriksson	Autonomous Devices	1
26	AD202	Self-Driving Cars: The Road to Autonomy	Buckle up for a ride into the future of transportation. Learn about the	Prof. Thiago Silva	Autonomous Devices	2

◄ ►   College of the Future - Courses   +

Figure 13.2   The Excel data I'll be using in this project

13.2.2 *Getting to know the JSON data format*

You see later in this chapter that the driver behind a data-driven web page is JavaScript, which can grab the contents of a file, process the data the file contains, display that data on the web page, and enable you to set up controls to perform searches, filters, and other data manipulations. The starting point for all this is the file that JavaScript reads. JavaScript can work with multiple file types, but the easiest and most convenient for our purposes is the JSON (JavaScript Object Notation) format. JSON (it's pronounced like the name *Jason*) is one of the most common ways data is handled on web pages.

One of the main reasons JSON is so popular is that the data is plain text, so it can be created and edited using a garden-variety text or code editor. In the next two sections, you learn how to convince ChatGPT to automatically create JSON data from an Excel file so you don't need to get your hands dirty with JSON code for this project. However, if you'd like to know how to work with JSON data directly, the rest of this section provides the details.

As I mentioned, JSON data is plain text. However, that text must be configured using the correct JSON syntax. Here's a general look at the syntax for JSON data:

```
{
    "property1": value1,
    "property2": value2,
    ...
    "propertyX": valueX
}
```

What you have here is a set of one or more property–value pairs. For this project, the property–value pairs come from the original Excel data as follows:

- The name of each property comes from the heading of a column in the range of Excel data.

- The values assigned to the properties come from a single row in the Excel range.
- Each property name is surrounded by double quotation marks (").
- Each value is usually a string surrounded by double quotation marks, but it can also be a number or any other JavaScript data type.
- The property–value pairs are separated by commas.
- The block of property–value pairs is surrounded by braces ({ and }).

Here's some example JSON data, which corresponds to the first row of the Excel data shown earlier in figure 13.2:

```
{
    "Course ID": "AI101",
    "Title": "The Art of Chatting: Building Conversational AIs",
    "Description": "Dive into the quirky world of chatbots and virtual
companions. Learn how to design AIs that can outwit humans in a battle of
banter, negotiate pizza toppings, and philosophically ponder the existence of
the internet.",
    "Instructor": "Prof. Kaitlyn Wong",
    "Department": "Artificial Intelligence",
    "Semester": 1
}
```

This is just a single row from the original Excel range. For ranges that have multiple rows, ChatGPT will generate an array of JSON objects: a comma separates each JSON object, and the entire set of data is surrounded by square brackets ([and]). Here's a partial example:

```
[
    {
        "Course ID": "AI101",
        "Title": "The Art of Chatting: Building Conversational AIs",
        "Description": "Dive into the quirky world of chatbots and virtual
companions. Learn how to design AIs that can outwit humans in a battle of
banter, negotiate pizza toppings, and philosophically ponder the existence of
the internet.",
        "Instructor": "Prof. Kaitlyn Wong",
        "Department": "Artificial Intelligence",
        "Semester": 1
    },
    {
        "Course ID": "AI102",
        "Title": "Robot Overlords 101: An Introduction to AI Ethics",
        "Description": "Explore the moral dilemmas of our future robot
overlords. From deciding who gets the last piece of cake to governing a small
island, this course tackles the hard ethical questions.",
        "Instructor": "Prof. Thiago Silva",
        "Department": "Artificial Intelligence",
        "Semester": 2
    },
    {
        "Course ID": "AI103",
        "Title": "Dreaming in Code: AI for Creative Minds",
```

```
        "Description": "Unleash the power of AI to create art, music, and
literature. Learn how algorithms can be inspired by dreams and how to
interpret the surreal artworks produced by silicon brains.",
        "Instructor": "Prof. Anika Singh",
        "Department": "Artificial Intelligence",
        "Semester": 3
    },
...
    {
        "Course ID": "AI402",
        "Title": "Ghost in the Machine: AI and Paranormal Research",
        "Description": "Investigate the uncanny valley with AI. Learn how
artificial intelligence is used to explore paranormal activities, communicate
with spirits, and debunk or prove age-old myths.",
        "Instructor": "Prof. Sven Eriksson",
        "Department": "Artificial Intelligence",
        "Semester": 1
    }
]
```

ChatGPT needs some data to work with, of course, so getting your Excel data uploaded is the subject of the next section.

13.2.3 *Uploading your Excel file to ChatGPT*

The first step to converting your Excel data to JSON format is to upload the Excel spreadsheet file to ChatGPT.

NOTE   As I write this, the capability to upload files is only available to ChatGPT Plus subscribers.

Here are the steps to follow:

1 Sign in to your ChatGPT Plus account.
2 Launch a new ChatGPT 4 chat session.
3 On the left side of the message text box, click the Attach Files icon (the paperclip; refer to figure 13.3) to display the Open dialog.

> 📎 Message ChatGPT...

Figure 13.3   Click Attach Files (the paperclip) to upload your Excel file.

4 Locate and select the Excel file that contains the data you want to convert.
5 Click Open. ChatGPT uploads the file, and an icon for the file appears in your chat, as shown in figure 13.4.

Figure 13.4 **The uploaded Excel file appears as an icon in the chat transcript.**

With your Excel file attached to the chat, you're ready to prompt ChatGPT to convert your data to the JSON format.

13.2.4 *Prompting ChatGPT to convert your Excel data to JSON*

ChatGPT—or, at least, the version of the chatbot you get with a ChatGPT Plus subscription—has excellent and robust data-processing capabilities. Those include

- Extracting the data from an Excel spreadsheet file
- Converting that data to the JSON format
- Writing the converted data to a JSON file (which uses the .json file extension)

As with all things ChatGPT, you enable these capabilities using a prompt. When you're ready to write your prompt, note that there are several common scenarios to consider:

- *The Excel data you want to convert to JSON resides either in a named range or in a named table.* In this case, you can use the range or table name in your prompt:

  ```
  In the uploaded Excel file, please convert the range named "Crypto" to
  JSON format and output the result as a JSON file.
  ```

- *The Excel file contains a single worksheet, and that worksheet contains nothing but the range of data you want to convert to JSON.* In this case, a prompt such as the following should do the trick:

  ```
  In the uploaded Excel file, please convert the range to JSON format and
  output the result as a JSON file.
  ```

  This is the prompt you can use for the example Excel file included with this chapter's sample files.

- *The Excel file contains multiple worksheets, but the range you want to convert is in the first worksheet.* When you don't specify a worksheet, ChatGPT automatically converts a range in the first worksheet, so you can use a prompt such as the following:

  ```
  In the uploaded Excel file, please convert the range to JSON format and
  output the result as a JSON file.
  ```

- *The Excel file contains multiple worksheets, and your range is not in the first worksheet.* In this case, your prompt needs to specify the name of the worksheet that contains your data:

In the uploaded Excel file, please convert the range in the worksheet named
"My Data" to JSON format and output the result as a JSON file.

When you submit your prompt, ChatGPT goes to work analyzing the Excel file, extracting the data, and converting that data to JSON format. When this work is complete,
ChatGPT lets you know and offers a download link for the resulting JSON file, as shown
in figure 13.5. Click the link to download the JSON file to your computer.

**Figure 13.5   When ChatGPT has converted your Excel data to JSON, it offers a link to download
the JSON file.**

It's a good idea at this point to take a quick look at the downloaded JSON file to make
sure ChatGPT got things right. Double-click the file to load it into whatever app is the
default on your computer for this file type. You should see your data in the JSON format; figure 13.6 shows an example.

```
1   [
2       {
3           "Course ID": "AI101",
4           "Title": "The Art of Chatting: Building Conversational AIs",
5           "Description": "Dive into the quirky world of chatbots and virtual companions. Learn how to design AIs that can
                outwit humans in a battle of banter, negotiate pizza toppings, and philosophically ponder the existence of the
                internet.",
6           "Instructor": "Prof. Kaitlyn Wong",
7           "Department": "Artificial Intelligence",
8           "Semester": 1
9       },
10      {
11          "Course ID": "AI102",
12          "Title": "Robot Overlords 101: An Introduction to AI Ethics",
13          "Description": "Explore the moral dilemmas of our future robot overlords. From deciding who gets the last piece of
                cake to governing a small island, this course tackles the hard ethical questions.",
14          "Instructor": "Prof. Thiago Silva",
15          "Department": "Artificial Intelligence",
16          "Semester": 2
17      },
18      {
19          "Course ID": "AI103",
20          "Title": "Dreaming in Code: AI for Creative Minds",
21          "Description": "Unleash the power of AI to create art, music, and literature. Learn how algorithms can be inspired
                by dreams and how to interpret the surreal artworks produced by silicon brains.",
22          "Instructor": "Prof. Anika Singh",
23          "Department": "Artificial Intelligence",
24          "Semester": 3
25      },
26      ]
```

Ln 1, Col 1   JSON C   4 Spaces

Figure 13.6 It's a good idea to view your JSON data to make sure ChatGPT got it right.

If the JSON file contains incorrect data, the most likely problem is that ChatGPT processed the wrong range in your Excel file. Create a new prompt that uses more specific identifying info for the data, such as the worksheet name or the range or table name. If that doesn't work, open the spreadsheet file in Excel, define a name for the range, upload the revised Excel file into the ChatGPT chat, and then craft a prompt that refers to the range name you defined. Once you have your JSON data file, it's time to learn how to extract that data and display it on the web page you're going to create.

13.3 Fetching and displaying the JSON data

At the moment you have a JSON file, and later you'll have a web page created by ChatGPT. How do you get that JSON data onto that web page? That's a JavaScript task, so when it comes time to prompt ChatGPT for your page's JavaScript code, you begin with the following request:

`Fetch the contents of the file filename.`

This tells ChatGPT to generate code that extracts the content of whatever's in the file named `filename`. For example, for this project's `college_courses.json` file, the prompt would look like this:

`Fetch the contents of the file college_courses.json.`

> **NOTE** The JavaScript method that extracts the contents of a file is called `fetch`, so the use of the verb *fetch* in the request is deliberate.

The resulting JavaScript code loads all the JSON data into memory, so the next step is to ask ChatGPT to generate JavaScript code to write that data to the web page. For example, suppose your web page code includes an empty `article` element, and you want all the data to appear in that element. One common scenario is to display each record in the data as a separate `section` element. So, your prompt would start like this:

`For each record fetched from the JSON file, add a section element to the article element and populate the section element with the following:`

You'd then specify the elements you want to use to display your data. For example, you might use a third-level heading for a record's title, if it had one. Similarly, you might use a paragraph element if the record had a long text item.

Here's the prompt for this chapter's project:

`For each record fetched from the JSON file, add a section`
`element to the article element and populate the section`
`element with the following three elements:`
`  * A third-level heading that includes the record's "Title" text.`
`  * A div element with the text "Course ID: ", the record's "Course ID" value,`
`a line break, the text "Instructor: ", the record's "Instructor" value, a line`
`break, the text "Department: ", the record's "Department" value, a line break,`
`the text "Semester: ", the record's "Semester" value, and a line break.`
`  * A paragraph element that includes the record's "Description" value.`

The resulting JavaScript code will loop through all the retrieved JSON records and write each of them to the page.

Once you have your JSON data fetched and displayed, it's time to learn how to manipulate all that data on the web page you're going to create.

13.4   *Searching, sorting, and filtering the course catalog*

It's entirely possible that you may want to display your JSON data on the web page and leave it at that. That's probably the case if your database is relatively small, say a couple of dozen items or fewer. But if your data consists of dozens, hundreds, or even thousands of records, just throwing all that information into a web page isn't going to cut it. Why? Because it's extremely unlikely to be useful—and very likely to be frustrating—for anyone who tries to view it.

If you have quite a bit of data, you need to have mercy on your visitors by offering them one or more of the following ways to manipulate the data: searching, sorting, and filtering. The next three sections take you through the details.

13.4.1   *Searching the data*

When searching, the user types a word or phrase that represents the data they want to see. Submitting the search text replaces the full database with only those records that contain text that matches the search word or phrase.

A web page search component is almost always a text box. So, in your ChatGPT prompt for the HTML code, you need to include such a text box. Here's an example:

```
A text box with the ID "Search" and the placeholder "Search".
```

Here, a *placeholder* is a word or phrase that appears in the text box to let the user know what they're supposed to enter. As soon as the user starts typing text in the box, the placeholder disappears. Note, too, that including an ID value for the component makes the JavaScript code easier to read.

When you prompt ChatGPT for the JavaScript code, you need to include how you want the code to handle search text. Generally, you ask JavaScript to monitor the search field and, when the user starts typing, replace the displayed JSON records with just those that match the typed text. Here's an example prompt:

```
When the user types text in the "Search" text box,
repopulate the article element with just the records
that include the search text in any field.
```

This example assumes that you want to apply the search text to every field in your JSON data. You may want to consider a couple of exceptions:

- If there are one or more fields you don't want to include in the search (such as a field that contains numeric data), add except the X and Y fields to the end of your prompt (where X and Y are the names of the fields you want to exclude).

- If you only want to apply the search to one or more fields, replace `any field` in the prompt with the `A` and `B` fields, where `A` and `B` are the names of the fields you want to search.

Searching is probably the most common (and arguably the most useful) data-manipulation feature, but you need to know about two others, the first of which is filtering.

13.4.2 *Filtering the data*

With filtering, the user displays a subset of the JSON data, usually by choosing one of the unique values that appear in a particular field. For example, in this chapter's project, users can filter the course data based on the unique values in the `Department` and `Instructor` fields.

A web page filter component is usually a drop-down list containing the unique items from a particular field, so in your prompt for the HTML code, you need to ask for such a component. Here are the two prompts used in this chapter's project:

```
A drop-down list with the ID "Department" and the initial value "Department
(All)".
A drop-down list with the ID "Instructor" and the initial value "Instructor
(All)".
```

Note that the prompt applies ID values to each list and also populates each list with an initial value. In both cases, selecting this initial value from the list repopulates the web page with the full database.

When you ask ChatGPT to generate your JavaScript code, you first need to include that you want your drop-down lists to be populated by the unique values in the corresponding data fields. For example, here's a prompt that populates the Department drop-down list with the unique values from the `Department` field:

```
Extract all the unique "Department" values and use them to populate the
"Department" drop-down list.
```

Next you specify how you want the code to handle the user selecting an item from a list. The general idea is that JavaScript monitors the list, and when the user selects an item, the code replaces the displayed JSON records with just those that match the selected list item. Here's an example prompt for the `Department` field:

```
When the user selects an item from the "Department" list, repopulate the
article element with just the records that match the selected department. If
the user selects the first item in the list, repopulate the article element
with every record imported from the JSON file.
```

The final data-manipulation technique is sorting, which is covered in the next section.

13.4.3 *Sorting the data*

With sorting, the user controls the order of the displayed records, usually by specifying a field in some way. The page then reorders the records alphabetically (if the field contains text) or numerically (if the field contains numbers). In this project, users can sort the course catalog on the `Department` and `Title` fields.

A web page sort component is usually a drop-down list containing the names of the sortable fields. When you ask ChatGPT to generate your page's HTML code, you need to ask for such a component. Here's an example from this chapter's project:

```
A drop-down list with the ID "Sort" and the values: "Sort by Department" and
"Sort by Title".
```

When you prompt ChatGPT for the JavaScript code, you need to include how you want the code to handle the user selecting an item from this list. The general idea is that JavaScript determines which item was selected, sorts the records based on that field, and then redisplays the sorted records on the page. Here's an example prompt from our project:

```
When the user selects "Sort by Title" from the "Sort" list, sort the
displayed records on the "Title" field and then repopulate the article
element with the sorted records. When the user selects "Sort by Department"
from the "Sort" list, sort the displayed records on the "Department" field
and then repopulate the article element with the sorted records.
```

At this point, you know all that's required to successfully prompt ChatGPT to build a course catalog. The following section takes you through the process.

13.5   *Crafting the prompt for the course catalog*

This chapter's project is a course catalog page that fetches and then displays all the data in a separate JSON file. The page includes controls for filtering, sorting, and searching the data. This project assumes you already have a title, subtitle, and logo; know which fonts you want to use for the page headings and text; and have a color scheme ready to apply. Head back to chapter 3 to learn how to prompt ChatGPT for title, typeface, and color suggestions.

To start your prompt, tell ChatGPT that you want to construct a web page and that you want it to generate the code for you:

```
I want to build a web page for a course catalog. I don't know how to code, so
I need you to provide the code for me.

First, write the HTML code for a web page that includes the following:
```

Now outline the page content, item by item, including the following (refer to figure 13.7):

- A header that includes an image on the left, a logo on the right, and a title and subtitle in the middle
- A navigation element that holds two drop-down lists for filtering, another drop-down list for sorting, and a text box for searching
- A main element that contains an empty article element
- A footer that includes a copyright notice

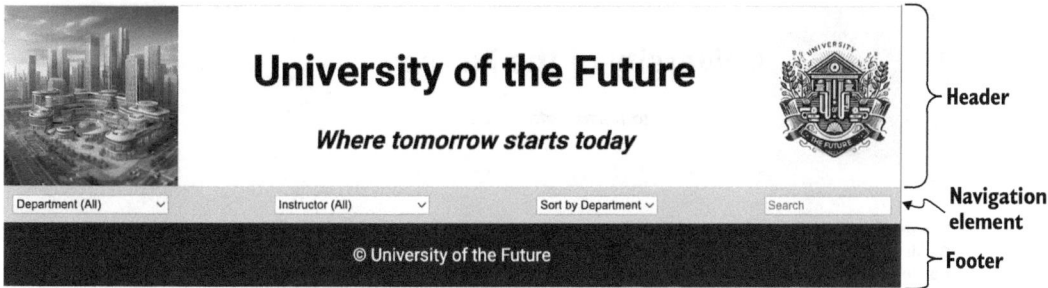

Figure 13.7 The elements of the course catalog page before the data is rendered

Figure 13.7 does not show data because, as I discuss shortly, the empty `article` element is only populated via the JavaScript code that you ask ChatGPT to generate.

Next, ask ChatGPT to generate the CSS:

`Second, in a separate file please write the CSS code for the following:`

You then specify the page formatting, including the following:

- The page background color and text color.
- The type sizes you want to use for the headings and page text.
- The fonts to use for the headings and regular page text.
- Which elements should be Flexbox containers. In this project, these will be the header, the navigation element, the article element, and each section element.

Finally, you instruct ChatGPT to provide the JavaScript code:

`Third, in a separate file, write the JavaScript code for the following:`

You then spell out what you want JavaScript to do, including the following:

- Fetch the content of the JSON file.
- Populate the drop-down lists that require unique values from a particular field.
- Write all the JSON data to the web page using text and HTML components that you specify.
- Handle a selection from a filtering drop-down list.
- Handle a selection from the sorting drop-down list.
- Handle when text is typed in the search box.

I used OpenAI's ChatGPT app to submit my prompt to GPT-4. The generated code produced the page shown in figure 13.8.

Figure 13.8   My course catalog

If you like the look of your page, you can skip the rest of this chapter and deploy the code to the web (refer to appendix B for deployment instructions). However, if you want to understand the generated web page code, keep reading to get a closer look.

13.6   *Examining the course catalog code*

If you'd like to have at least some idea of what ChatGPT generated on your behalf, the next three sections provide you with a brief look at the HTML and CSS code that underlies the course catalog page shown in figure 13.8, as well as the JavaScript code that populates the page data and handles the various data-manipulation controls.

> **NOTE**   The generated HTML and CSS code for my course catalog are available on this book's website (www.manning.com/books/build-a-website-with -chatgpt) and in the book's GitHub repository: https://github.com/paulmcfe/ websites-with-chatgpt.

The code annotations that follow should help you understand how the course catalog works and can make it easier to modify or customize your own code.

13.6.1   *Examining the HTML*

Here's an annotated version of the HTML code that ChatGPT produced for my course catalog:

```
<!DOCTYPE html>
<html lang="en">
<head>
```

```
    <meta charset="utf-8">
    <meta name="viewport"
        content="width=device-width, initial-scale=1">
    <title>University of the Future</title>
    <link href="https://fonts.googleapis.com/css?family=
        Roboto:400,700&display=swap" rel="stylesheet">
    <link rel="stylesheet" href="styles.css">
    <title>Ampersand Photography</title>
</head>
<body>
    <header>
        <img src="images/header.png" alt="Header Image">
        <div>
            <h1>University of the Future</h1>
            <h2>Where tomorrow starts today</h2>
        </div>
        <img src="images/logo.png" alt="University Logo">
    </header>
    <nav>
        <select id="Department">
            <option value="all">Department (All)</option>
        </select>
        <select id="Instructor">
            <option value="all">Instructor (All)</option>
        </select>
        <select id="Sort">
            <option value="department">Sort by Department</option>
            <option value="title">Sort by Title</option>
        </select>
        <input type="text" id="Search" placeholder="Search">
    </nav>
    <main>
        <article></article>
    </main>
    <footer>
        &copy; University of the Future
    </footer>
    <script src="script.js"></script>
</body>
</html>
```

Annotations:
- Helps the page display properly on mobile devices
- Loads the Roboto font from Google Fonts
- Tells the web browser where to find the CSS code
- Site's header image
- Site title — Page header
- Page title
- Site logo
- Department filter drop-down list
- Instructor filter drop-down list — Navigation element
- Sort drop-down list
- Search text box
- Empty article element
- Page footer
- Tells the web browser where to find the JavaScript code

Note that the HTML code includes the following line:

```
<link rel="stylesheet" href="styles.css">
```

This tag tells the web browser where to find the CSS code, which I describe in the next section.

13.6.2 *Examining the CSS*

Here's an annotated version of the CSS code that ChatGPT produced for my course catalog:

```
body {
    margin: 0;
    background-color: white;
    font-family: 'Roboto', sans-serif;
    font-size: 20px;
    color: black;
}
```

Styles the page background color, the margin, and the text size, color, and font

```
header {
    display: flex;
    justify-content: space-between;
    align-items: center;
    max-height: 200px;
}
```

Styles the header as a Flexbox container

```
header img:first-of-type {
    height: 100%;
}
```

◄—— The left header image takes up the full header height.

```
header img:last-of-type {
    max-height: 150px;
}
```

◄—— Sets the maximum height of the right header image

```
header h1 {
    font-size: 48px;
    text-align: center;
}
```

◄—— Styles the page title font size, style, and alignment

```
header h2 {
    font-size: 28px;
    font-style: italic;
    text-align: center;
}
```

Styles the page subtitle font size, style, and alignment

```
nav {
    display: flex;
    flex-wrap: wrap;
    justify-content: space-between;
    background-color: lightgray;
    padding: 10px;
}
```

Styles the nav element as a Flexbox container

```
article {
    display: flex;
    flex-wrap: wrap;
    gap: 20px;
    justify-content: flex-start;
    margin: 20px;
}
```

Styles the article element as a Flexbox container

```
section {
    display: flex;
    flex-direction: column;
    justify-content: space-between;
    flex-grow: 1;
    flex-basis: 200px;
    max-width: 300px;
}
```

Styles the section elements as Flexbox containers

```
h3 {
    font-size: 24px;
}
```

◄—— Sets the font size of the course titles

```css
footer {
    background-color: navy;
    padding: 24px;
    text-align: center;
    color: white;
}
```

Styles the footer

In the HTML code listing from earlier in this chapter, note the following line near the bottom:

```html
<script src="script.js"></script>
```

This tag tells the web browser where to find the JavaScript code, which I annotate in the next section.

13.6.3 *Examining the JavaScript*

If you're careful, it's fine to make small tweaks to the HTML and CSS code. However, I strongly suggest you leave ChatGPT's JavaScript code alone. The code is complex, and an injudicious edit could render the course catalog unusable.

If you happen to know a bit of JavaScript, however, you may be interested in how ChatGPT coded the fetching, displaying, and manipulating of the JSON data, so here's an annotated version of the JavaScript code that ChatGPT generated for my course catalog:

```javascript
document.addEventListener('DOMContentLoaded', () => {
    fetch('college_courses.json')
        .then(response => response.json())
        .then(data => {
            populateDropdowns(data);
            populateArticles(data);
        });

    document.getElementById('Department')
        .addEventListener('change', function() {
        filterData();
    });

    document.getElementById('Instructor')
        .addEventListener('change', function() {
        filterData();
    });

    document.getElementById('Sort')
        .addEventListener('change', function() {
        sortData();
    });

    document.getElementById('Search')
        .addEventListener('input', function() {
        searchData(this.value.trim());
    });
```

Runs the function code that follows once the page has loaded

Fetches the data from the JSON file

Runs the function that populates the drop-down lists

Runs the function that populates the article

Listens for changes to the Department drop-down

Listens for changes to the Instructor drop-down

Listens for changes to the Sort drop-down

Listens for text input to the Search text box

```
});

function populateDropdowns(data) {
    const departments = new Set(data.map(course => course.Department));
    const instructors = new Set(data.map(course => course.Instructor));

    departments.forEach(department => {
        document.getElementById('Department')
            .add(new Option(department, department));
    });

    instructors.forEach(instructor => {
        document.getElementById('Instructor')
            .add(new Option(instructor, instructor));
    });
}

function populateArticles(data) {
    const article = document.querySelector('article');
    article.innerHTML = '';
    data.forEach(course => {
        const section = document.createElement('section');
        section.innerHTML = `
            <h3>${course.Title}</h3>
            <div>
                Course ID: ${course['Course ID']}<br>
                Instructor: ${course.Instructor}<br>
                Department: ${course.Department}<br>
                Semester: ${course.Semester}<br>
            </div>
            <p>${course.Description}</p>
        `;
        article.appendChild(section);
    });
}

function filterData() {
    fetch('college_courses.json')
        .then(response => response.json())
        .then(data => {
            const departmentValue = document
.getElementById('Department').value;
            const instructorValue = document.
getElementById('Instructor').value;

            let filteredData = data;
            if (departmentValue !== 'all') {
                filteredData = filteredData
.filter(course => course.Department===departmentValue);
            }
            if (instructorValue !== 'all') {
                filteredData = filteredData.
```

Runs the function code that follows once the page has loaded

Populates the Department and Instructor drop-downs with the unique values from those fields

Populates the article element with course data

Filters the data when the user selects an item in the Department or Instructor list

```
filter(course => course.Instructor===instructorValue);
            }
            populateArticles(filteredData);
        });
}
```

Filters the data when the user
selects an item in the
Department or Instructor list

```
function sortData() {
    fetch('college_courses.json')
        .then(response => response.json())
        .then(data => {
            const sortValue = document.getElementById('Sort').value;
            data.sort((a, b) => {
                if (sortValue === 'title') {
                    return a.Title.localeCompare(b.Title);
                } else {
                    return a.Department.localeCompare(b.Department);
                }
            });
            populateArticles(data);
        });
}
```

Sorts the
data when
the user
selects an
item in the
Sort list

```
function searchData(searchText) {
    if (!searchText) {
        fetch('college_courses.json')
            .then(response => response.json())
            .then(data => {
                populateArticles(data);
            });
        return;
    }

    fetch('college_courses.json')
        .then(response => response.json())
        .then(data => {
            const filteredData = data.filter(course =>
                course.Title.toLowerCase().includes(searchText.toLowerCase()) ||
                course['Course ID'].toLowerCase().includes(searchText.toLowerCase())
||
                course.Instructor.toLowerCase().includes(searchText.toLowerCase()) ||
                course.Department.toLowerCase().includes(searchText.toLowerCase()) ||
                course.Description.toLowerCase().includes(searchText.toLowerCase())
            );
            populateArticles(filteredData);
        });
}
```

Searches the
data when the
user types
something in the
Search text box

If you like, you can use the HTML and CSS annotations from the previous two sections
to help customize your web page code, as I describe in the next section.

13.7 Customizing the course catalog

Using the previous section's annotations as a guide, here I'm going to take you through
a few relatively simple code customizations you can make by opening the HTML and

CSS files in your text editor. If your page isn't close to what you want, however, you're better off rewriting your prompt and submitting it to ChatGPT in a new session.

The HTML code in this project is minimal because most of the page is generated via JavaScript. So, I have just a couple of suggestions:

- Feel free to add more sorting fields by adding new items to the Sort drop-down list. Just remember to prompt ChatGPT to generate the JavaScript code to handle sorting on the new fields.
- In the footer section of the HTML code, you can add links to your social media accounts, as I describe in chapter 4.

Now, here are a few customization ideas for the CSS code:

- To use another page background color, specify a different color keyword for the body element's `background-color` property.
- To use another background color for the header and footer, specify a new color keyword for the `header` and `footer` elements' `background-color` property.
- To use a different color for the page text, specify a different color keyword for the body element's `color` property.
- For any font size value, you can change the number to increase or decrease the font size. Just make sure you leave the `px` unit in place.
- For any padding or margin value, you can change the number to increase or decrease the padding or margins. In each case, be sure to leave the `px` unit in place.
- To make your page code more accessible, consider converting all px measurements to rem measurements. 1 rem is by default equivalent to 16 px, so 20 px is 1.25 rem, 24 px is 1.5 rem, 32 px is 2 rem, 48 px is 3 rem, and so on. The rem unit is more accessible because it measures font sizes relative to the default font size the browser user has defined in their browser settings.

13.8   *Where to go from here*

My goal in this book has been to show you that although it appears magical that ChatGPT can generate sophisticated web page code on request, the real secret is converting your web page vision into a detailed and specific prompt that tells ChatGPT exactly what you want. You've seen many examples of such prompts in this book, and along the way, you've learned everything you need to know about web page construction and design. That's great news because it means you now have the knowledge and experience to create almost anything you want on the web. When you're ready to build something bold and beautiful, ChatGPT will be there for you to turn that dream into a reality. It's all just a prompt away.

Summary

- To convert Excel data to JSON, make sure the data resides in a range or table and that each column has a unique heading.

- JSON is a set of one or more comma-separated property–value pairs surrounded by braces ({ and }), where the property names are surrounded by double quotation marks. Text values are also surrounded by double quotation marks.

- If you have a ChatGPT Plus account, you can upload your Excel file to a chat and then prompt ChatGPT to convert your data to JSON and output the result as a file you can download.

- You ask ChatGPT to generate your web page code with an empty element (such as an `article` element); you then use JavaScript to populate it with the JSON data.

- The most common data-manipulation techniques on web pages are searching, filtering, and sorting. You can prompt ChatGPT to generate the JavaScript code to implement each technique.

- For the best results, your page prompt should be as specific as possible, including colors, font sizes, and heading levels.

- Save the generated HTML to the index.html file, the generated CSS to the filename suggested by ChatGPT in the HTML code, usually styles.css, and the generated JavaScript code to the filename suggested by ChatGPT in the HTML code, usually script.js.

Getting ready to build web pages with ChatGPT

Aside from the introductory material in chapter 1, this book's focus is on showing you how to convince ChatGPT to help you build web pages without having to learn how to code them yourself. I hope you find that the book's web page ideas and the prompts used to generate them are useful to you, either directly or as stepping-off points to explore on your own.

Using ChatGPT as a web coding assistant is nowhere near as complex as learning to code pages yourself, but it does require a bit of setup and a modicum of infrastructure. This appendix is all about taking you through the few things you need to know and the few tasks you need to do before you can successfully get ChatGPT to help you turn your website ideas into something real. After going through a mercifully short list of requirements, you learn how to set up an optional ChatGPT or Microsoft account. You also learn how to test your code before deploying it and how to work with HTML and other web page files.

A.1 What you need to get started

One of the best things about using ChatGPT to help you create web pages is that you can get started with very few requirements and without spending a nickel of your hard-earned money (unless you want to). In fact, I can summarize everything you need to get up and running in a list that's a mere four items long:

- *Internet access*—Although you can use the ChatGPT mobile app offline, the OpenAI app (https://chat.openai.com), Bing Copilot (https://bing.com and then click Copilot), and Microsoft Copilot (https://copilot.microsoft.com)—any one of which you need to use for easy access to the code generated by ChatGPT—are online-only, so you need internet access.

- *Web browser*—You can access the OpenAI app and Bing Copilot using any recent version of a major browser (such as Chrome, Safari, Edge, or Firefox). But to use Microsoft Copilot, you need to use Chrome or Microsoft Edge, with support for Firefox and Safari in the works as I write this.

- *Text editor*—After you copy the code generated by ChatGPT, you have to paste it somewhere, and that somewhere is almost always a file opened in a text editor. Yep, you can use the default text editor that comes with your computer (Notepad for Windows or TextEdit for macOS), but here are some code-friendly editors to consider:
  - *Notepad++*—Available for Windows only, and it's free: https://notepad-plus -plus.org
  - *Nova*—Available for Mac for $99, but a free trial is available: https://nova.app
  - *Sublime Text*—Available for both Windows and Mac for $99, but a free trial is available: www.sublimetext.com
  - *Visual Studio Code*—Available for Windows and Mac, and this one is free, as well: https://code.visualstudio.com

- *Web hosting account*—Once you've saved the ChatGPT-generated code to a web page file, your final step is to deploy the file to the web. To do that, you need an account with a web hosting provider. I talk about setting up web hosting accounts and deploying your web code in more detail in appendix B. If you don't have a web host, you can still view your pages locally by using your web browser's File > Open command to open each page's saved HTML file.

NOTE   If you're going to use your own photos on your web pages (check out chapter 10), you may need a photo-editing app for tasks such as cropping, enhancing colors, and changing the image size and file format. The Photos apps that ship with Windows and macOS can handle these simple operations, but for more in-depth chores, you'll want higher-end software such as Adobe Photoshop (www.adobe.com/products/photoshop.html) or GIMP (www.gimp.org), which is free.

Yep, that really is all you need, and none of these items have to cost you any extra cash (assuming you'd be paying for internet access even if you weren't using ChatGPT to create web pages). The one exception you may want to make is to pay for a ChatGPT subscription, which I discuss in the next section.

A.2 *Understanding ChatGPT account access*

ChatGPT is a product of OpenAI, which is backed by Microsoft. So, it would seem reasonable to expect that you'd need either an OpenAI account or a Microsoft account to converse with ChatGPT. Is that true? Surprisingly, the answer is no, not unless you want one. So, should you get an account for ChatGPT access? Here are the scenarios to consider:

- *Maximizing privacy (no account)*—Many people are loath to send private data to large corporations (such as OpenAI and Microsoft), so accessing ChatGPT without an account makes the entire process a bit more private. You can access the Open AI ChatGPT app without an account, but you're restricted to using GPT 3.5. To use ChatGPT without a Microsoft account, you need to access Copilot via Bing. Note, however, that without a Microsoft account, you're restricted to just 10 responses from ChatGPT per session (versus the 30 responses per session you get when you're signed in with a Microsoft account).

- *Getting free access to GPT-4 (Microsoft account)*—GPT-4 is (at least as I write this) the latest and greatest large language model (LLM) from OpenAI, so it's the one most people want to use, especially for generating web code. You can pay OpenAI to get access to GPT-4 (as I discuss in the last of these bullets), but an alternative is to navigate to Microsoft Copilot, which uses GPT-4 as its LLM. To get the most out of Bing Copilot (and to access the separate Microsoft Copilot site at all), create a Microsoft account and use it to sign in—or use your existing Microsoft account if you're a Windows user. To create a Microsoft account, go to https://account .microsoft.com, click Sign In, and then follow the steps.

- *Getting free access to GPT-3.5 (free OpenAI account)*—GPT-3.5 is a fantastic AI model that produces reliable and useful web page code. If you want free access to GPT-3.5 and for some reason aren't able (or don't want) to use Copilot to get free access to GPT-4 (as described in the previous bullet), you can set up a free OpenAI account. Having an account gives you access to some extra ChatGPT features that aren't available to people who use ChatGPT without an account (as described in the first bullet). To create a free OpenAI account, go to https:// openai.com, click Sign Up, and then follow the steps.

- *Getting paid access to GPT-4 (ChatGPT Plus subscription)*—If you want to use GPT-4 and for some reason aren't able (or don't want) to use Bing Copilot or Microsoft Copilot to get free access to GPT-4 (as described in an earlier bullet), you need to set up a subscription to ChatGPT Plus, which as I write this will set you back US $20 per month. To set up a ChatGPT Plus subscription, create a free OpenAI account (as described in the previous bullet), access the ChatGPT app (https:// chat.openai.com), click Upgrade in the lower-left corner (refer to figure A.1), and then follow the steps.

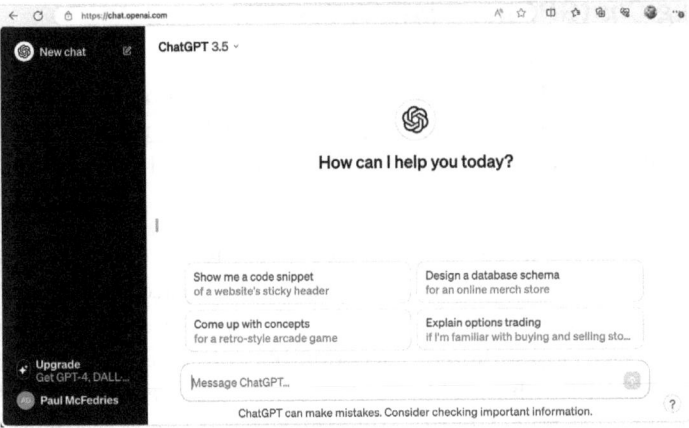

Figure A.1   To set up a ChatGPT Plus subscription, click Upgrade in the ChatGPT app sidebar.

A.3   Testing your code

ChatGPT has been trained on an unfathomably large amount of programming code, which is why it's (usually) so good at generating the web page knickknacks you ask for. But ChatGPT isn't infallible, which means it will sometimes produce HTML, CSS, or JavaScript code that either doesn't do what you asked or is broken in some way. A professional coder can usually examine the generated code and understand not only *that* the code is wrong but also *why* it's wrong. You're reading this book because you're not a professional coder, so how will you know whether ChatGPT has coughed up some errant code?

The answer is that you get a web browser to render the code and then examine the result to see if the code works like it's supposed to (or at all). One way to get a web browser to render ChatGPT code is to run the full prompt-copy-save-deploy cycle. That process isn't particularly onerous, but neither is it trivial, so it seems like overkill if you just want to know, say, whether the ChatGPT-generated code for a form works as intended.

A better and faster method is to test only the code generated by ChatGPT, which you do by copying the code and then pasting it into one of the available online coding playgrounds. The next two sections provide the details.

A.3.1   Copying data from ChatGPT

Once ChatGPT has finished generating your code, your first step is to copy that code to your computer's Clipboard. (The Clipboard is a special memory area that your computer uses to store the most recent item you've copied.) How you go about this depends on which method you're using to access ChatGPT:

- *OpenAI ChatGPT app*—Click the Copy Code button in the upper-right corner of the code window (as shown in figure A.2).

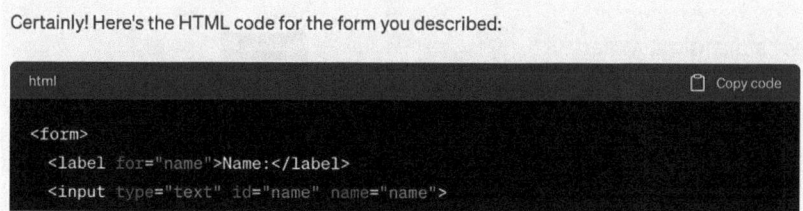

Figure A.2   **In the OpenAI ChatGPT app, click the code window's Copy Code button to copy the generated code.**

- *Microsoft Copilot*—Click the Copy button that appears above and to the right of the code (as shown in figure A.3).

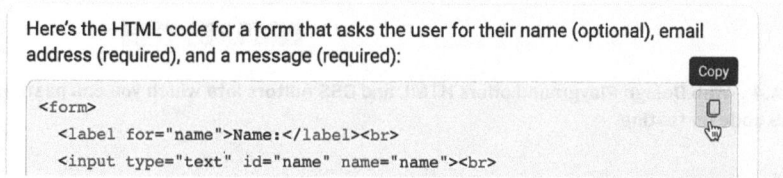

Figure A.3   **In Copilot, click the Copy button to copy the generated code.**

> **WARNING**   Your computer's Clipboard can store only one copied item at a time. If you copy something else before pasting your ChatGPT code (as I describe in the next section), that code will be wiped out of memory, and you'll have to copy it all over again.

A.3.2   *Pasting data into an online coding playground*

With your ChatGPT-generated code copied to your computer's Clipboard, the next (and final) step is to paste the code into an online web coding playground. A *playground* is a website that accepts HTML, CSS, and often JavaScript code and then displays how that code will render in the web browser. By using a playground to test your code, you avoid the hassle of saving your code to a file and then deploying the file to a web host, which is too much work when you just want to see whether a page section or component is working properly.

Here are a few web coding playgrounds to check out:

- *Web Design Playground*—This is a companion website for my book *Web Design Playground*, which teaches HTML and CSS for beginners. As shown in figure A.4, the website offers a "sandbox" that includes HTML and CSS editors into which you can paste ChatGPT-generated HTML and CSS code. Click Run Code, and the bottom results area shows how the code looks in the browser. Navigate to https://webdesignplayground.io/new to try it out.

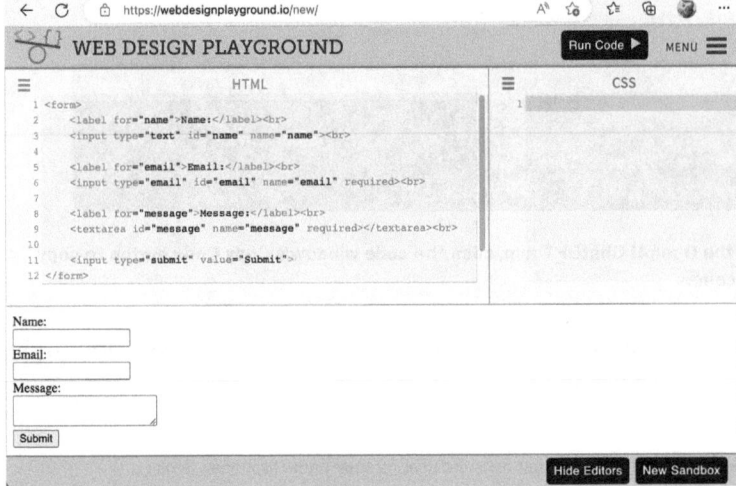

Figure A.4   Web Design Playground offers HTML and CSS editors into which you can paste HTML and CSS code for testing.

- *WebDev Workbench*—This is a playground I built to help web developers test HTML, CSS, and JavaScript code. As shown in figure A.5, the Workbench offers HTML, CSS, and JavaScript tabs into which you can paste ChatGPT-provided HTML, CSS, and JavaScript code. Click Run, and the bottom results area shows how the code looks in the browser. Navigate to https://webdevworkshop.io/wb to check it out.

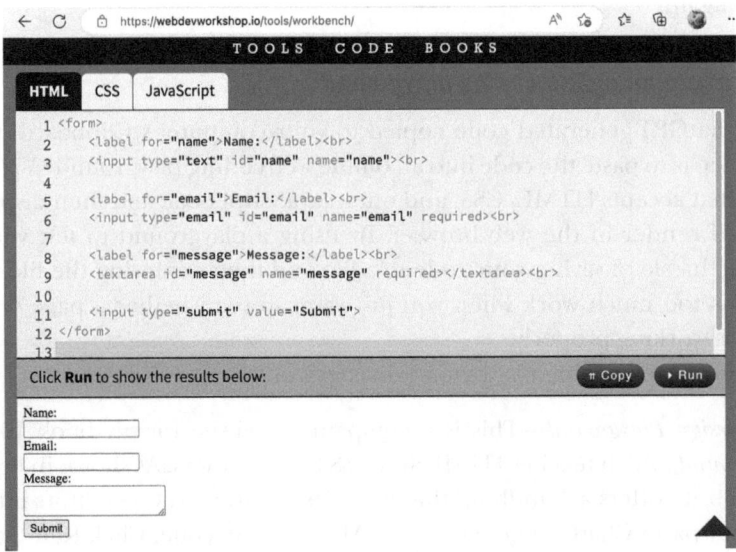

Figure A.5   WebDev Workbench offers tabs for HTML, CSS, and JavaScript into which you can paste ChatGPT code for testing.

- *CodePen*—This is a popular site for testing web page code. You create a "pen" that includes editors for HTML, CSS, and JavaScript code, as shown in figure A.6. A few seconds after pasting, the rendered result appears automatically in the lower frame. Navigate to https://codepen.io and then click Start Coding to give it a try.

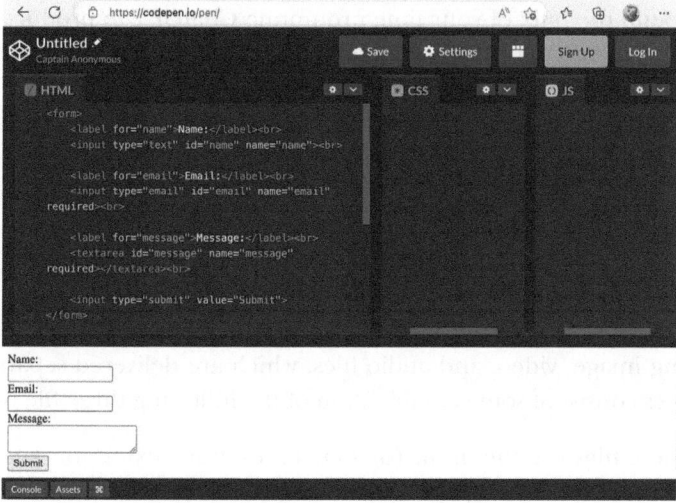

Figure A.6   CodePen offers editors for HTML, CSS, and JavaScript. Paste your ChatGPT code into the appropriate editor to test the code.

All of these playgrounds work in more or less the same way:

1   Copy your ChatGPT code.
2   Navigate to the playground.
3   Click inside the editor that corresponds to the type of code you're testing (for example, use the HTML editor for HTML code).
4   Click the button that runs the code (or, in the case of CodePen, just wait a few seconds).

NOTE   If ChatGPT generates HTML code that also includes CSS code (between `<style>` and `</style>` tags), it's best to copy the CSS separately (ignoring the `<style>` and `</style>` tags) and paste it into the playground's CSS editor. Similarly, if ChatGPT generates HTML code that also includes JavaScript code (between `<script>` and `</script>` tags), copy the JavaScript code separately (leave out the `<script>` and `</script>` tags) and paste it into the JavaScript editor. To avoid the extra work of extracting CSS and JavaScript from generated HTML code, include in your prompt that you want ChatGPT to output the HTML, CSS, and JavaScript separately. ChatGPT should put the HTML code in an HTML window, the CSS code in a separate CSS window, and the JavaScript code in a separate JavaScript window.

As you work with ChatGPT, it's a good idea to keep your favorite playground open in its own browser tab. That way, as soon as ChatGPT generates new code for you, you can immediately copy-and-paste the code into the playground to check that it works.

A.4   *Working with web page files*

Although you'll spend the bulk of your time prompting ChatGPT to produce the web page code and text you want to put online, at some point you need to get that code into one or more files that you can deploy. To help with this "save" portion of the prompt-copy-save-deploy cycle, the rest of this appendix tells you what you need to know.

A.4.1   *Understanding the different types of web page files*

One of the amazing and surprising things about the web is that everything you see, from the humblest home page to the mightiest megacorp website, has nothing but simple text underlying it. How do I know? Because every web page consists of one or more files, and all the file types supported by the web are variations on the text file theme. (Here I'm ignoring image, video, and audio files, which are delivered separately.) In fact, most web pages consist of some combination of the following three file types:

- *HTML*—These files use the .html (or sometimes .htm) extension and provide the basic structure of a web page. All websites include at least one HTML file (usually named index.html).
- *CSS*—These files use the .css extension and provide the overall look of a web page by defining style rules for things like fonts, colors, borders, and layout.
- *JavaScript*—These files use the .js extension and add interactivity to a web page.

When you use separate files this way, you need to reference them from your HTML file, which you learn how to do shortly. For now, though, you need to learn how to paste ChatGPT-generated code into a web page file.

A.4.2   *Pasting ChatGPT data into an HTML file*

A simple web page may use a single HTML file that includes CSS and JavaScript code. The CSS code goes between `<style>` and `</style>` tags in a special header section of the page, and the JavaScript code goes between `<script>` and `</script>` tags, usually near the bottom of the HTML file. Here's the general layout of such an HTML file:

```
<!DOCTYPE html>
<html>
<head>
    <style>
                                    ◄——— CSS code goes here.
    </style>
</head>
<body>
                                    ◄——— HTML tags and text go here.
    <script>
                                    ◄——— JavaScript code goes here.
```

```
    </script>
</body>
</html>
```

You use this code as a starting point for all your simple web page projects. (You learn how to get ChatGPT to generate a similar template in chapter 6.) With this template in place, here's where you paste code generated by ChatGPT:

- *CSS*—Paste the code below the `<style>` tag but above the `</style>` tag.
- *HTML*—Paste the code below the `<body>` tag but above the `<script>` tag. The various page components need to appear in the file in the same order that you want them to appear on the page. I give you more specific placement instructions in the chapters where you generate page components.
- *JavaScript*—Paste the code below the `<script>` tag but above the `</script>` tag.

Remember, however, that this all-code-in-one-file approach is really only suitable for the simplest web pages. When your pages get a little more complex, you'll want to create separate files for the CSS and JavaScript, as I describe next.

A.4.3 Referencing CSS and JavaScript files in an HTML file

Putting your CSS and JavaScript code in separate files makes your HTML file simpler and cleaner and also enables you to apply the same CSS and JavaScript code to multiple web pages, which can be a real timesaver. Assuming you've already saved your CSS and JavaScript code in separate .css and .js files, respectively, add references to the files in any HTML file where you want to use the CSS and/or JavaScript code:

```
<!DOCTYPE html>
<html>
<head>
    <link href="styles.css" rel="stylesheet">       Use the <link> tag to
</head>                                              reference a CSS file.
<body>
    HTML tags and text go here
    <script src="code.js"></script>                 Use the <script> tag to
</body>                                              reference a JavaScript file.
</html>
```

Here are the specifics:

- *CSS*—Between the `<head>` tag and the `</head>` tag, add a `<link>` tag, and set the `href` attribute equal to the name of the CSS file surrounded by quotation marks.
- *JavaScript*—Just above the `</body>` tag, add a `<script>` tag with its `src` attribute set to the name of the JavaScript file surrounded by quotation marks, and then add a `</script>` tag.

To reuse a CSS or JavaScript file in multiple HTML files, include the same `<link>` tag or `<script>` tag in those files.

A.4.4   *Saving your work*

Once you've made any changes to an HTML, CSS, or JavaScript file, you should save your changes right away to avoid losing your work. Here are a few notes to bear in mind when saving new files for the first time:

- Be sure to use the correct file extension: .html for HTML files, .css for CSS files, and .js for JavaScript files.
- If your site consists of a single HTML page, name that page index.html. If your site consists of multiple pages, name the home or main page index.html.
- Don't use spaces or unusual symbols in your filenames. Use only alphanumeric characters, dashes (-), or underscores (_).
- For most web hosts, filenames are case sensitive, meaning that, say, index.html, Index.html, and INDEX.html would all be treated as separate files. It's best to stick with all-lowercase letters in your filenames.
- Keep the filenames as short as possible without becoming obscure. The name about.html is better than a-few-words-about-this-project.html, but nlsup.html is worse than newsletter-signup.html.
- Be sure to save all the files associated with a single website—meaning not only all your HTML, CSS, and JavaScript files but also all your image, video, and audio files—in a single folder. This makes your life much easier when it comes to deploying your site, as I describe in appendix B.

Deploying your site

I'm not spilling any great secret or espousing any esoteric knowledge when I say that the key feature of a website is the "web" part of the word. That is, although you're free to create and preview as many HTML files as you want on your computer, those files don't add up to an honest-to-goodness website until they're deployed to the web for your friends, family, and even total strangers to see. Getting HTML, CSS, JavaScript, images, and other files from your computer to a web host is known as *deploying* your site.

The great news about the types of websites you learn to build in this book—that is, websites that use only static HTML files that don't require access to a full-blown web server—is that the simplicity of these files means there are web hosts out there that will deploy your site free of charge. These sites make their money from big-time corporations and professional web developers, so it's nothing to them to host a basic personal website. In this appendix, you learn how to deploy your website to two such web hosts: Netlify and Cloudflare. For good measure, I also give you general instructions for deploying your files to other web hosting providers.

B.1   Deploying to Netlify

Netlify is a company that offers big businesses and professional developers a cloud-based development platform for building and deploying web apps. Happily, Netlify also supports individuals and hobbyists by offering a free tier that enables anyone to put up a page or three with no hassle. The only restrictions are that you're limited to a maximum of 500 websites and 100 GB of bandwidth. (*Bandwidth* is the amount of data per month that your sites transfer to web browsers. And 100 GB is a *lot* of bandwidth.)

B.1.1   Setting up a Netlify account

To get up and running with Netlify, you need an account. Here are the steps to follow:

1 Send your favorite web browser to https://netlify.com.
2 Click Sign Up.
3 Click Sign Up with Email.
4 Type your email address, type the password you want to use, and then click Sign Up. Netlify sends a verification message to your email address.
5 Open your email app, click the Netlify verification message, and click the verification link. Netlify verifies your account and then displays a series of questions.
6 Run through the questions, click Continue to Deploy, and then click Skip This Step for Now.

Netlify drops you off at the Team Overview page. From here, you can upload your files using one of two methods: drag-and-drop or a dialog. The next two sections take you through both methods.

B.1.2   Uploading your files via drag-and-drop

Usually, the quickest way to get your website files to Netlify is to use your mouse to drag the website folder to the upload area. Here are the steps to follow:

1 On your computer, open File Explorer (Windows) or Finder (macOS).
2 Navigate to the folder that contains the subfolder you want to upload.
3 Sign in to Netlify (if you haven't done so already), and click Sites in the left sidebar.
4 Arrange the browser window and the File Explorer (or Finder) window so they're side by side (or at least so you can see the upload area in the browser and the subfolder you want to upload in File Explorer or Finder).
5 Drag the subfolder from File Explorer (or Finder), move your mouse pointer into the browser window and over the upload area (as shown in figure B.1), and drop the subfolder. Netlify uploads the subfolder and its contents and then deploys the site.

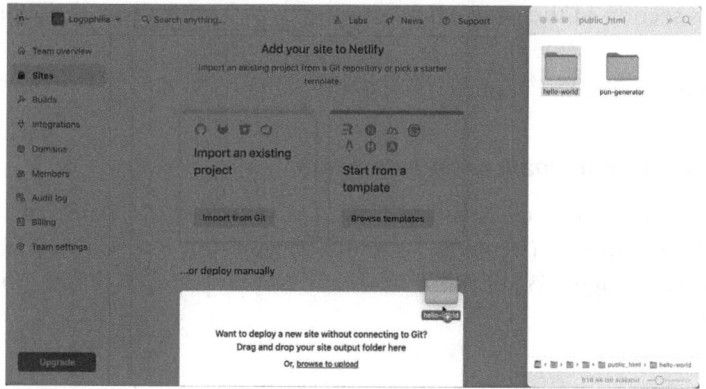

Figure B.1 Drag the website folder to the Netlify upload area.

6 In the Deploy Success! dialog (shown in figure B.2), click Get Started. Netlify displays your account overview page.

Figure B.2 Netlify displays the Deploy Success! dialog once your website is deployed.

7 In the Sites section of the page, click your new site. Netlify displays the Site Overview page.

8 Click the link to view the deployed site in the web browser.

B.1.3 Uploading your files using a dialog box

The drag-and-drop method isn't ideal if you have a relatively small screen or if your mouse skills aren't up to the task. That's fine because Netlify also enables you to upload your website folder using a dialog. Here are the steps to follow:

1 Sign in to Netlify (if you haven't done so already), and click Sites in the left sidebar.

2 Click Browse to Upload.

3 In the dialog that appears, select the project folder, and then click Upload.

4 If your web browser asks you to confirm the operation, click Upload. Netlify uploads the subfolder and its contents.

5 In the Deploy Success! dialog, click Get Started. Netlify displays your account overview page.

6 In the Sites section of the page, click your new site. Netlify displays the Site Overview page.

7 Click the link to view the deployed site in the web browser.

B.1.4 Changing your site's subdomain or domain name

By default, Netlify gives your deployed website a custom domain name of the form *wacky-name-a1b2c3*.netlify.app (figure B.3 shows an example). You see your site name on the Site Overview page. To get there from any Netlify page, click Sites in the left sidebar and then click the site.

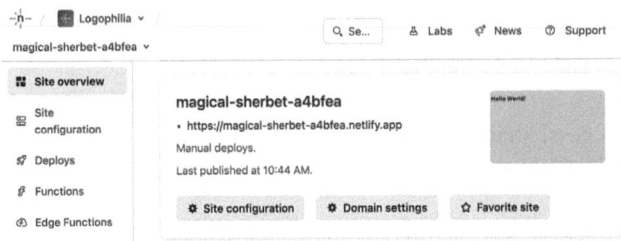

Figure B.3   The Site Overview page shows the name Netlify assigned to your site.

You might like the oddball name supplied randomly by Netlify, but if you'd prefer a domain name that reflects the content of your site, you need to use one of the following methods to change the domain name:

- *Changing the subdomain name*—If you want to keep the netlify.app domain name and just change the subdomain (the wacky-name-a1b2c3 part), open the Site Overview page, click Domain Settings, click Options in the Production Domains section, and then click Edit Site Name. Type the subdomain you prefer, and then click Save. If Netlify tells you the site name has already been taken, try again using a different name.

- *Changing the domain name*—If you already have a domain name or want to purchase a new one with Netlify, open the Site Overview page, click Domain Settings, and then click Add a Domain in the Production Domains section. Type your existing or new domain, click Verify, and then follow the instructions that appear.

B.2 Deploying to Cloudflare

Cloudflare is best known as a networking company that specializes in helping large websites avoid or get out of cyberattacks, such as *distributed denial of service* (DDOS) attacks that barrage a website with massive amounts of junk data. But Cloudflare also offers web hosting via a service called Pages. This service is ostensibly targeted at web developers, but it's also available for the likes of you and me. Best of all, a Pages account is free and offers no restrictions on the number of sites and the amount of bandwidth they use.

B.2.1 Setting up a Cloudflare Pages account

To get started with Cloudflare Pages, you first need to follow these steps to set up an account:

1 Navigate to https://pages.cloudflare.com.
2 Click Sign Up.
3 Type your email address, type the password you want to use, and then click Sign Up. Cloudflare sends a verification email to your email address.
4 Open your email app, click the Cloudflare verification message, and click the verification link.

Cloudflare verifies your account and then displays your Cloudflare dashboard. You're ready to create a new Cloudflare application for your website, as described in the next section.

B.2.2 Creating a new Cloudflare application

In Cloudflare, a Pages website is called an *application*, and you deploy it as part of Cloudflare's Pages feature. You begin the deployment by creating a new Pages application, as outlined in the following steps:

1 Sign in to Cloudflare if you haven't done so already.
2 In the navigation menu on the left, under Workers & Pages, click Overview. The Overview page appears. If you haven't yet deployed a Pages project, skip to step 4; otherwise, continue with step 3.
3 Click the Create Application button, shown in figure B.4. The Create an Application page appears.

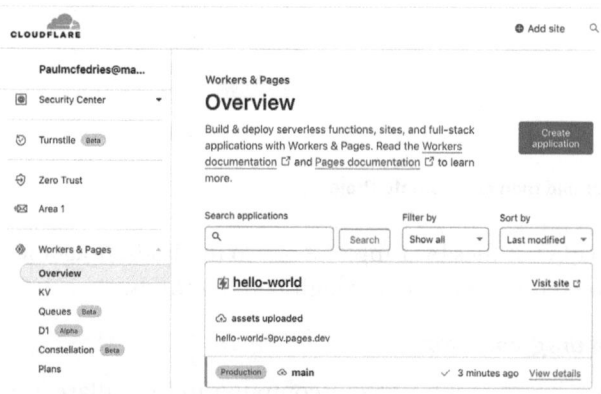

Figure B.4   In the Workers & Pages Overview page of Cloudflare, click Create Application.

4   Click the Pages tab, as shown in figure B.5.

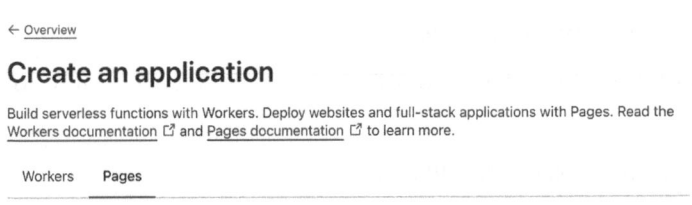

Figure B.5   **In the Create an Application page, click the Pages tab.**

5   Scroll down to the Create Using Direct Upload section, and then click Upload Assets (refer to figure B.6). The Deploy a Site by Uploading Your Project page appears.

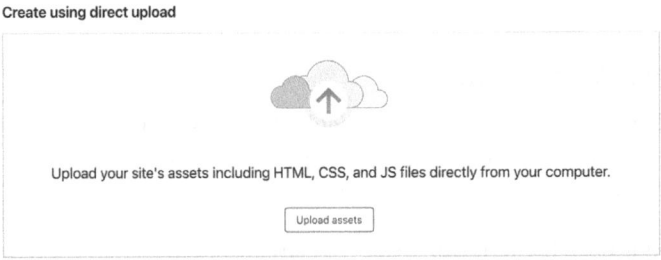

Figure B.6   **Click Upload Assets.**

6   Type a name for your project, and then click Create Project (refer to figure B.7). When your project is ready (it takes a few moments), Cloudflare displays an upload area.

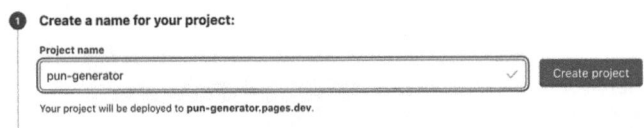

Figure B.7   **Name your project and then click Create Project.**

From here, you can upload your files by using one of two methods: drag-and-drop or a dialog box. The next two sections take you through both methods.

B.2.3   *Uploading your files via drag-and-drop*

Often, the easiest way to get your files from your computer to Cloudflare is to use your mouse to drag the website folder to the upload area. Here are the steps to follow:

1 On your computer, open File Explorer (Windows) or Finder (macOS).

2 Navigate to the folder that contains the subfolder you want to upload.

3 Arrange the browser window and the File Explorer (or Finder) window so they're side by side (or at least so you can see the upload area in the browser and the subfolder you want to upload in File Explorer or Finder).

4 Drag the subfolder from File Explorer (or Finder), move your mouse pointer into the browser window and over the upload area, and then drop the subfolder. Cloudflare uploads the subfolder and its contents.

The final step is to deploy the site, as described in section B.2.5.

B.2.4 Uploading your files using a dialog box

If you're working with a small screen or your mouse skills aren't that sharp, you may prefer to upload your files to Cloudflare using a dialog box. Here's how it's done:

1 In Cloudflare's upload area, click Select from Computer.

2 Click Upload Folder.

3 In the dialog that appears, select the project folder, as shown in figure B.8, and then click Upload.

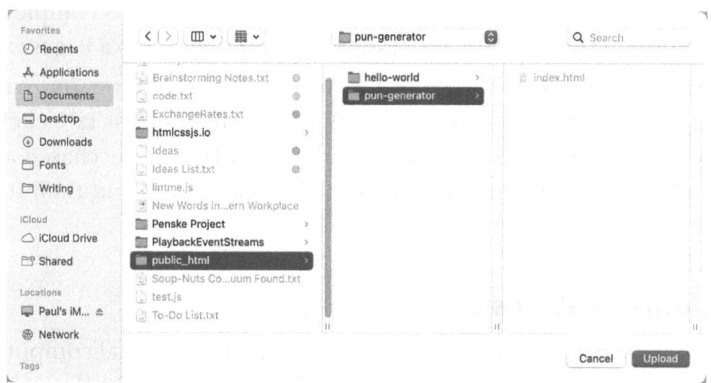

Figure B.8   Select the website folder.

4 If your web browser asks you to confirm the operation, click Upload. Cloudflare uploads the subfolder and its contents.

The final step is to deploy the site, as described in the next section.

B.2.5 Deploying the site

With your files uploaded, you're ready to deploy the new site. You do that by clicking the Deploy Site button. Cloudflare deploys the site and then displays the Success! message, as shown in figure B.9. Click the link to view the deployed site in the web browser.

Figure B.9   Cloudflare displays the Success! message when your site is deployed.

B.2.6   Changing your site's domain name

Cloudflare gives your deployed website a custom domain name of the form *folder-name -a1b2*.pages.dev (where *folder-name* comes from the name of the website folder you uploaded). You can change this name to your own domain name as follows:

- *Domain name purchased from Cloudflare*—In the left sidebar, click Domain Registration, click Register Domains, type the new domain name you want to use, click Search, and then follow the instructions. Once the purchase is complete, follow the instructions in the next bullet to assign the new domain to a Pages website.
- *Domain name you already own*—From the Worker & Pages Overview page, click the website you want to work with, click the Custom Domains tab, click Set Up a Custom Domain, type the domain name you own (if you purchased a domain with Cloudflare, type that domain name), click Continue, and then follow the instructions.

B.3   Deploying to other web hosts

Other services can host your website; they store your files on a special computer called a *web server*, which accepts and responds to web browser requests for the page and its associated files. To use such a service, you need to sign up with one that offers space on its server. Because the service in effect plays host to your files, it's called a *web hosting provider* or *web host*.

B.3.1   What to look for in a web host

When you evaluate a web host, what criteria should you use? The answer depends on the type of website you want to set up, but the following criteria are the most common:

- *Maximum bandwidth*—The maximum amount of your data per month that the host will transfer to web browsers. In most cases, you pay extra for data that exceeds your monthly maximum. Some web hosts offer unlimited bandwidth.

- *Total disk space*—The amount of hard disk storage space you get on the web server. At a minimum, total disk space is usually a few hundred megabytes, which is more than enough for a simple site.
- *Number of websites*—The number of root folders you can set up.
- *Number of email addresses*—The number of email addresses included with the hosting service.
- *Domain name hosting*—Whether the web host also hosts domain names that you've previously purchased from a domain name registrar. Some hosts sell domain names, and others offer free subdomain names of the form *yourdomain .webhostdomain*.com.
- *FTP support*—Support for the *File Transfer Protocol* (FTP), which is the internet service you use to transfer your files to the web host. Almost all web hosts support FTP, but some offer only proprietary file-transfer services.

As a rule, the cheaper the web host, the fewer of these features you get. Before you start looking for a web host, make a list of these features and decide what you need and what's optional. That may be difficult for something like maximum bandwidth because bandwidth is determined in part by how popular your site becomes, but make your best stabs at each one for now. When you're looking for a web host, you have three main choices:

- *Your internet service provider* (ISP)—The company or institution you use to access the internet may also offer a web hosting service. Many ISPs offer free web hosting for simple personal websites, and some organization networks include a web server you can use. In most cases, the hosting includes features such as bandwidth and disk space at the lower end of the scale.
- *Free web hosting provider*—Many services will host your web pages without charge. The catch is that you usually have fairly severe restrictions on most hosting features, particularly bandwidth and disk space, and you almost always get only a single website. Some free web hosts also display ads, although that's becoming rare these days.
- *Commercial web hosting provider*—If you want a reasonable set of features for your web presence, you need to shell out money to rent space with a commercial web hosting provider. Note that I'm not talking about big bucks. Popular providers such as Bluehost (www.bluehost.com), GoDaddy (www.godaddy.com), and Host-Gator (www.hostgator.com) offer feature-packed hosting, usually for less than $5 per month. If you think you'll be getting into web design beyond creating a basic home page, you should consider a commercial web host.

When you've signed up with a web host, it usually takes anywhere from a few minutes to a few hours before everything is ready. When your hosting service is good to go, it's time to get your stuff online.

B.3.2 *Uploading your files*

With your HTML and CSS files coded and validated, your support files (such as images) in place, your folders set up, and your web host ready to serve your stuff to a waiting world, all that remains is to send your files from your computer to the web host's server—a process known as *uploading*. How you go about uploading your files depends on the web host, but the following three methods are by far the most common:

- *FTP*—Most hosts offer support for FTP uploads. First, you need to get yourself an *FTP client*, which is a software program that connects to your web host's FTP server and offers an interface for basic file chores, such as navigating and creating folders, uploading files, and deleting and renaming files. Popular Windows clients are CuteFTP (www.globalscape.com/cuteftp) and Cyberduck (https://cyberduck.io). For the Mac, try Transmit (https://panic.com/transmit) or FileZilla (https://filezilla-project.org). When you've downloaded the software, check your web host's support pages for information on how to connect to the host's FTP server.

- *cPanel*—Many web hosts offer an administration tool called cPanel that presents a simple interface for hosting tasks such as email and domain management. cPanel also offers a File Manager component that you can use to upload files and perform other file management chores.

- *Proprietary*—Some web hosts offer their own interface for uploading and working with files. See your host's support page for instructions.

Whatever method is available, upload all your website files and folders to your root folder on your host. Then load your site into your favorite web browser to make sure everything's working okay. It wouldn't hurt to try your site in a few different browsers and on a few different devices to be sure it works properly for a wide variety of users.

Learning a few ChatGPT best practices

Web developers know that creating web pages is a craft that's as much art as technology, as much design as it is coding. My main assumption with this book is that you don't want (or don't have either the time or the inclination) to become a web developer. So, the craft that you learn in this book is the craft of prompting ChatGPT to generate the code and text you need for the web pages you want to put online.

A big part of cajoling ChatGPT into doing your web page creation chores is using your prompts to lay out what you want with as little ambiguity as possible. That's the goal behind all the prompts you see in the book. However, prompting ChatGPT is an art, which means there are lots of subtle ways to improve your prompts to get better results. You may find (fingers crossed!) that this book's prompts provide good enough starting points for getting ChatGPT to help build your website. If so, great! If not, however, don't despair. As this appendix shows, there are quite a few tips, tricks, and best practices you can use to get ChatGPT to generate high-quality web page code and text.

C.1   *Ask ChatGPT to adopt a persona*

One surprising feature of ChatGPT is that it can adopt a specified persona—for example, a teacher, a consultant, or a data analyst—during a conversation. Telling the model "who" it is not only gives ChatGPT an overall perspective from which to generate its output but also places the conversation in a more specific context, which usually helps the model formulate more targeted results.

For web page creation, you can start your conversations with example persona prompts such as the following:

- *You are a web design consultant.*
- *Act as a senior web developer.*
- *Provide code that a front-end web engineer would create.*
- *You are a website marketing manager.*

TIP   For assistance writing your persona prompts, see the GitHub repository called Awesome ChatGPT Prompts: https://github.com/f/awesome-chatgpt -prompts.

Of course, you can also ask ChatGPT to assume any persona that suits your needs, which is especially handy when asking for help to generate web page text.

C.2   *More detail is better than less*

If you leave important information out of your prompt, ChatGPT will try to guess what you want, which is almost certainly not going to produce quality results! Don't be afraid to add salient details to your prompts to give the transformer part of ChatGPT something to chew on.

For example, consider the following prompt (from chapter 1):

```
Write web page code to display "Hello World" in a large font.
```

The use of the word *large* here is vague, so ChatGPT will guess what size you want for the text. For example, in chapter 1, I showed some ChatGPT-generated code that formatted the text in a 48-pixel font. However, if you know you want the text displayed in a 72-pixel font, add that to your prompt:

```
Write web page code to display "Hello World" in a 72-pixel font.
```

Here's some example code generated by ChatGPT from this prompt:

```
<!DOCTYPE html>
<html>
<head>
    <title>Hello World</title>
    <style>
        h1 {
            font-size: 72px;
        }
```

```
    </style>
</head>
<body>
    <h1>Hello World</h1>
</body>
</html>
```

> **WARNING** One of the ways a large language model (LLM) such as ChatGPT is trained to produce outputs that aren't (or aren't *always*) boring or run-of-the-mill is to add a soupçon of randomness to the process. This randomness also means, first, that ChatGPT doesn't necessarily generate identical results from identical prompts and, second, that sometimes ChatGPT seems to go out of its way to not understand your prompts. For the latter, it's almost always the best strategy to clear the current conversation and start over.

Detail is generally your friend when prompting ChatGPT, but if you find the model timing out, getting confused, or producing incomplete results, too much detail may be the culprit. In that case, try breaking your detailed prompts into two or more less-detailed prompts.

C.3   *Set an output length*

When you're working with ChatGPT to generate text, depending on the prompt, ChatGPT may output a result that's long and/or detailed. That long-winded result may be exactly what you want, but web page components are often restricted in how much text they can accommodate. For example, you may want a product description to be only large enough to fit a card component; similarly, you may want the answers to some frequently asked questions to be on the succinct side.

So, when prompting ChatGPT to generate website text, you'll often want that text to have a maximum length. It may be 200 words, 3 paragraphs, 4 sentences, or 5 bullet points. Whatever the length, be sure to include it as part of your prompt. Some examples:

- Provide an answer to the question "Why was Jerry Lewis so popular in France?". Make the answer 100 words or less.
- In three paragraphs, write a buyer's guide to cubic zirconia jewelry.
- List ten fun things to do in the Broad Ripple neighborhood of Indianapolis.

> **TIP** Chances are, ChatGPT will ignore your suggested output length in its first response! This is particularly true for lengths expressed in words, paragraphs, and sentences. Once the response is complete, run a follow-up prompt asking ChatGPT to reduce the answer to the length you specified in the original prompt.

Setting an output length is an example of a *constraint*, which refers to any aspect of the prompt that limits ChatGPT's response in some way. Here are some example constraints to play around with:

- `Write your output in the style of` *X* (where *X* is an author or publication).
- `Write the text in a manner that's` *X* (where *X* is an adjective or adjectival phrase such as *academic, casual,* or *accessible to a 10-year-old*).
- `Make the text` *X* (where *X* is an adjective such as *vivid, lively,* or *humorous*).

Constraining your requests is a great way to get ChatGPT to write more interesting text.

C.4   *Delimit extra text input with triple quotation marks*

If you're providing extra text input for ChatGPT to use, surround the input with triple quotation marks and include that fact in your prompt. For example, in a previous project, I'd asked ChatGPT to write a short biography of the poet Walt Whitman. I copied that biography and then pasted it into the following prompt:

```
Create a limerick from the text surrounded by triple quotation marks.

"""Walt Whitman (1819-1892) was an American poet, essayist, and journalist,
known as one of the most influential poets in the American canon. He was
often called the "father of free verse" because of his unconventional use of
form.

Whitman was born on May 31, 1819, in West Hills, New York. His family moved
to Brooklyn when he was a child, where he attended public school before
leaving at age eleven to work in a series of jobs such as office boy,
printer's apprentice, and teacher.

In 1841, Whitman turned his interests to journalism and founded the "Long
Islander," a weekly newspaper. He continued to write and edit for various
periodicals throughout the 1840s and became known for his progressive views,
championing issues like workers' rights and women's suffrage.

Whitman's groundbreaking poetry collection "Leaves of Grass," first published
in 1855, was unlike any poetry that had been seen before in its free
verse form and candid content. This volume, which he revised and expanded
throughout his life, explored themes of democracy, sexuality, death, and the
individual's place in the universe.

During the American Civil War, Whitman worked as a government clerk
and volunteered as a nurse in an army hospital in Washington, D.C. His
experiences with wounded soldiers and the realities of war deeply impacted
him and influenced much of his later work, notably his poem "O Captain! My
Captain!" mourning the death of President Lincoln.

Whitman continued to write and publish his work until his death on March 26,
1892, in Camden, New Jersey. His innovative style and uniquely American voice
have made him a staple in the study of American literature."""
```

ChatGPT rose to the challenge with the following ditty:

```
In New York, a poet named Whit,
Whose verse was a free-forming hit.
From "Leaves of Grass" sprang,
A new style Whitman sang,
In America's canon, he sits.
```

Including example text is particularly useful when you'd like ChatGPT to generate new text using your own writing style. For example, you can say something like this:

```
Using the same style as the text surrounded by triple quotation marks, write
a short essay on the nutritional benefits of eating rutabagas.
"""Include a few paragraphs of your own writing here"""
```

When including example text in your prompt, bear in mind that most ChatGPT queries are limited to about 500 words (about double the number of words in the earlier limerick prompt). Remember (as I explain in chapter 7) that you can use Copilot to work around this limitation by navigating to a page that includes the text you want ChatGPT to reference and then using the Copilot sidebar to write your prompt.

C.5 An example is worth a thousand prompts

If you're asking ChatGPT to output something unusual or esoteric, the model may not get what you want. To point ChatGPT in the right direction, include two or three examples of the type of output you're looking for. Here's an example:

```
Create a dozen unique insults of the form "Not the Xest Y in the Z",
replacing X, Y, and Z with related terms. For example: "Not the sharpest
knife in the drawer", "Not the quickest bunny in the forest", "Not the
brightest crayon in the box."
```

> **TIP** The prompt shown here is an example of a *template prompt*, where you give ChatGPT an overall pattern (`"Not the Xest Y in the Z"`) that includes one or more placeholders (`X`, `Y`, and `Z`) and tell ChatGPT how you want it to replace each placeholder.

However, before spending time coming up with examples, it's usually best to try the prompt on its own without any examples. ChatGPT has been trained on such a large quantity of text that it often gets even obscure requests the first time.

C.6 Flip the conversation direction

Most of your ChatGPT conversations are one-way affairs that have you asking the model to perform some tasks and the model (hopefully) completing the request successfully. If you're not getting quality results, it's probably because you're not giving ChatGPT prompts that are good enough for it to figure out what you need. Do you know who may be able to figure out the correct prompts to use? ChatGPT! That is, instead of constantly pestering ChatGPT for output, turn things around and get ChatGPT to ask *you* to provide the info the model needs.

Here are some example prompts:

- ```
  Ask me whatever questions you require me to answer for you to
  create an "About" page for my website.
  ```
- ```
  I want to create a web page card for a product. I would like you to
  ask me questions until you have enough information to generate the
  HTML and CSS code for the card.
  ```
- ```
  I want you to help me write a short story. What information do you
  need from me? Ask me one question at a time, please.
  ```

Note that in each case, the prompt includes a specific outcome, goal, or result. This is important because it enables ChatGPT to generate the appropriate questions.

C.7   *Ask ChatGPT to refine your prompts*

One of the problems you'll run into when using ChatGPT to generate web page code is that, not being a web developer yourself, you can't be sure that your prompts are worded correctly, that they're asking the right question, or whether they're seeking something that's just not possible. One of the main goals of this book is to give you enough example prompts that you become familiar with a wide range of what you can request from ChatGPT. However, if you find yourself in new territory, go ahead and prompt ChatGPT as best you can. If the results aren't what you want, ask ChatGPT to refine your prompt for you:

- ```
  Can you suggest a better version of my previous prompt?
  ```
- ```
  Is there anything missing from my previous prompt that would help
  you generate a better response?
  ```
- ```
  In the following conversation, each time I ask you to generate
  some code, suggest a better version of my request and ask me if I'd
  prefer to use that version instead of the original.
  ```

It may also help if you provide some context. For example, if you're trying to create more accessible web pages, let ChatGPT know so that its improved prompts can take that goal into account.

C.8   *Ask ChatGPT to create steps for you to follow*

If you want to learn how to perform some complex task (for example, to deploy your website to a web host not covered in this book), you can ask ChatGPT to provide you with the steps to follow to accomplish that task. For this kind of prompt, you usually need to give ChatGPT the following tidbits:

- The goal or task you're trying to accomplish
- What information related to that goal or task you already know, or what steps you've already performed

- What steps are required to accomplish the goal or task
- The details of any steps that deal with information you don't yet have or steps you haven't yet performed

Here's an example prompt that asks ChatGPT for the steps required to publish a website to Vercel:

```
I want to deploy my website to Vercel. I know I need a Vercel account. I
have completed my website and all the files are in the my_app folder on my
computer. What steps are required to deploy my website to Vercel? Please
provide detailed information for each step I haven't yet completed.
```

A similar idea is to ask ChatGPT to tell you how to use the web page code that it generates for you. For example, if ChatGPT gives you some code but you're not sure where the code is supposed to go in the HTML file, ask ChatGPT to tell you where to place the code in the file.

C.9   Ask ChatGPT to provide and rate alternatives

With all but the simplest designs, there are always multiple ways to code a web page or page component. After ChatGPT provides its initial output, you can always click Regenerate Response to get another block of code, but how do you know which response is the one you should use? Ask ChatGPT, of course! That is, you can ask ChatGPT not only to provide alternative approaches to what you're trying to accomplish but also to rate those approaches. Here are some examples:

- ```
  I want to add a responsive dropdown menu to my web page. If there
  are multiple ways to accomplish that goal, list the three best
  methods.
  ```
- ```
  List up to four ways that I can add a navigation bar to my web pages
  and tell me the pros and cons of each method.
  ```
- ```
  Tell me the most popular ways to get form data emailed to me and
  compare and contrast each method.
  ```

Depending on the prompt, you may prefer to use Copilot, which can use a web search to help it rate each alternative.

C.10   In Microsoft Copilot, choose the appropriate conversation style

If you're using Copilot, be sure to choose a conversation style that's suitable to your task:

- *More Creative*—This style is best when you want Copilot to stretch its wings, so to speak, and generate text or ideas that are less conventional and more imaginative or inventive. This version of Copilot can generate truly wild text but is prone to claiming its fanciful output is fact, so *caveat emptor*. This style has an input limit of 4,000 characters.
  ```

- *More Precise*—This style is best when you want results that are concise, uncompli- cated, and to the point. This style has an input limit of 4,000 characters.
- *More Balanced*—This is the default style, and it presents Copilot as a friendly, informative assistant with results that straddle the line between inventiveness and straightforwardness. This style has an input limit of 2,000 characters.

When generating web page code, it's usually best to try the More Precise style, which creates code that's relatively free of unnecessary embellishment.

C.11 Troubleshooting ChatGPT's errors

How ChatGPT does what it does isn't a big mystery, and it's certainly not magic, but it *is* extremely impressive, as you learn throughout this book. However, that impressive- ness doesn't mean ChatGPT is infallible—far from it. Yes, fortunately, most of the time the response you get from ChatGPT is code that not only matches what you asked for but also works properly (meaning when you display the code in a web browser, you see the content and style you asked for). However, it's crucial to understand that although lots of people call ChatGPT "AI," it's not even remotely intelligent. It can—and, alas, often does—churn out code that's inaccurate, mistaken, or sometimes downright non- sensical. And, worse, ChatGPT will present this "bad" code with the same cheerful confidence with which it presents its "good" code. ChatGPT simply doesn't know the difference between the two.

So, that leaves you with a big problem: given that you don't know (and presumably don't want to know) how to code web pages, how can you "fix" whatever code prob- lems ChatGPT creates? Happily, you're not stuck, because you have a few ways to get ChatGPT to help fix its own problems:

- Ask ChatGPT to regenerate its response. Sometimes a second or even a third try is required to get things right.
- Modify your prompt. If your original prompt was simple, try adding more detail; if your original prompt was complex, try breaking it into multiple prompts that are simple and/or focus on a single task.
- Ask ChatGPT to generate one or more prompts that it thinks are suitable to the output you're looking for.
- Tell ChatGPT that the code it generated doesn't work, and ask it to fix the prob- lem. You'll be amazed how often this helps!

My hope is that you won't have to switch to troubleshooting mode all that often because ChatGPT really is good at churning out web page code.

index